WAR IN THE TWENTIETH CENTURY
NO FLIGHT FROM THE CAGE

We arrived at Sagan in the evening of the following day. Stalag Luft 3, which we could see as we straggled down the road from the station, had a forbidding bleakness. Long wooden huts huddled together in tidy rows. The wind whipped the sand around the spindly legs on which the barracks perched, scuffled it through the wire, beneath the ugly, squat sentry-boxes, across the sandy, stump-punctuated wasteland surrounding the camp, into the frigid pine trees that loomed beyond.

Calton Younger has lived in England since 1949. He is the administrator of a group of grant-making charitable trusts and the author of Ireland's Civil War, A State of Disunion, Arthur Griffith *(a biography), and a novel* Less Than Angel.

Also in this series

WAR IN THE TWENTIETH CENTURY

NO FLIGHT FROM THE CAGE

Calton Younger

with an Introduction by
General Sir John Hackett

Star
A STAR BOOK
published by
the Paperback Division of
W. H. ALLEN & Co. Ltd

A Star Book
Published in 1981
by the Paperback Division of
W. H. Allen & Co. Ltd
A Howard and Wyndham Company
44 Hill Street, London W1X 8LB

First published in Great Britain by
Shakespeare Head Press Ltd, 1956

Reproduced, printed and bound in Great Britain by
Hazell Watson & Viney Ltd, Aylesbury, Bucks

ISBN 0 352 30828 1

To Dixie Deans
and to
Dick and Toby

INTRODUCTION

by General Sir John Hackett

No Flight from the Cage chronicles the passage of a human spirit
through some of the darker corridors of war-time. It is an
exploration of the life of a prisoner of war in German hands in
World War II, corralled with thousands of others in the POW
camps of the Reich. The writer was a young Australian serving in
the RAF, like so many of his countrymen. He was shot down in a
Wellington bomber over France in 1942 and was captured after a
brief period on the run to spend three years behind the wire.

This is a book which deserves to be read and re-read as the
impact of World War II fades from the memories of those who
lived through it, and as it becomes no more than a frequently
overlooked and minor aspect of history to those who did not
experience this terrible cataclysm. This is the story of the development of a young man – sensitive, intelligent and courageous –
under the pressures and deprivations of life in a POW camp. It is
the story of the development of others around him and of the
relationships that evolved between them – often with a previously
unknown intensity – creating situations as unfamiliar as they were
difficult and painful. It was a totally different life from anything
that could be called normal by those who were forced to lead it,
and it is very difficult for anyone who has never been a prisoner of
war to imagine. The camp in which the 'kriegies' were enclosed
was another planet, light-years away from this one. To observe its
details in high definition is a chastening experience which is both
saddening and uplifting.

Until the tide turned for the Germans, physical conditions were
by no means bad for the British prisoners. Red Cross parcels came
in freely, and there was an abundance of chocolates and cigarettes
with which to buy small comforts or bribe the guards. Mail came
in freely too – including letters from wives and girlfriends who
could wait no longer. The author was rejected by his fiancée in this
manner, but shortly afterwards he was adopted as a pen-friend by
a woman he had never met, and when the war ended they married.

Though some in the camps kept their emotions tightly buttoned
up, brooding in silent despair to the point of madness or even
suicide, most POWs expressed their feelings with a freedom rare
among people of their own kind outside the wire: 'one gave way to
almost any emotion quite unashamedly . . . in a prison camp there
could be no sham'. Nor could there be anything but strict
observance of a totally unyielding code of conduct. In such a close-
knit society of deprived men whose possessions were few and
valuable, stealing was a very serious crime. As the war dragged on
and conditions grew worse almost daily, theft was punished with
increasing severity. The stealing of food, always a serious offence,
now became a very grave crime indeed and men were savagely
beaten for it by their comrades. On one occasion a man found
guilty of theft was flung into a full cess-pit that served thousands.
Towards the end of the war food, long limited to an occasional

crust of bread and thin vegetable soup, grew very scarce indeed. Men were driven to grim expedients, such as scouring cook-house refuse to pick out barely edible swede-parings.

Captivity sharpened personal characteristics. Among men of such high quality as were commonly found in aircrew on active service – pretty well everyone in the camps described had been shot down in action – it is not surprising to find a positive and constructive approach. Among these men who came into captivity healthy in mind and spirit there was a common determination to make the best of it all, a refusal to be downcast. The atmosphere was a self-consciously creative one, an expression of a refusal to accept defeat. Men studied the arts and sciences, history, literature and foreign languages. They taught each other, painted, wrote, made music and did much in makeshift theatres. They played games with huge gusto, displaying national characteristics which were often very puzzling to their captors. A surprising thing in this big group of men segregated for so long without women is the apparently total absence of homosexuality.

The airmen did not like the Army much: they were different people living in a different culture. For other Europeans – Poles, French, Yugoslavs and many others – they felt curiosity but little fellow-feeling, and for Americans there was impatience and an often thinly-veiled dislike. The prisoners' relationship to their captors is complex and fascinating. Sometimes there was a degree of trust and good humour, more often suspicion, malice, self-importance and bad temper. Hun-baiting was good fun, but dangerous to take too far: it could make life more difficult for your friends, it could make escape attempts more hazardous. Not everyone wanted to escape. For many the war was indeed over: they were civilians only waiting to be returned to their civilian lives. For others not to try to escape was unthinkable, though very few succeeded.

One of the most interesting aspects of the whole experience, and certainly one of the outstanding themes of Calton Younger's account, is the emergence of camp leadership. What is likely to be remembered most clearly by many readers is the outstanding performance and personality of Dixie Deans, the Sergeant who became Camp Leader of the NCOs' compound at Stalag Luft III and whose name was before long held in high regard not only throughout the prison camps, but also among Germans, in the British Air Ministry, and in the Red Cross organization in Geneva. There was respect and affection for this man as remarkable as it was widespread. This book is worth reading, apart from all else, to get to know Sergeant Dixie Deans.

No Flight from the Cage not only throws light on a curious and almost completely self-contained culture, the culture of the prison camp in war-time, it is also an adventure in the exploration of the human spirit whose total effect is both sobering and uplifting. The writer was young and the writing sometimes shows this, but there is never any doubt of his complete sincerity – nor of his courage and compassion.

CHAPTER

1

Plaster trembled on the walls of Gonesse and tumbled in a spatter on to the cobblestones. In a doorway a young couple huddled, as if sheltering from the rain, and above their heads, caught in the slanting light from the full moon, a piece of broken guttering quivered like a palsied arm. A few kilometres away our bombers were blasting the Gnome Rhone factory. I should have been loosing my bombs, too; instead they had blown up the Wellington with three of the crew, and I, having watched without comprehension my parachute blow across the fields, was walking through Gonesse to the country. A motor-cycle combination bumped noisily down the road, and the driver and passenger glanced back, but did not stop. Two soldiers came towards me, but I dared not go furtively across the moonlit road.

"Heil Hitler."

"Heil Hitler." I saluted as they had, and was thankful that I was wearing a collar and tie, and a cap.

Near Le Bourget I heard the last of our bombers leave the target. The sound of its engines was lost in the night. I was lonely. Absurdly I took comfort from the road along which I was walking for, with its spindly trees, it resembled the avenue of Hobbema's familiar picture.

I saw more Germans later in the day from the upstairs window of the ante-natal clinic at Sevran. They were parading in the street, and at first I thought they were a search-party, but it was a routine parade at the end of their day. The French women standing at the window beside me watched with cool contempt, but I was afraid, afraid of the Myth.

At daybreak I had hidden behind a hedge in the churchyard and there lain until the evening, sleepless, with only Horlicks tablets to eat, and nothing to drink but the rain licked from the leaves. The ladies of the church were preparing for the Festival of Motherhood, and a young woman who came to throw some dead flowers behind the hedge saw me, and fled.

It was thought that I was a drunken German, and a lively old lady came fearlessly to send me packing. Unable to follow her diatribe, I smiled and said: "*Je suis un aviateur Anglais.*" She fetched her daughter, Hélène Buvelot, who spoke some English, and I was taken into the clinic, fed, and put to bed, in spite of the fact that several suspected collaborators knew where I was.

When I had slept for an hour Hélène, with much difficulty, awakened me, and explained that the Germans had found my parachute and were not far away. Her husband, Jean, and the young French poet, Jean Lelong, were waiting to guide me into the country. And so, wearing a mackintosh and béret, and carrying a haversack with a little food, rum, wine, matches and a torch, I followed my friends into the dark street.

They led me to a wood and gave me directions to reach a deserted house, but, in the darkness, after stumbling through brambles and undergrowth, I missed my way by a little, and the house I found was not the one they had intended. When they came with more food the following day and could not find me, they thought never to see me again. Meanwhile I crouched behind some junk on a veranda while, within a few feet of me, a woman did her week's washing.

Rumour reached the Germans that Madame Buvelot had been seen with a strange man whom she had found hiding in the churchyard, but somehow her story of having helped a drunken German convinced her interrogators. Jean Buvelot confided his experience to a close friend, and, to his delight, found himself enlisted in the underground movement. Jean Lelong made the incident the subject of a poem which was published after the war in the second volume of his poems, *Croisière*. When Paris was liberated he wrote to the R.A.F. to inquire my fate, and so I was able to find these brave people again. Grandma who, in her eighties, is lively and charming as ever, delights in reminding me that she had once believed that I was a drunken German.

More than a week after I left Sevran I was trying to find a way through the town of Provins, after the curfew, when I was arrested by French police. Too late they decided that I was not a German trying to deceive them; their sous-préfet had telephoned German headquarters.

Two German feldwebels came to the police station to take charge of me. At last I was in the presence of men of the Myth. They were awesome figures, jack-booted, steel-helmeted, and, because I was frightened, I nicknamed them Hawkeye and Dirty Dick. Hawkeye was perhaps six feet six inches in height, with an immense nose, a Modigliani neck, and protruberant eyes. When he removed his steel helmet his bald head emerged like a tortoise from its shell. The other man was swarthy with a single black bar of eyebrow and a heavy prickling of twelve-hour beard.

"*Pour vous la guerre est finis*," growled Hawkeye. In one language or another it was the conventional overture to the new prisoner.

I wanted to run immediately we left the police station, but the sous-préfet was just behind, and Hawkeye's hand closed on my wrist.

My arrival at headquarters brought all the young Germans from their beds and, looking very boyish in their pyjamas, they stood in the doorways staring at the terrorflieger. I tried to look casual, tough. An oberfeldwebel offered me a cigarette. Hawkeye, who was trying to put through a telephone call to Paris, objected. They argued briefly, then

Hawkeye capitulated. News of my capture was passed to the authorities in Paris.

After a night in a narrow stone cell, which did not seem to have been occupied since the French Revolution, I was escorted to a car, and, from something which Hawkeye said in stern French, I concluded that I was to be shot. My stomach contracted violently, and I wished that I had risked breaking away the previous evening. He guessed that I had not understood, and in a kindly voice repeated what was, in fact, a warning of the consequences of trying to escape. Rifles were stowed on the ledge behind the back seat; Hawkeye, Dirty Dick, a driver and myself got into the car, and we travelled to Paris.

Free for eight days, I had believed that, by being patient and careful, I could walk home. Now, as the car flashed past the kilometre stones, each of which I had reached laboriously in the darkness, I was miserable at my failure. I glimpsed a farmhouse where, a few days before, I had been shaved by the village barber, and I began to worry about the inquisition which awaited me in Paris. How had I lived for eight days, they would want to know; who had helped me? At Provins the wife of a police officer had taken charge of my civilian clothing and haversack, when I told her that French people had given them to me, and disposed of them a moment before the Germans had taken me into custody. For that I was grateful.

"That was quite a good effort to get so far in a week. You were helped of course?" I was in a cell beneath Luftwaffe headquarters, and the interrogation officer, speaking English with an Oxford accent, had chosen to come to me immediately I had eaten a good meal which, after subsisting for over a week on half an orange, or a slice of bread each day, I had needed. "No one helped me."

He laughed. "You must have eaten. Who did help you? No harm will come to them, I assure you, but—well, we're interested."

"The first bloody Frenchman I ran into handed me over," I told him bitterly, as he persisted in ignoring my denials. Perhaps he was convinced, but I do not think so. I believe that he did not enjoy the task, and either did not feel that he could take advantage of my naivety, or hated the thought of French people being done to death.

"You took a great risk, you know," and he did not seem so relentless, now. "You might easily have been shot as a spy."

But he became exasperated when I would not answer questions about the squadron. In Africa British officers were refusing food and water to obstinate prisoners, he alleged. "We might consider ourselves entitled to adopt similar measures."

"You speak English beautifully," I countered. "Were you educated in England?"

"I was three years at Oxford."

"Those British officers might well have been your friends, then. Do you believe that story?"

He conceded the point, then asked: "Do you know Sergeant Loder? But of course you do. Your rear-gunner." Godfrey alive! It was unbelievable. "Pilot Officer Jones, Sergeant Mellowes and Sergeant Houghton, I regret to say, lost their lives."

Although the aircraft had exploded, and I had baled out so low that anyone jumping after me must have hit the ground before a parachute could open, I had still hoped that the others might have escaped. For hours, lying alone in barns, I had tried to believe that the miracle might have happened. In a hundred exhausting dreams I had seen the flames stream from the wing like a scarlet and obscene banner, had seen the serene half-smile on Russ Jones's face when I clipped on to his harness the parachute that he knew he should never be able to use.

Another aircraft from my squadron also had been shot down; only the rear-gunner, John Holborow, had escaped.

We three, all Australians, were the only survivors from the seven aircraft lost that night from a force of seventy-two, many of which had not reached the target.

I was relieved when three guards arrived to escort me to Germany, for I had feared that another interrogation officer might be sent to probe my story further. No question had been asked about my route to Provins; Sevran had not been mentioned. The Germans had believed Hélène Buvelot's improbable tale, though I knew nothing of her questioning, then, and they had accepted my denials. It seems incredible that they did not try to link our lies. In my pocket was proof enough that I had been in contact with French people.

As our train drew out of the Gare de l'Est I lit my pipe. In my pouch was the harsh, aromatic tobacco given me by Hélène Buvelot; suddenly, one of the guards asked me whether it was French or English tobacco.

"English," I bluffed, realising at once how easily the interrogation officer might have trapped me. Auguste took the pouch, sniffed appreciatively. Yes, English without doubt; the French was a very inferior weed, he vouchsafed.

We got on well together. Auguste told me that he, Stefan and Theodor had escorted Loder and Holborow to Frankfort-on-Main, the previous week. They referred to Godfrey as my comrade with the huge moustache, and to John as my comrade with the enormous shoulders. I had once seen Holborow force those shoulders through an aperture little more than six inches wide to escape from the turret of a Wellington that crashed and burned.

Always my guards apologised when they ate in front of me. I had no rations, having in my ignorance scorned to bring the loaf of rye bread, sour to the tongue, which had been given to me in the cell.

As we neared Frankfort the train filled, and a station-master, angrily puffed up in a resplendent uniform, tore to shreds the magical paper which, until now, in spite of many arguments had kept other travellers from our compartment.

"No German woman is going to stand in the corridor while an English swine has a compartment to himself," thundered the station-master, and I thought that an English station-master, in similar circumstances, might well have said the same sort of thing.

Soon I was wedged between Stefan and a very fat lady who listened interestedly, but without rancour, to the stories he told her of the carnage our bombs had caused in Paris. Airmen passing through the Cologne area were stoned and spat at, but, in these days of June, 1942, the middle-aged Germans in the compartment had not experienced bombing from the air, and they did not hate us. Schooled in hatred, the Hitler Youth boys in the corridor fingered their sheath knives as if they longed to skin me alive. I wondered if Auguste, Theodor and Stefan had once been in the Hitler Youth, with virginal legs projecting from tiny trousers—like sticks of celery.

Arriving at Frankfort my guards became officious, but I refused to go any further without eating, and led the way to the refreshment-room. Larry Gains, a Canadian sergeant-pilot, and an officer who was a navigator had just finished a grim railway journey from Greece, and were standing glumly near a barrier. They grinned when I waved, and set out to persuade their guards that if another prisoner was entitled to a meal so were they.

We sat at a long table, and Stefan brought bowls of soup. Opposite was a civilian who might easily have stepped from a Low cartoon. His hair was clipped short from the narrow ledge of forehead to the fat rolling over his collar. His head close to the plate, he blew noisily on his spoon, then sucked up the soup. Occasionally he looked up; his aqueous eyes glared through heavy lenses. When he finished his meal he sat grumbling to himself.

Until I saw my guards exchanging glances, like old maids unexpectedly overhearing a smutty story, I thought that I was the reason for his displeasure. Presently Stefan spoke to a man in a black uniform, and a moment later the grumbler, with the mien of a terrified pug, was fumbling for his identity card. His fingers, thick with panic, could not find his waistcoat pocket. The man in black waited silently.

Suddenly I was sorry for the man. I did not know what treason he had uttered, but I did not doubt that the same grumbles were heard in thousands of English pubs every night of the week.

We went to Dulag Luft by tram. A pretty girl next to me was reading Thackeray's *Vanity Fair*, and I wanted to ask her what she thought of it, but had not the courage. Larry Gains and his companion were on the same tram. When we alighted a feldwebel like a little grey penguin took charge of us. Auguste, Stefan and Theodor said good-bye, briefly, and walked away. Our strange companionship had ended; I was sad that, apparently, it had meant so little to them. The feldwebel motioned with his pistol, and we trudged up the hill.

2

THE cells at Dulag Luft engendered a sense of utter blankness, a feeling of being emptied. There were none of the traditional bugs to tame, not even nails in the door to count. There was a bed, and a table and chair. I was ordered to strip. My clothes were taken away to be searched, and I was given a Polish uniform that was rough on my skin, and clogs in which I could hardly walk.

I remembered having been warned of this camp when a bogus Red Cross officer gave me a questionnaire to fill in. When I refused he completed it himself, accurately, and did not carry out his threat to keep my parents in ignorance of my fate.

"These are members of your squadron recently shot down. The names with crosses after them are dead." He handed me a list. I knew them all but did not comment. Most of the names were marked with neat crosses, among them that of Jack Shearer. Ten of us had been together from the beginning of our Air Force training. Already three were dead and I was a prisoner. "Ten Little Navigators . . ." we once had sung.

"The others," said the German, "you will join in the main camp—when you have finished your solitary confinement. If you are reasonable it won't be long."

In turn I was visited by an officer wounded in Crete, who professed to be interested in "G", the first of the radar navigational aids, only because he wanted to fly as a civilian pilot after the war, and by the official interrogation officer, a very smooth gentleman whose expiscatory attack made one feel that one's reticence was perverse and stupid. "They know so much, they may as well be told the rest," was my reaction, and it was with some desperation that I stuck to the regulation reply: "I'm sorry. I can't answer any questions."

Solitary confinement would not end yet awhile, I thought, but I was wrong. There had been three "thousand-bomber" raids, and, while the casualty percentage was not high by Bomber Command standards, many more prisoners than the Germans were prepared for were arriving, on an average thirty or so from about two hundred and fifty airmen lost on this kind of raid, and the interrogation cells filled and were emptied rapidly.

The cooler, a large converted house, was just outside the camp into which, with half a dozen others, I was now led. There were no barred windows here. Long, low barracks were set in a barren compound with wire fences around it. I was behind the wire, and behind it, except when moving from one prison camp to another, I was to remain for almost three years.

After solitary confinement conversation was essential to rehabilitation, and this doubtless the Germans knew. Unable to locate the hidden microphones, we went outside to talk. Some of my new friends, shot down in Holland, had been imprisoned first in an old stone gaol in Amsterdam. One of them had been in a cell where some earlier occupant had carved deeply into the wall those lines of Lovelace's: "Stone walls do not a prison make, nor iron bars a cage." Beneath, a later inmate had graven with pungent irony: "Well, they are a bloody good imitation."

I was sketching Peter Buttigieg when Group Captain Massey limped up, and sat beside us. A veteran of World War I, he had been booked to lecture in U.S.A., and was getting experience of flying conditions over Germany when his aircraft was shot down. Rumour had it that he was found hiding with a sergeant air-gunner in a chicken house.

If this was true I am sure he lost not a shred of his commanding presence.

Peter Buttigieg was born in Malta, but brought up in Gibraltar. Unhappy at home, he ran away when he was fourteen, and joined the crew of a small ship, but, learning that his shipmates were smugglers, became frightened, and, off the Spanish coast, leaped into the sea and swam ashore. He walked for some days until he reached Gibraltar. A second time he ran away, and signed on in a yacht belonging to an eccentric Englishman, who, he believed, was later shot for espionage in Spain.

On this vessel he sailed round the Mediterranean area. In Oran he was arrested for murder when the finding of an unrecognisable body in the harbour coincided with the sudden disappearance of his employer, who, shortly afterwards, cabled from Lisbon. Later, when his mother was desperately in need of money, Peter himself became a smuggler. In Spain he was pressganged into Franco's army, but escaped.

At the outbreak of war he was in command of a target-towing boat off Gibraltar, but relinquished the job to sign on an oil tanker. Off the South American coast he helped to refuel the *Ajax*, *Exeter*, and *Achilles* for the *Graf Spee* battle. On the return journey a torpedo sliced off the bow of the ship, but the crew brought it safely into Gibraltar where it was destroyed by French bombs dropped as a reprisal for Dakar.

Buttigieg decided to go to England and signed on a Swedish ship bound for Liverpool. Off the Bristol Channel the freighter was blown up by a mine. For eleven hours he clung to some driftwood, was picked up and taken ashore where he promptly joined the R.A.F.

The rear-gunner in a Manchester set ablaze by a night-fighter, he stayed long enough at his guns to destroy the attacker before baling out at low altitude. He was still only twenty-three.

When there were seventy officers and N.C.O.s in the main camp we were marched to the station. Next to me in the train a Canadian navigator sat studying a tiny compass. His hands had once been badly burned; the skin was discoloured and taut over the bones. His battle-dress was stained a dirty yellow from dinghy-released fluorescence. Partially paralysed, he hunched in his corner, his long hair shot forward over a suddenly jutting brow. All his facial bones were sharp, especially the long jawbone. The mouth was belligerently drawn, and he wore a small moustache that did not quite belong. I asked him his name.

"Thomas Breech Miller," he answered in a powerful, almost harsh voice with a firm Canadian accent. "Call me T.B." His smile was quick, friendly.

Many months previously his aircraft had been shot down by an intruder over England, and crashed in flames. Of the crew of six only Miller was conscious; the rear-gunner was thrown clear. Though he could smell his own flesh burning, somehow Miller dragged one man from the blazing wreckage, went back, and back again, until he had rescued all four. He spent five months in hospital and was awarded the George Medal.

Discharged from hospital he had flown again to Germany. Homeward bound the Halifax was pounced on by a night-fighter and sent spinning from 11,000 feet into the North Sea. Miller, who had been helping the pilot fight the spin, found himself, paralysed, floating on his back. The rear-gunner, unhurt, clambered into the dinghy, released when the impact burst open the wing, and was able to pull Miller out of the water. Two days later they were picked up by a German E. Boat. Now, T.B. was sitting beside me planning to escape. He had recovered the use of his limbs, but his back had not yet become unstuck.

Bored, we organised parlour games like Twenty Questions. The man sitting immediately opposite me played with little zest, as if he found the occupation childish. Fresh-faced, but pale, with handsome features, a fine head, and smooth dark hair, Dick Vernon was, I decided, "a supercilious product of the English Public School system", but in spite of my arrogant verdict I found myself wanting to like him. In him I thought I sensed hostility.

Dick, son of a Southampton doctor, educated at Uppingham, had been shot down exactly a week before. His Lancaster, with mines in the bays, was raked by a flak ship and blew up, hurling him from his turret to the Baltic 800 feet below. For an hour he tried to climb on to a floating wheel, but it flopped over on to him each time he grasped it. He tried to drown himself, but his flying suit, ballooning, kept him afloat, and a German launch, searching for survivors from another aircraft, found him. The two pilots were rescued from the wreckage of the machine; the other four members of the crew were dead.

Dick became aware of the man beside him, a chunky little Canadian with slightly bowed legs and an infectious chuckle. Cyril H. Tobias was 26, six years older than Dick. He came from Morden, Manitoba, where his father kept the store, and where, he said, all windows were closed against dust if ever a car passed through. Until the war he had been reading for a degree in Agricultural Science, playing a saxophone in a dance band to pay his way. There was something basically honest in Toby which appealed to Dick.

Toby joined in the quiz with hilarious guesses which he ridiculed the next moment, for he was never happy unless he could laugh at himself. But, underlying the humour was frustration. Nineteen times he had captained a Hampden over Germany. Then, transferred to Manchesters, he had been sent as a second pilot to gain experience, a wasteful move for he needed not operational but flying experience on the new type of machine.

On the way to the target the aircraft was shot down. "I just sat on my backside and twiddled my thumbs all the way," he complained. "If I'd only retracted the undercart it would have been something. As it was I was utterly futile."

Although he laughed about it, his uselessness on that ill-fated trip was something he never forgot; it coloured the whole of his prisoner-of-war life, and indeed the frustration of it and of the subsequent wasted years is with him to this day.

We arrived at Sagan in the evening of the following day. Dulag Luft was small, and in a way intimate. Stalag Luft 3, which we could see as we straggled down the road from the station, had a forbidding bleakness. Long wooden huts huddled together in tidy rows. The wind whipped the sand around the spindly legs on which the barracks perched, scuffled it through the wire, beneath the ugly, squat sentry-boxes, across the sandy, stump-punctuated wasteland sur-rounding the camp, into the frigid pine trees that loomed beyond.

Passing through the main gate, we marched into the Vorlager where the German administrative offices, the sick-bay, the cooler, the Red Cross stores, and the shower hut and delouser were situated. From this outside compound gates led into the two prison lagers, one for officers and one for N.C.O.s, which were separated by a wooden fence. A third lager, abutting the N.C.O.s' compound, contained the German quarters. Russian prisoners had their own pen in a corner of the Vorlager.

It was dusk and we could not recognise friends in the crowds lining the warning wire of the inner compounds, but I heard my name called and recognised Godfrey's voice.

We were locked in a reception hut in the Vorlager for the night as there was not time to search and sort us before it was dark. Guards patrolled outside. A party of prisoners from the N.C.O.s' compound, also under guard, brought cans of tea. They were on short rations, and this brew for the new "kriegies" was a sacrifice. Godfrey had wangled his way into the tea-party, his new, blond beard giving him the mien of a Viking.

"What's on, fancy dress ball?" I asked him.

He laughed. "Boy, it's good to see you. I wrote home and said I was the only survivor. Where are the others?"

"They've had it."

"I thought maybe you'd got home after all."

He really meant it; his imagination had prevailed over what he had actually seen. After cutting him free from his parachute, which had hooked on to a gargoyle on the town hall somewhere, the Germans had taken him to the wreckage of the aircraft; he had seen the bodies of the other three, though they were not recognisable, and he had picked up my navigation log which he was able, subsequently, to destroy. He had given the names of the three killed, and mine also, assuring the Germans that there was a fourth body somewhere in the wreck. Yet he had been able to persuade himself that we "might have got home after all".

Next morning we were searched. Fountain-pens and cigarette-lighters were forbidden, and my pen was forfeit. I was given a numbered ticket as if I had handed in an article to a railway cloakroom. My battle-dress was confiscated, the Germans declaring that the Australian blue made it easy to transform the uniform into civilian clothing. Loder's, too, had been taken from him. In the prisoners' clothing store I was given a new, but ill-fitting R.A.F. uniform. Disgruntled, I joined the waiting N.C.O.s' party. Some of the men were asking a German feldwebel questions. How often could they write home? When would their parents know that they were safe? The German held up his hand. "Any questions you have will be answered by Sergeant Deans. Now march."

Who was Sergeant Deans, I wondered, and why had the German spoken with that inflexion of respect?

We were near the gate, now. The sentry was swinging it open. Beyond stood hundreds of prisoners, eager to greet the newcomers. We passed into the throng. I saw only a confusion of bearded faces, shaven heads, queer, home-made hats, and sunburnt shoulders. Shouts and roars of laughter greeted men who were recognised by old inhabitants.

Someone, Jack Stephenson from my squadron, shouted my name, but I could not see him. The thick dust got in my nostrils. I shouldered my way through the crowd. Behind me I heard the gate thud, heard the wild interrogation, the cynical laughter. I felt a little sick. Suddenly a cigarette was pressed into my hand. Automatically I stopped while the donor lit it. I caught his arm. "How long have you been down?"

"Over two years." He disappeared into the crowd.

CHAPTER

3

WHAT had Churchill said in his last speech? Had we seen preparations for the invasion of the Continent? Was it true that convoy losses were crippling, that we were retreating in Africa? We did not know. And the old prisoners who poured into Block 40, offering cigarettes with their questions, knew that we did not know.

We had been too absorbed in the business of survival, had thought little of a future beyond tomorrow's dawn, and the report of twelve aircraft lost at Mannheim, or seventeen at Hamburg had had more significance for us than the more momentous of war announcements.

How long did we give the war? For the first time we thought about it, but the answer came pat. Twelve months. The old kriegies smiled agreement. And we put it at twelve months, old prisoners and new, because twelve months of imprisonment was as much as any man could bear to contemplate. Years already spent in captivity could be written off, but no one was prepared to write off more than twelve months of his future.

The old kriegies did not want to know how we were shot down, but they listened, knowing that we were still shocked, and incredulous of our own experiences, and hoping that they might hear a familiar name mentioned, an old haunt recalled.

Dixie Deans subscribed to the general view that the war would not last longer than twelve months. At the same time he recognised it as a delusion, as a creed in which, for sanity's sake it was necessary to have faith. His job demanded realism, and he proved that he had realism when he made a calendar which covered a period of from September 1940 to May 1945.

On September 10th, 1940, Deans had captained a Whitley, one of six aircraft to attack Berlin. It was his twenty-fifth operation and it was only because of his experience that he had been asked to fly that night, for he was a tired man. He had flown over Germany only a few hours earlier, and, to enable him to snatch a little sleep, another pilot had tested his aircraft. When he took off for Berlin he hated the idea of the ordeal ahead. Yet there was nothing he could have done to prevent the flak from crippling his machine. Hit over Berlin the aircraft lolloped to the Dutch border before the crew were compelled to abandon her.

Now he was Camp Leader of the N.C.O.s' compound at Stalag Luft 3, and already his name was well known in prison camps throughout Germany; his reputation stood high in Geneva, and in the Air Ministry. When we new prisoners were called in turn to his office, and I came face to face with him for the first time, I learned the reason for the respectful tone of the feldwebel when he had spoken of Sergeant Deans.

The straight, nuggety figure of James A. G. Deans, born in Glasgow on January 25th, 1914, one felt contained a tremendous power, his vigorously sculpted face nobility. The work of camp administration and external relations allowed him little respite, yet any man could take to him a personal trouble, and know that when he came away at least some of the burden was transferred to the sturdy shoulders of the camp leader. At such times he smiled, a crooked little smile that held a wealth of understanding. When he laughed, which perhaps was not often, he did so with gusto, his great voice booming. In the presence of fools, of men who had let down their comrades, of German officers who mouthed empty promises, his expression became harsh and his voice rough with anger.

Sometimes he was spoken of as "the king", or "the Führer", but mostly, and inevitably, it was "Dixie". In the officers' compound there was the service hierarchy, and between the pilot officer and the group captain was a gap which even common hardship could not bridge altogether. The Senior British Officer, to whom Deans was responsible in so far as insularity permitted, was in fact the highest ranking officer, and Group Captain Massey now took over from Wing Commander Day.

But Deans was an elected leader, and he kept order by the sheer weight of his personality. There were men his senior in rank, but they, like everyone else, were loyal beyond belief. In the prison community there was the constant suspicion of men with any kind of privilege; always the scandalmonger was there to whisper accusations, to cry "Rackets". The obvious man to decry was the camp leader, but in three years I never heard a murmur against his benevolent despotism.

When I stood at his table he regarded me steadily, and I felt that in those few silent moments he isolated my every virtue, laid bare my every weakness, and gently pushed aside my every pretence; revealing nothing of himself save his strength.

To each man's story he listened patiently and carefully. Hundreds of men, each believing that his was a unique experience, had told him their stories. They were all variations on a theme, but Deans never betrayed any lack of interest.

Most men, realising the magnitude of his task, recounted their experiences without too much emphasis on irrelevant if exciting details, and in this they were helped by Deans himself, for he had a way of drawing out the salient. His was a threefold interest. Firstly he had to determine whether the story was genuine; there was always the possibility of the Germans introducing an impostor. Then he wanted the sort of information which would be of value to the authorities at home, and he possessed the means of spiriting such information back to England. Finally he wanted clues to the fate of men listed as missing, not only those had recently failed to return from operations, but also those whose names appeared on inquiry lists sent from Geneva.

When the interview was done he explained that we could make allotments from our pay if we wished, and his office assistants made the necessary arrangements.

"I do appreciate your allotment," wrote a new prisoner's fiancée, some time later. "Please increase it as the chap I go with is only a private on 5s. 6d."

The business of learning to live this hyper-gregarious existence was not easy. You talked, ate, slept, and walked with the same men, even sat beside them in the latrine. You looked back on the days of solitary confinement almost with longing. There were times when the impossibility of being alone, even for a few minutes, drove you almost to madness.

Some, in time, developed a kind of inward solitude, enviable, yet dangerous, for the mind involuted was likely to become hazed in a miasma of self-sympathy. The melancholic was pitiful but he was a burden, and sometimes a menace.

In Hut 40 cameraderie grew slowly, but with great certainty, as coral is built; men drew upon qualities which were innate but never before needed to the same degree, and the tiny skeletons of ephemeral kindnesses created a structure of unyielding tolerance.

Initially we had formed ourselves into groups or "combines" of ten who pooled rations and shared chores, but dissension and differing tastes soon led to smaller groups. Combines of two, three, or four worked best, and the combine system was perhaps the most important factor in camp life. The combine was the substitute for the family unit. A few men, however, chose to be lone wolves, but, paradoxically, were known as "one-man combines".

Dick, Toby, Ken Gaulton and Johnny Farquhar decided to work together, Haworth, Johnson and Welsh to form a second unit. That left T. B. Miller, Peter Buttigieg and myself to work things out. I was disappointed at being left out; my compatriot, Gaulton, and the puckish Toby both appealed as partners and Dick had become strangely important in my life. Peter, already working on plans to escape, elected to be a lone wolf, so the lovable T.B. and I joined forces.

T.B. was an extraordinary figure, his one garment being a winter singlet from the armholes of which protruded thin, vein-corded legs. The neck was sewn up, and the bulk of the garment was rolled down over his middle and tied with a piece of string. He walked barefooted, head prognathically forward, shoulders hunched, hair flopping over his eyes; always he carried a tin into which he put cigarette-ends scooped up from the sand. He had no false pride, but when I went scavenging with him invariably I glanced to see if anyone was watching before stooping to pick up a butt. The garnerings we smoked, in turn, in my pipe.

Smoking on *appell* was a crime, and those who transgressed were detected almost unfailingly by "Smoky Joe", a lean, hoop-shouldered German whose face was immobile save for the twitch of his Hitler moustache as he tautened his spiky nose to catch the aroma of tobacco. T.B. was an easy catch.

Summarily sentenced to a week's solitary confinement with its concomitant of bread-and-water diet, he was given half an hour to report to the main gate. Mindful of his slogan: "Every little bit of nutriment counts," I prepared him a meal, using most of the week's rations, and he was still eating when the guards, tired of waiting for him, came and collected him.

Escape was in many minds, but it seemed impossible. Designed to hold air-crew prisoners, Stalag Luft 3 was a new and reputedly unbreakable camp which even the old kriegies were still summing up. The only escape attempt had been in the early days of its occupation when a party of prisoners in charge of a "guard" marched out of the camp—to the astonishment of "Nobby" Hall an acquaintance, who was just coming through the gate after travelling from another camp—but were detected when the "guard" misunderstood a facetious remark shouted after them by a German N.C.O. and gave the wrong answer.

But it was not long before Peter Buttigieg found his way into the presence of the Escape Committee, who sanctioned his modest plan but could not assist his preparations. These were crude. If he succeeded in getting out of the camp he intended to masquerade as a Spaniard, relying on his fluency in the Spanish tongue and some letters, purporting to be from relatives in Spain, to support his story. The letters, which he drafted himself, were mainly long recitals of family woes. They were naïve, as Peter himself was naïve, but they had an authenticity no other prisoner in the camp could have matched.

One morning, Peter said a quick good-bye to a few friends. When the bread van went out of the compound he was clinging, face upwards, under the chassis. At the gate the guard looked perfunctorily under the van, but did not see him, and, in the same way, Peter might have got through the main gate. Unexpectedly, however, the van drove into the officers' compound adjacent, and stayed there for twenty minutes. In all the weeks Peter had watched, it had never done that.

Refusing to be beaten, he held on as he had held to that piece of driftwood in the Bristol Channel, and probably with equal incentive. But he must have weakened a little; his body sagged, and the guard at the officers' gate discovered him as the van drove out.

Not unnaturally, it was supposed that he was an officer, and he did not deny it. Bewildered German counters found the officers' numbers correct, and the officers, guessing the truth, quite enjoyed the extra roll-calls for which they had to turn out.

Peter was still grinning when he came out of the cooler fourteen days later. That same day he began his tunnel.

RED CROSS parcels, intended only to supplement prison fare, were all-important. The German bread was compounded of rye and sawdust, the potatoes were bad, and the daily issue of vegetable or grain did not go far. The morale of the camp fluctuated according to the number of parcels in store, and the rumours which travelled quickest, and occurred most frequently, concerned trucks of parcels alleged to be arriving.

In our first three months at Sagan the issue was half a parcel per man. It did not seem much, but without it life would have been grim. Few of us realised then the magnitude of the work the International Red Cross had undertaken, or how much we owed to its delegates, Dr. Marcel Junod and Mlle Odier who had persuaded the warring navies to allow the safe passage of ships carrying the Red Cross flag, in spite of the problems involved in arranging the penetration of blockades and the circumventing of minefields.

When the Red Cross food began to come in sufficient quantities to enable a fairly regular issue of a parcel per week belts were slipped back a notch, and kriegies got off their bunks and began to take an interest in the various activities of the camp. There were some chronic "pitbashers", defeatists who dozed in their bunks throughout the day, but most people wanted more from life than that, even from prison life.

Two more parties arrived from Dulag Luft, and the camp was declared full—many months before it had been anticipated. From this time most new prisoners went to Stalag 8B at Lamsdorff from which camp, only a short time previously, R.A.F. prisoners had been transferred, together with those at Stalag Luft 1, Barth, near Stettin, to Sagan.

We were at the gate with the others when the new men arrived, and joined in the jeering, questioning chorus. It was kriegy tradition, and no man upholds tradition with more fervour than he who is newly acquainted with it.

Doug. Hurditch, when I called his name, looked surprised and did not see me at first. Despite the ordeal of the past weeks, Hurditch looked debonair, as he always did.

Over the North Sea his Wellington had been attacked by a night-fighter, and the rudder shot away. Until the second attack he was managing without, but when he lost the port motor he was helpless. Every member of the crew except himself was wounded. The machine was losing height, and swinging towards the coast. Beneath them stretched tide-deserted sand and the shallows of the retreating sea. Hurditch gave the order to bale out, and "Bluey" Maher, the wireless operator, jumped. Immediately afterwards, unable to maintain a safe height, Hurditch rescinded the order and decided to try a belly landing. A superb pilot, he nursed the machine through the darkness and gently on to the beach. As soon as his crew were a safe distance from the aircraft he fired a Verey pistol into the petrol tank.

There was no question of his attempting escape; he had wounded men to look after. Colin Campbell, the rear-gunner, dreadfully injured by cannon fire, was carried by Hurditch, assisted by his walking wounded, to a Dutch farm-house where a girl, still in her teens, took them into her most capable hands and gave what aid she could.

Her father went for the Germans, and the wounded were taken to hospital. Campbell's legs were amputated, but, to the great grief of Godfrey Loder who had shared a room with him on the squadron, and in training days before that, he died a few weeks later. The others, after perfunctory treatment, went to Dulag Luft, and on to Sagan, with Hurditch.

The last had not been heard of Bluey Maher whom they had thought too badly injured to fight his way through the shallows. With both legs almost severed at the ankles, with shrapnel wounds in the arm, chest and head, wiry little redhead that he was, he had swum and crawled a quarter of a mile to the beach. German doctors wanted to amputate both legs but he would not allow it, and, shrugging their shoulders, they left him to take the consequences. In time, with the aid of spring straps, he was able to walk without crutches.

I was eager for news of the squadron, but what Hurditch had to tell was tragic. Ten aircraft had been lost in just over a week, half the squadron wiped out. Among the missing was Hugh Brodie, another of the ten of us who had been together for so long. "Ten little navigators . . ." Again I remembered the half-humorous, half-rueful parody we had composed in the classroom at O.T.U. Somehow I knew that the brilliant, sensitive Brodie, until the war senior history master at Melbourne Boys' High School, would not be seen again. Strangely, four of the ten were old boys of that school.

Hugh had never doubted that he would die over Germany. In his kit they found a poem, and with it a letter, addressed to the boys he had taught, in which he asked that any injustices he had committed be forgiven, any shortcomings on his part be overlooked.

The poem, which he showed to me a few days before I was shot down, moved me deeply. "An Airman's Prayer"—his prayer—was not that he might be spared death, but:

> Almighty and all-present Power,
> Short is the prayer I make to Thee;
> I do not ask in battle hour
> For any shield to cover me.

The vast, unalterable way,
From which the stars do not depart,
May not be turned aside to stay
The bullet flying to my heart.

I ask no help to strike my foe;
I seek no petty victory here—
The enemy I hate I know
To Thee is also dear.

But this I pray, be at my side
When death is drawing through the sky.
Almighty God, who also died,
Show me the way that I should die.

Periodically the Germans decided that the camp was not quite full; there was room for two more in each hut, they would say. Sometimes N.C.O.s' commissions came through and they were transferred to the officers' compound, others, troublesome to the Germans, were moved to strafe camps, a few, losing their reason, went to mental hospitals.

There were amongst us numerous Polish, French, Belgian and Dutch airmen, some of whom had disappeared from their homes in occupied countries, or escaped from concentration camps, making their way to England to fly with the R.A.F., and they were apt to be marched away in the early mornings, to be taken to Berlin dungeons. Somewhere the wheels of German Intelligence had turned and a P.O.W. record was linked with a report of a young Belgian or Frenchman who had got out from under the German boot. The young man having tumbled back into German territory from an English aeroplane, the Germans were anxious to know what to enter on the blank page of his dossier.

In divers ways, therefore, vacancies occurred and new prisoners did trickle in. With the advent of Flight Sergeant

A. F. P. James the camp, to its astonishment, was bludgeoned from its summer somnolence.

A Spitfire pilot, "Jimmy" James was a brisk, cocky little man with a back as straight as the edge of a door. His face was narrow, with cleanly moulded features, burn-scarred, but not badly, in expression cold and shrewd. His hair was crisp and cut short. An Australian serving in the R.A.F. he had enjoyed a varied career. He claimed to have fought in China and in Spain, to have purchased aeroplanes for China in Russia. He had been for a time in the permanent Royal Australian Air Force. Because he was an outrageous egotist he was dismissed by many as a "line-shooter". Yet I do not think that he was ever tripped up, and personally I was never disposed to doubt the veracity of his brilliantly told stories.

Not surprisingly, he did not enjoy—nor did he court—popularity; he even fostered the story that he had been shot down by another Spitfire pilot. The latest James aphorism went round the camp twice as fast as rumour. He usually had his way. On one occasion, when we were locked in the barracks for some misdemeanour, James coolly walked through the cordon of guards.

"Put that gun down, my man," he snapped at the feldwebel who had a pistol levelled at his chest. The German flushed, and his finger tensed.

"James has had it this time," someone remarked with no great sorrow. But the slim little man berated the feldwebel to such purpose that a moment later he was being bowed through the gate on his way to lodge a complaint.

For six months Godfrey and I had been trying to get back our battle-dresses. We happened to mention it to James. "You shall have them back, this afternoon," he promised, and so we did.

His undoubted influence with his captors was resented by some, and there was even a threatening demonstration against him. For this there was no justification whatever, and the explanation was probably the one most commonly suggested, that he had served in Spain with one of the German officers.

He carried his fine intellect, his incredible memory and devastating repartee into the camp Debating Society which, despite a high standard of oratory, attracted little support. The protagonists were mostly university men enjoying the cut and thrust of argument in a quiet, almost monastic way.

The ebullient James changed all that. His was not the only strong personality, and there were some fierce clashes, notably with Peter Thomas, an Oxford law student prominent in all the intellectual pursuits of the camp. As accounts of the first battle were bruited about the camp, interest flared, and the following week the newly-built theatre, the "Stalag Stage", bulged. From that day it was necessary to queue for the Debating Society meetings, though James, who had breathed fire, if not life, into the Society was repatriated within a few months of his arrival.

The camp theatre was an imaginative work. An ordinary hut, set aside for use as chapel and theatre, was transformed by hard work and ingenuity. Tons of earth were excavated so that the floor could be stepped, a stage was constructed, comfortable seats were built from Red Cross crates, and "Mad John" Murrell painted some fine murals.

The Germans were helpful, though at times enforcing cessation of work as a reprisal for some camp offence. They usually were co-operative when they saw a chance of diverting energies into harmless channels. Their attitude was made plain by their reaction to escapes or attempts to escape. The theatre would be shut, the library closed, sports equipment confiscated. Such reprisals were punitive, but they were also an indication that, in the German mind, the recreational facilities of the camp had failed in their purpose, although they had never created but only countenanced those facilities.

Banning, confiscating, prohibiting, restricting, all coming

under the heading of reprisals, were frequent. We paid in mass for the transgressions of the few, but the penalty was not always unjust, for those who had not sinned in most cases condoned and applauded. Not always unjust, but there were times when the trouble was not of the prisoners' making.

Some of the Poles were resourceful model-makers, and one barrack housed a collection of beautifully worked scale model aircraft, replicas of contemporary British and German types. These were suspended in flying positions from the ceiling. German searchers ripped them down and trampled upon them.

The editor of the *Daily Recco*, the camp wall-newspaper, wrote a bitterly ironical article on the theme of German's vaunted culture which "Slim", a pallid, slight German, who had lived for too long in England not to appreciate the satire, chanced to read. He ran to fetch the Commandant, leaving the paper on the wall. Evidently the Commandant was to see it for himself. But that old gentleman was unlikely to emulate Slim's undignified run, and the editor, Dennis "Streak" Adams, a Sydney journalist, worked fast.

When Slim returned with the Commandant the whole paper had been done again, all by hand, and an innocuous leader replaced the original provocative one. After the first moments of discomfiture Slim did convince the Commandant that he had not imagined the insult and the paper was banned. But the Commandant may have had doubts, or perhaps he felt, for he was a fair-minded man, that the article had been justified, for the ban was soon lifted.

Delaying the mail as a reprisal was first used on orders from the High Command. Letters to and from German prisoners in Australia were not reaching their destinations, and, until this was remedied, no letters would be allowed us. This sounded grim, but the camp postmen went out as usual to drink tea—which they supplied—with their censor friends, and returned to the compound with uncensored letters, some but five or six days old.

Whether more U Boats were sunk so that fewer of our mail-carrying ships went down, or whether Australian bumble-dom really had been dilatory and had been prodded into action by the reprisals against us, it is impossible to say, but the High Command announced that the position had improved and ordinary mail service was resumed. The letters I valued most through the next months were those from my fiancée which had escaped the censor.

During the mail ban the *Daily Recco* had to discontinue its popular column of extracts from letters, mostly humorous though the humour was often adventitious. For example a mother attempted to enclose English clothing coupons in a letter to her son. They had been removed by the censors in England, but the letter explained that they had been intended for the purchase of slippers in a German store, none having been obtainable in the local shops.

But tragedy came in the mails, too, and one wondered why men were willing, even anonymously, to divulge things that must have hurt. Often the letters themselves were posted up, and perhaps it was a saner course to ridicule one's misfortune than to nourish it in self-pity.

Letters from fiancées, even from wives grown tired of waiting, were made public, and how hackneyed became the phrase: "I know you will forgive me." Such letters were known as "Mespots". The term had enjoyed pre-war currency in the R.A.F., men isolated in Mesopotamia having been jilted in such numbers that a "Mesopotamian letter" came to have a special connotation. The inevitable contraction stuck.

CHAPTER
5

PETER BUTTIGIEG'S tunnel was detected in a little over a
week, when it was nearly under the wire. He had
chosen to tunnel from one of the latrines, thirty feet
from the German compound, which meant that he would
still have to find a way out of the German hutments.
Naked, he lowered himself into the cesspit, where, standing
waist deep, he chiselled his way through the two-foot-thick
brick wall, a task made more difficult because of the
proximity of a sentry-box.

Once through the brick, he hacked into the soil, burrowing
tirelessly, each day lengthening his dank little hole into which
seeped the horrible gases of the cesspit. When the probe of a
ferret found the burrow Peter was just preparing to go down,
and was able to get away without losing any of his equipment, inadequate as it was.

The ferrets, or moles, belonged to the Abwehr, the
Security Section. Shrewd men and dangerous, though not
always unamiable, they carried out their work all too
effectively, their chief ally the careless or indiscreet prisoner.
Constantly they prowled the compound, even crouched
under hut floors, or, at night, near the windows, listening,
always listening.

When a ferret entered a barrack the first person to see him
cried a warning. Sometimes it was "Ferrets up!" but
"Moles up!" carried much better. For a time "Huns up"
was a popular cry, but to this the Germans took exception,
and anyone who used it found himself in the cooler. One
man escaped the cooler by giving his name and number as

Whitehall 1212. A few of the administrative Germans frequently visited the barracks to drink tea with prisoner acquaintances. They were mostly harmless, but no German was cultivated unless it was, in some way, of advantage to ourselves.

The senior feldwebel, Popeye—because of a stonily protruding glass eye—was well liked. He was often in the block leader's small room where John Valentine and his three Dutch room-mates plied him with tea or cocoa, and allowed him to pollute their air with his evil-smelling cheroots. All four spoke German, and through them I obtained Indian ink for my drawing.

Ink was forbidden, and if found was confiscated, yet, once a drawing was done it could be pinned on the wall with impunity. A German officer asked if he might see my sketchbook in which were many pen-and-ink drawings and cartoons. Probably he had heard of the book from Popeye. He looked through it, seeming genuinely amused, and asked if he might borrow it to show his brother officers. I was surprised when the book came back, surprised, too, when he said that the cartoons had been enjoyed in the officers' mess; one would have thought kriegy humour would evoke little response in the German.

Popeye, until the war, had been the proprietor of a second-hand furniture business. Broadly built, stolid as a piece of his own stock, he was, I believe, an honest man and a kind one. The "Moles up" call did not distinguish between the genuine ferrets and the administrative staff, and Popeye was always a little annoyed when he was heralded in this way. "Please. Please," he begged at last, "for me not 'Moles up,' but '*Achtung, Deutsch feldwebel* approaches'."

Even Popeye's visits were sometimes embarrassing for the "canary" had begun to sing. The "canary" was the code name for the radio. The original "canary" which had nested in a piano accordion had been discovered, and was now an object of curiosity in a German museum. Another receiving set had been built, the job taking several months, by John Bristow, the wireless operator of a Blenheim shot down in 1941. The hiding-place was changed frequently. Sometimes the set was housed in a gramophone, sometimes in a model ship or aeroplane, once even in a jam tin which had a false tray containing jam in the top. Collaborating with Bristow was Harry Young, a B.B.C. engineer, who worked out the technical details.

Until now we had had only German news, and we had not learned the scale of reductions which the old kriegies applied to enemy claims. It was not a good time to be subjected to German propaganda. Rommel had our troops on the run in North Africa, the Germans were investing Stalingrad, and, in the Far East, the Japs were cock-a-hoop. Each day a German radio bulletin was posted in the barracks, each day German newspapers and magazines poured into the camp. Weekly *The Camp* was issued. Printed in Berlin and distributed to prison camps throughout Germany, this newspaper, some of whose staff and most of whose contributors were British prisoners of war, was an insidious form of propaganda. Alongside the harmless outpourings of verse and "News from the camps" was a column, written by a German commentator, which was undiluted poison. A friendly column, its theme was the tragedy of natural friends like Germany and Britain fighting each other.

Subtly this man worked to lower morale in the camps, for the despondent prisoner is always easier to manage. Doubtless contributors to *The Camp* had no thought of assisting the enemy; in fact, that was what they were doing. Dixie Deans asked that no one in the camp should forward material, and no one did.

Countering the intromission of German propaganda, the acquisition of a new canary had a tremendous effect on morale. The news was taken down in shorthand and transcribed, and readers visited the barracks. If a German was in the vicinity the reader would miss the barrack; so it was that Popeye's visits were inconvenient at times. Any eagerness to send him away might have evoked suspicion.

Obtaining parts for the radio was a vexing problem. Bristow needed a coil, and the opportunity to get one suddenly presented itself. The German corporal who supervised the cookhouse had a portable telephone which he could plug into a wall socket. One day he forgot to take the instrument with him when he left the cookhouse, and Bristow got his coil.

The Commandant threatened immediate reprisals if the coil was not returned. Deans promised an urgent investigation, but subsequently reported failure. There was some suggestion, he told Von Lindeiner, that the coil might have been spirited into the officers' compound, and his proposal that he should be allowed to consult senior officers to see if they could assist was warmly approved.

It chanced that, immediately after the crime, Wing Commander Harry Day, whose record was already thick with black marks, had led a contingent of officers and N.C.O.s to a new camp at Schubin, and Deans and the officers agreed that he should be blamed. The quick-witted Day could be relied on to produce something.

When Group Captains Massey and McDonald, their interpreter, Flying Officer Murray, and Deans met the Commandant at their routine weekly conference Von Lindeiner accepted the verdict of the "Court of Inquiry", and was not surprised to learn that the culprit was the intransigent Day. He would write to his opposite number at Schubin, and request him to recover the stolen coil.

In the middle of the next conference an orderly stamped in, saluted theatrically, and laid a small parcel on the table. It was from Schubin. "Wings" Day had guessed at once what had happened, and had handed a broken condenser to the Schubin Commandant. Von Lindeiner did not know the difference, or, perhaps, having saved his face, he did not care, and pronounced that he was pleased with the way in which the unfortunate business had been cleared up. Group Captain Massey and Dixie Deans were smiling, but rotund Group Captain McDonald guffawed, almost too heartily.

Following the Dieppe raid, of which the canary first gave us news, a German officer read to us, at roll-call, a brief report of an attempted "invasion" by Allied forces who had discovered for themselves the impregnability of the "Atlantic Wall". Even in those days of 1942 we half expected the invasion, especially as we knew of Russia's growing impatience for a second front.

A consequence of the raid was the manacling of R.A.F. prisoners at Stalag 8B, the Germans alleging that some of their soldiers, taken prisoner and shackled by the raiders, had later been jettisoned from the boats. Their bodies were washed ashore, the hands still tied. Because the R.A.F. were non-working prisoners the reprisals were directed against them. Von Lindeiner was said to have rejected the order to manacle prisoners under his command, but at Lamsdorff the men had their hands tied for many months.

Three Canadian soldiers, captured at Dieppe, came into Block 40. Anti-aircraft gunners, they were bewildered to find themselves in an Air Force camp. German anti-aircraft personnel came under Luftwaffe command, and a German officer had assumed that the English had a similar system.

In the belief that soldiers would be better informed than airmen of the planned strategy of the war, prisoners from all over the compound came to interrogate the three. All amiable stoutness, "Tubby" Underwood said firmly and disappointingly that there would be no invasion for a long time, and himself settled down to learn the mouth-organ.

We had to believe him; Dieppe had been at best an experiment, not a very successful one, it seemed. We began to realise the futility of merely passing time; we must make use of it.

In the camp were men of diverse talents, of a variety of callings, from all segments of the globe, and groups of men had seen the opportunity which was theirs. Students could learn languages, take London University Matriculation examinations, even the Intermediate examinations for some degrees. Institutes of secretaries, accountants, bankers, sent syllabuses, arranged examinations. All this needed co-ordination, and Eddie Alderton, dark, vital, former Manchester University man, assembled a staff, arranged time-tables—a heart-breaking job because of classroom space limitations—supervised the issue of books and materials received through the Red Cross, and, in time, was the head of what became a remarkable university.

In the autumn of 1942 a batch of several hundred prisoners was transferred to Stalag Luft 1 at Barth. The men were mostly volunteers, and among them were T. B. Miller and Peter Buttigieg. Some had been at Barth before moving to Sagan, and preferred the old camp, others wanted a change of scenery, and there was a core of would-be escapers who hoped for an opportunity to get away during the journey, or that Barth might be an easier camp to crack.

T.B.'s going was a blow to me, and I was tempted to go, too. But there were strong rumours that the officers were to be moved, the two compounds merged, and the vacant huts filled by the R.A.F. N.C.O.s at present held at Lamsdorff. I was hoping that Bill Nettle, my squadron room-mate, might be among them, for that he was missing I knew— another of the ten, of whom, now only two remained. But Bill was dead, and, in any case, ultimately the Germans reversed their rumoured plans, moved us away, and made Stalag Luft 3 a camp for officers.

The Barth party straggled out of the camp; their possessions were in kitbags on their shoulders, in oddly-shaped, precariously-tied bundles, and in Red Cross boxes fastened to their belts or dangling like shopping parcels from their fingers. I caught a last glimpse of T.B., his gaunt body

43

hunched under his pack. Beside him was wistfully smiling Peter Buttigieg. They went through the gate together.

I was without a combine partner, but, a week later, Johnny Farquhar withdrew from the four-man combine and I was asked to replace him. Then Ken Gaulton transferred to Hut 56 where most of the Australians lived, leaving Dick, Toby and me together. I moved into the top bunk which first T.B. and then Ken had occupied, next to Dick with whom my friendship had been developing steadily, the earlier antipathy dissolved.

Prison friendship is not easy to analyse or to explain. It has an intensity possible only where men are thrown together in such a way that they cannot avoid each other, cannot choose when they will meet, when separate. Even the husband-wife relationship is not so taut, is less absorbing, less demanding.

You could have friends in other barracks, it is true, and these relationship were more everyday, but at the same time you had to live with a group of men. It was not possible to be in propinquity with all of them, but it was almost essential to have someone to whom you could come with your ego naked, someone in tune with your every mood, who knew every crevice of your mind. Such a one shared with you your hours of melancholy, nursed you in illness, and accepted, without complaint, the spite you felt in your heart for the other fellows, but which, to preserve the peace, you vented upon him.

Some men never achieved this bitter-sweet comradeship, and their lives were the more difficult for lacking it. Mostly only two men were involved, but at times three, or even four, achieved a near-perfect understanding. We were three, but Dick was the pivot. Toby and I, staunch friends even today, were never quite so close as each of us was to Dick.

CHAPTER
6

THE first U.S.A.A.F. prisoners arrived. Their immense kitbags were stocked with three or four uniforms, a range of footwear, a variety of headgear—including baseball caps—shirts innumerable, even handsomely framed photographs of "the girl back home".

Had they baled out with their kitbags under their arms? Or piled them into a dinghy in the North Sea? The Americans took the R.A.F. cracks good-humouredly. The explanation was simple. On a flight from America, carrying neither navigator nor radio, but relying on the master plane of the formation, in cloud they had lost the formation. With no idea of their position, they had flown "by guess and by God", and God had left them to guess. They had missed England altogether, and crash-landed in Holland.

Within weeks I felt sorry for these two American boys, for now their countrymen, shot down in some of the bloodiest air battles of the war, were arriving in ever-increasing numbers, and, as always, the inexperienced, the uninitiated, did not quite belong. The two had only their sorry little story of a mundane blunder to set alongside dramatic accounts of fierce aerial combat, and the unsympathetic guffaws of their compatriots must have been harder to bear than the mirth of the R.A.F. which, if as loud, had a somewhat more refined quality.

The Americans told their stories well, uninhibited by the tradition of understatement for which the R.A.F. was noted —in itself a subtle form of boasting, no less effectual for being not brazen—and with a wealth of detail which promptly provoked accusations of "line shooting" from British prisoners.

But this was a new kind of air war which we had yet to understand. Heavily armed Fortresses and Liberators, sacrificing bomb load for armour, and flying in formation, did exact a terrible toll of enemy fighters. But many of their own squadrons were decimated. The Americans were inordinately brave, but it was not until the introduction of long-range fighter escorts that the slaughter was reduced to the point where achievement was measurable and—later— immeasurable.

In Block 40, where there were now nationals of twenty-three different countries, the Americans were well represented. One, Don Bevan, was a New York *Daily News* staff artist. Aged twenty-two, he had had stage experience in "Summer stock", before making art his profession. He had worked on the Superman strip, and in Hollywood on the full-length animated cartoon, *Gulliver's Travels*. Bevan was determined to seek fame after the war, and thought he might do it by stunt caricatures of celebrities whose indignant squawks he hoped would be well publicised. I suggested that, in the meantime, he should send caricatures of his fellow Americans back to home-town papers. I had already sent work home to Australian papers.

In a post-war letter he told me that in the American camp to which ultimately he was transferred from Sagan he had renewed his interest in the theatre, and had written and produced plays. It was in this field that, eventually, he was to achieve the success he sought, for he was part author of *Stalag 17*, which had a long run on Broadway and was also a success as a film. In London the play, unfortunately, was a flop.

Bevan and I were doing a great deal of work together, and I went with him to caricature the cast of *Home and Beauty*, the camp hit of the moment. Backstage the stars posed for us. Immaculate in the play, they were now just four ordinary kriegies, as scruffy as we.

The *Home and Beauty* husbands were Peter Thomas and Cyril Aynsley, each of whom has distinguished himself in his own profession since the war. Aynsley scooped most of Fleet Street with his story of Bernard Shaw's death, and he was a *Daily Express* war correspondent in Korea. Thomas was one of a crew all of whom were able to bale out of a Whitley destroyed by flak near Dortmund. It was rare for an entire crew to survive. He is now a successful barrister, son-in-law of Basil Dean, and Conservative M.P. for Conway.

Both were fine actors, and Aynsley had recently given a clever interpretation of Shylock in a production of *The Merchant of Venice*, playing him sympathetically as a subtle affront to the Jew-hating Nazi officers who attended.

With Bevan driving me my work improved, but sometimes, enraged by criticism, I would tear up all my drawings. Friends rushed to salvage what they could, and Dick took charge of my sketch-books, so that I came to depend on him to keep them safe. One day, to test me, he left them where they were. Faced with this challenge I tried to catch his eye, knowing that if I did so laughter would end my pique, but he was reading with a great show of nonchalance, and sadly I tore up my precious books, page by page.

One sulked, or lost one's temper, or gave way to almost any emotion quite unashamedly. In ordinary life we present a façade to the world, are ashamed of emotionalism, afraid to transgress the recognised code. But in a prison camp there could be no sham. One could not have Queen Anne at the front without revealing Mary Anne at the back.

Until the advent of hypnotism—which was introduced by Mike Riordan, another young American—other ways of mental escape had been devised. Godfrey Loder, for instance, would shuffle in a narrow circle, keeping his eyes focused on the electric light bulb, until he collapsed, and unconsciousness was induced in another, more dangerous game. A willing victim lay upon his back, and, after he had inhaled deeply several times, someone knelt violently on his chest. He went out like a spirit lamp in a gale. The coma lasted seconds only, but it was said that, in this state, the most delightful dreams were experienced.

Godfrey submitted himself to the experiment, and his expression of horror when he came round so appalled us that the practice was discontinued. He thought that he had passed out in a Yorkshire pub, and when he realised where he was the shock was almost more than he could bear.

The M.O. quickly put a stop to the new craze. Probably he was tired of dressing cigarette burns, which were the proof of hypnosis, but, apart from that, he felt that it was an unhealthy occupation for the prisoner mind. There were enough melancholia cases on his hands, already.

More common than cases of minds unhinged by acute melancholia was subnormality in some form, the shutting up of part of the mind because it was being hurt; sometimes even the features coarsened as the brain dulled. One man, however, had quite lost his reason. Having been missed at roll-call he was discovered with his wrists cut, in a latrine, and, shortly afterwards, he tried during the night to knife a fellow prisoner. He was admitted to a mental hospital but discharged three months later.

When he re-entered the camp he walked straight from the main gate to the back fence and climbed over the wire. The first fence he crossed safely, but he became entangled in the coils of wire between the fences. The guard patrolling that stretch fired several shots at him but he was not hit. No one doubted that he had fired to kill, and angry prisoners abused him.

Technically the *posten* was within his rights; a prisoner was seemingly bent on escape. But he must have known that only a madman would attempt such a suicidal venture. It is not easy to justify the man's action, but there is in all of us a primitive fear of the demented, and rising panic is difficult to curb. Panic, too, might explain misses at point-blank range. Against such extenuation can be set the fact that at the time he aimed the gun the guard must have seen that the prisoner was helpless in the prehensile claws of the wire.

IXIE DEANS read the citation, and then pinned the ribbon of the Distinguished Flying Medal on the tunics of two men shot down after successfully attacking the target of the famous Augsburg daylight raid. German officers stepped forward and congratulated the decorated prisoners, embarrassed perhaps and yet sincere, for the Germans did admire bravery. Twice at least, with the Swiss acting as intermediaries, awards were made to prisoners on German recommendation. One was a Conspicuous Gallantry Medal to Jock McGarvie who swam for twelve hours towing his navigator, a non-swimmer, when their aircraft crashed into the sea ten miles from the coast.

The practice of "Jerry baiting" was carried on zestfully by many prisoners, but it was for the most part crude, schoolboy stuff, which, vitiating our own dignity, only encouraged the Germans to a deeper belief in their superiority. That the Germans tolerated so much of it was sometimes surprising, but they were wise enough to know that contempt was their best answer.

To outwit the Germans, to embarrass them or humiliate them by subtle means was altogether different; the moral ascendancy was ours, and it was a surer ascendancy when they were left wondering whether we had hoodwinked them, or whether they had themselves been clumsy. At roll-call Deans always gave the impression that he considered the parade was a German affair, and that he was present to take over when the situation was beyond German control. One crackling command from Deans brought immediate silence, horseplay, indulged in on a fantastic scale, ceased, a rabble was transformed into a military assembly. German punishment and threats of punishment never achieved this.

When the counting was done, Deans took the parade completely into his control, and he used the occasion to make domestic announcements. Sometimes he made known to the parade the complaints and the demands of the Detaining Power, and went on to comment upon them with noteworthy fairness, commanding our acquiescence when the German case was with justice, counselling reflection if he considered that it was not his province to decide for us, and denouncing openly the unreasonable demand.

It was at that moment when the German officers awaited the formality of the parade's dismissal that Deans invested the two men of Augsburg. No doubt the situation was one which the officers would have preferred to avoid, but they won the admiration of the prisoners by their sporting acceptance of it, although, concomitantly they must have been aware, as we were, that their authority had been diminished.

Good sportsmanship was demonstrated by a German officer in a quite remarkable way on another occasion when two prisoners were brought before him for misbehaving on *appell*. They had been playing a game of imaginary bowls, they explained. The officer thought their antics on the imaginary green savoured too much of lack of discipline, and sentenced them to seven days solitary. The kriegies then pointed out that it was Hitler's birthday and asked for an amnesty, whereupon the German officer suspended the sentence if they would agree, on the "word of an Englishman", to spend the next day tidying up the camp. The men kept their word, and the German officer made no attempt to check that they had done so.

The Germans were inclined to belittle our discipline. Prisoners arrived late on *appell*, some with greatcoats pulled hastily over pyjamas; most dressed with the utmost casualness, and behaved as if they had had no military training whatever. Deans had not much sympathy with this conduct, but did not wish to interfere. The *appells* were for the convenience of our captors, and there was no reason why we should make their task any easier. Indeed it suited us to maintain a chaotic type of roll-call, for there were times when the confusion enabled us to conceal the absence of men who, we hoped, were many miles away. Nevertheless Deans wanted the Germans to know that we could impose discipline upon ourselves when we chose. A national day of prayer having been ordered by the King in England, Deans decided that the subjects of the King who were incarcerated in the N.C.O.s' compound at Stalag Luft 3 should observe the day. He obtained permission to hold a Church Parade, and to invite some of the senior British officers.

Shaven and shining, with boots gleaming and caps at the correct angle, with uniforms brushed, and ties set neatly, we marched, barrack by barrack, with all the precision we could remember from our "square bashing" days of years past, to the parade ground where the padres conducted a moving service. Many Germans saw the parade and palpably were astonished.

Group Captain Massey and Wing Commander Day walked slowly from the parade ground towards the gate, with Deans in attendance. Barrack leaders had their instructions, and knew exactly when to order their men to march. As the first squad overtook the officers the command came sharply: "Eyes left."

Massey and Day halted, came to attention, and saluted.

"Eyes left." The next barrack followed immediately afterwards.

"Eyes left." One after another the squads came down the road, and, even had they wanted to, our senior officers could not walk on. No troops were more punctilious in saluting than the Germans, and so they could make no protest, but the expressions of their faces proclaimed their realisation that they had witnessed an organised March Past of British prisoners in a German prison camp.

German officers and N.C.O.s often were discomfited, too, when they attended our shows and heard the prisoners sing with patriotic enjoyment "God Save the King", but they were forbearing until the day of the sports. Hundreds of British officers visited our compound to cheer their athletes against the N.C.O.s, and, afterwards, Group Captain Massey presented the prizes. Over two thousand prisoners were gathered around him, and, at the front, near the dais, stood some score of German officers.

The band, which had been producing jolly tunes all the afternoon, now played the first earnest notes of the National Anthem, commanding a great and respectful silence. I watched the Germans. Most of them stood to attention, two of them ostentatiously began a conversation, and two, after some hesitation, held their hands at the salute. When the music stopped those last two were angrily rebuked by fellow officers. From that time the National Anthem was banned, but we had achieved a signal victory.

The most impressive loss of face suffered by the Germans was begotten, inexplicably, by themselves. When teams of ferrets searched the barracks we were denied entry, and were thus compelled to trust the Germans to confiscate nothing but what we were not entitled to possess. The loss of these things we accepted philosophically, recognising that we had been outplayed in the game of hide-and-seek, but, after these searches, we began to find that cigarettes and chocolate had been pilfered, and Dixie Deans protested strongly to the Commandant when, a trap having been laid in Block 41, a German was caught stealing cigarettes.

Chagrined no doubt, the Commandant went too far in his measures to restore our faith in German integrity; he ordered that when a search had been completed the ferrets were to line up and allow themselves to be "frisked" by the barrack leaders. The practice might have continued, but too rich for silence was this joke. Invariably there was a jeering chorus, and the end came inevitably.

Deans then persuaded the Commandant to allow the barrack leader to remain in the hut while a search was in progress. Most of the Germans were honest, and the innovation was a welcome one, for honest men do not like to be suspected of knavery, even by their enemies.

Between the Commandant, the dignified, aristocratic Von Lindeiner, and the wise and indomitable Deans who was considerably less than half his age, existed a cordiality compounded of respect and something which was very nearly affection. Each recognised that the other had a duty as a military commander, a peculiarly specialised duty, and each knew that the duty was performed with honour and without malice.

We were as much aware of the magnanimity of the Commandant's rule as we were moved by the inspiration of Deans's governing. When Deans was unhelpful, as in the subtle campaign for moral ascendancy, the Commandant accepted it, as Deans accepted, and on occasion even supported, measures taken by the Commandant to maintain his lawful authority. On a personal basis Deans was not unwilling to please the elderly Oberst who, more than once, had resisted higher authority on our behalf.

So it was that when higher authority, in the person of a bulky General, inspected the camp, Deans was sympathetic when the Commandant asked for a good show. Almost wistfully he wondered if Deans might hand over the parade in the approved German style. Deans just smiled, and Von Lindeiner did not expect him to do it. But Deans learned the elaborate rigmarole, and, on the day, to the delight of the Commandant and the surprise of the General, was word perfect. On these occasions, when outside authority visited the camp, a kind of community spirit prevailed, drawing prisoners and guards together as teachers and pupils sometimes ally against the invasion of a school inspector.

The Commandant rarely wore jack-boots, those symbols of Nazi domination, preferring immaculately tailored trousers to riding-breeches, but the visiting General exemplified the vanity and the crudity of his kind. He had the flabbiness and the plethora of the self-indulgent; his greatcoat had an immense fur collar and a red silk lining, his chest, when he threw open his coat, we saw was loaded with orders and medals, his jack-boots were glossy and fitted tightly the calves, which seemed ill-made for the support of so gross a torso.

One felt that he was a brutal man, but he was genial during his inspection of the camp, and, as he went out through the front gate, he showed a great interest in the food parcels which our Red Cross representatives were hauling into the camp on a handcart. Noticing the Christmas labels, he asked what the parcels contained, and, with eyes glistening, hinted that he would like to have one. The hint was ignored, but Deans was sure that had the Commandant not been present the General would have made a firm offer for a parcel.

Each week a little food had been put aside to make memorable this Christmas which we persuaded ourselves was the only one we should spend in Germany. A whole year stretched ahead, and it was unthinkable that at the end of it we should still be prisoners.

For some that Christmas of 1942 was the fourth of their captivity, for men like Larry Slattery and George Booth who had been shot down in a Blenheim on the second day of the war, and we took comfort from the fact that, cheerfully, they faced another twelve months.

There could have been no better example than that of

Tipperary-born Laurence J. Slattery, for he had, and has still, a quiet, confident philosophy, and a sense of humour rich as the cadences of his voice.

Taken from the sea by a German merchantman, Slattery was treated for severe head injuries at Bremerhaven hospital before joining Booth, whose ankle had been broken, in the naval hospital at Wesermunde. There they were interviewed by German and United States radio commentators. Declining an offer to work for the German Ministry of Propaganda, Slattery was imprisoned first in the castle at Spangenburg, and then at Stalag 6B, Warburg, where he met legless ace, Douglas Bader, who was already causing the Germans not inconsiderable trouble. With Bader he had been transferred to Sagan in May 1942.

We were able to visit friends until late on Christmas Eve, for, instead of locking us in when darkness came, the Germans now allowed us to visit other barracks, or the latrines, until 9 p.m. Certain routes had to be followed, and these were marked in red ink on an exhibited plan of the camp. "The Red Line System" it was from its inception. No one seemed eager to take advantage of it on the first night; too often the Germans failed to inform all concerned. In fact, the dog handlers had not been warned, and when one brave man did venture towards the latrine he was mauled by dogs, fortunately not severely.

By Christmas Eve the system was functioning properly and it was extended until 11 p.m. As soon as a man walked into the open a searchlight beam fastened upon him, and followed him, often all the way. Always I felt defenceless, naked. There was ever the chance that a trigger-happy *posten* would take a shot. It would be an accident. There were *postens* who had lost families when the bombs fell. . . .

On Christmas morning the gentlemanly Hauptmann Pfeiffer, by profession a schoolmaster, came to each hut, and in his piping, toneless voice, wished us a Christmas "as happy as the circumstances allow". We did not doubt his sincerity although his face retained its customary blankness; there was no lighting up of the eyes behind the spectacles, no change in their transparent blueness—almost imperceptible in the white patch of face like washed-out ink-stains on a handkerchief. He did not even blink at the rather unconventional balloons, purchased from concupiscent guards, which ornamented our pine branch Christmas tree.

The Germans, too, had been making preparations for the Christmas period; they had been fattening rabbits in hutches made by French carpenters from our Red Cross crates. We had many uses for those boxes, but recently the Lager Officer had forbidden us to have them, and both the officers' compound representatives and ours protested indignantly when the Germans appropriated them. Were they so short of timber that they had to steal from their captives?

This brought an eruptive Major Jacob into the compound in search of Dixie Deans. Jacob, an unfortunate alloy of Prussian extremist and Nazi fanatic, a corseted, strutting little man, was the Lager Officer. Anger gleamed upon his spectacles, and upon the harsh red of his cheeks, and his polished jack-boots glinted as if they reflected the light of anger.

"Complaining British swine. Always it is something. Insults."

Deans heard him patiently. He had some respect for Jacob who, though inclined to be brutal, was a fair man, and, unlike some of his prevaricating colleagues, never made promises which he did not intend to honour. To requests for coal he was unusually sympathetic, but then he was, in addition to being an officer in the Luftwaffe, a Sagan coal merchant. Subsequently he was in trouble for charging himself, as Lager Officer, rather more for coal than, as merchant, he was entitled to ask.

Jacob ordered Deans to change into his "best blues", and

to accompany him into the Vorlager. There, in ceremonial atmosphere, the French prisoners were made to smash up the hutches while Deans, as official observer, stood not quite solemnly to attention.

The episode belonged surely to pantomime and did not escape a reference in *Aladdin*, written in collaboration by Tubby Dixon, who had written scripts for the B.B.C., and Ron Mogg, now of the *Daily Sketch*.

Twenty-four German officers attended the opening night at our invitation. Long before the show finished two of them walked from the theatre to the gate. The guard must have been convinced that they had not enjoyed the antics of Paddy Sheppard as Aladdin, for they were in a foul temper, and poured so much vituperation upon him that he was glad to hurl open the gate and watch them go. The sentry at the outside gate, shouted into incoherency, also was pleased when they went on their way. It was not unusual for a German officer to rage so that he literally foamed at the mouth, and always it terrified the lower ranks.

Neither of the bemused sentries asked the officers to produce their passes which was what the masqueraders, Allan Morris and George Grimson, had anticipated. Later, when the twenty-four officers arrived at the gate, the last two were arrested, the guard alleging that they were escaping prisoners. That he should decide the last two would be the escapers was typical of the German soldier's thought processes.

Morris and Grimson had escaped several times before. This time they were well into Southern Germany before a woman, suspicious because they had shown her a courtesy to which she was not accustomed, reported them, believing them to be two French officers whose escape had been publicised.

When they were brought back into the compound after serving twenty-one days' solitary confinement Morris and Grimson were paid the compliment of being required to report to the guard at the gate every two hours during daylight, and, at night, of having a guard enter their barracks at frequent intervals to check that they were still there.

The Escape Committee was now well organised, and frequent attempts to get away were made. Aborted tunnels honeycombed the camp, and it was saddening to watch savage scimitars of water from fire-hoses slash the earth along the line of a tunnel. Nothing was left of hope and the agony of effort but a rut in the earth.

Almost unfailingly the tunnels were located before completion. Sometimes it was the finding of fresh earth, sometimes the careless word overheard, but mostly it was the seismographs which led the Germans to the burrowing. Opinion was that the tunnels were not worth the effort, but for the many they offered the only chance.

The solution seemed to lie either in shortening the length of the tunnel, which involved finding a way of beginning in open ground, or in digging very deep so that the vibrations of the digging were lost in the earth. Ultimately both methods succeeded from this camp, the first by means of the wooden horse made famous by Eric Williams's best seller, the other by way of one of the three great tunnels, code-named Tom, Dick, and Harry, the history of which is related, with its tragic sequel, in Paul Brickhill's *The Great Escape*.

Nobody had an inspiration like the wooden horse. Perhaps one sees inspiration only in the plan which succeeds; there were clever ideas which did not come off because there was not that element of luck without which such ventures were bound to fail.

Even the Germans came to watch Charlie Honeychurch pole-vaulting the barbed-wire fence enclosing huts 39 and 40 which had been intended originally as reception barracks. He was an American in the Royal Canadian Air Force, small, swarthy, and bald, with a rarely eclipsed smile, and the pioneer's capacity for improvisation.

Up, up he went, the slim pole, mysteriously acquired, curving like a bow. Prisoners and guards grinned significantly at each other, appreciating half fearfully and half with delight that here was a man imperilling his virility, for although the fence was less formidable than the twin barriers of the compound perimeter, the possibility of vaulting which he was exploring, it was some eight or nine feet high, and the barbs were convoluted with malice. Honeychurch's idea, though very likely conceived in all seriousness, was never developed beyond the rehearsal stage, and never left the plane of farce.

Very different were the rehearsals of three men who, early in 1943, planned to cut through the wire. Night after night they made a way through unpredictable channels of darkness, between blinding banks of light radiating from the sentry-boxes.

And then came the night when they were no longer rehearsing, and on this occasion the darkness betrayed them, dissolving as a searchlight beam swivelled unexpectedly. They were caught like rabbits in the headlights of a car. From the sentry-box a petulant machine-gun crackled. Two men threw themselves behind a brick incinerator, and the bullets crashed into the brickwork. Their companion lay in the open. They dragged him to safety. The machine-gun stopped.

Crouching behind the incinerator, watched by their friends from the barrack windows, they examined their comrade. It was difficult to see in the warm pool of shadow thrown by the incinerator, although all about them was thin, fierce light. Quick footsteps. There would be no more shooting tonight. The Germans arrested them, and Joyce was moved to the sick-bay where, after making a partial recovery, he died of his wounds.

The deep snows of the winter were past. In a way that

was a pity for the only time there was beauty at Stalag Luft 3 was when the snow came. Then the grey sand, churned interminably by three thousand boots, was hidden, the fence transformed, with shining white particles fastened upon the ugly points, and the posts becoming dramatic columns of black and white.

Beyond the fence the containing forest became a pattern of magic, no longer a dark barrier that hid the world. Sometimes, when the wind went mournfully through the pines, we heard lonely seas, and watched the slow sway of the branches that seemed to grief abandoned. When there was no wind, and the trees were still, an aura of changelessness and agelessness reached out and encompassed us, and time had no passing.

After the snows had come the thaw, and the stench of the mud of the sterile earth. We floundered through it with tins of rations, with jugs of hot water, floundered through it to the parade ground and were rooted in it while we waited to be counted. Junkets of mud were trampled into the huts and found a way into clothing and blankets, and, sometimes, when you turned the page of a book, there was a hideous brown rash of it on the white pages.

We had been prisoners for nine months; novelty, if there had been any, had worn off. The ingenuity, the improvisings of the older kriegies no longer amazed us, their eccentricities we had accepted. But we were still adjusting ourselves, still trying to acquire the kriegy philosophy. It was a difficult period.

Not until long afterwards did I know that Dick and Toby had worried about my mental stability, nor did Toby know that Dick and I, anxiously, had discussed him. Dick retained a wonderful serenity; he became depressed as we all did, but one knew that he never allowed melancholy to possess him; it was some outside force assailing him and he considered it analytically and dispassionately.

Grieved to learn that my friend Stuart Wood had been killed in a Lancaster crash, in a morbid moment I tried furtively to strangle myself with a belt, and twice fell unconscious which allowed the belt to flow through the buckle, easing the pressure. No doubt that was as much as I had intended to do.

Wood's death left only one of the "ten little navigators". Two were prisoners, seven were dead. A few more months saw the end of the song for Stan Hicks died when a Mosquito crashed on take-off.

At regular intervals Toby wrote home asking for his saxophone, but his parents carefully avoided mentioning it in their letters; doubtless they thought it foolish to risk losing the valuable instrument. Finally he had his way; the saxophone arrived. He played a couple of trills, then put it away. The two rival bands, Johnny Fender's and Stan Parris's asked for his services, but he was not interested. He never played the instrument, and eventually sold it.

Toby liked hard work, manual work, and had we been compelled to work on farms, or in coal-mines, prisoner-of-war life would have seemed to him less intolerable. Characteristically, after the war he completed his degree, did agricultural research work for a time, then threw it all up to become a factory hand in Vancouver, dwelling in monastic seclusion in a Y.M.C.A. hostel.

As the weather warmed and the flies came in evil, black squadrons, gastro-enteritis became prevalent. I had not succumbed during the first summer, but now I got a nasty dose. The only cure was to eat nothing for five or six days. At night we queued for the overgrown baby's chair at the end of the hut, tense, sweating, fighting the horrible looseness of the bowels. Often a man cried out that he could not wait, but no one yielded a place, no one believed that the need of another could be greater than his own. Despair held in a sob, resignation contained in a curse intimated that the claim had been justified, but that it mattered no longer. The name coined for this malady was "the squitters".

When lice appeared in Block 40 the barrack was promptly fumigated. We burned our palliasses. Blankets and clothing went into the delouser for heat treatment. After a hot shower we sat nude, waiting for the trolleys with our clothes to be wheeled from the heat caverns. When they came we were ordered to dress quickly and the buttons burned the skin. We returned to the compound, feeling scoured, cleansed right through, as if we had taken part in some intensely moving religious ceremony.

CHAPTER

8

THE defeat of their renowned Afrika Korps shocked the Germans, and turned the knife in the gaping wound of Stalingrad, which had been reported in newspapers heavily edged with black. Remorselessly the R.A.F. and the U.S.A.A.F. punched at tender spots. In May the great dam busting exploit of 617 Squadron appalled the nation. The battle of Germany was mounting. Enemy fighters were shot down in swarms, especially by the daylight-operating Americans, but the cost was heavy. Prisoners became almost an embarrassment to the Germans who were throwing up more camps to hold them, and there was a constant ebb and flow of prisoners across the country. At last the rumours of months were confirmed, and we were caught up in the tide.

Our kit went first, after a perfunctory search. We had accumulated a surprising amount, but as transport was available we abandoned nothing. Each of us had a collection of long under-pants and thick singlets. Well, we were going north to the Baltic; combinations might be invaluable. Dick, Toby and I obtained a packing-case into which we spilled the overflow from our kitbags—letters and books, Toby's saxophone and skates, my manuscripts and a thick album of drawings, tins and nails, bits of wire, and two planks which might be useful—some time.

Among my letters was one which began: "Dear Sergeant Younger, You have been 'adopted' . . ." from an English girl I had never met. She would write twice a month as a wartime task, and send cigarette parcels as often as she could. Both promises were kept.

At the gate we were checked against our records. A sceptical German challenged my height and we stood back to back. Prisoners and guards were agreed that I was—as I should have been—eight centimetres taller than he.

In the Vorlager we were searched, and the Commandant addressed us. Be patient, he exhorted. We should not aggravate needlessly the anxiety of those who loved us, and were waiting for us, by attempting to escape. "To those who are young life is worth much," he concluded, "so do not risk it foolishly."

While he was talking to us George Grimson, listed to travel with a later party, was climbing over the wire. Dressed as a ferret, wearing earphones made from boot-polish tins, and using a home-made ladder, he was pretending to repair the seismograph wire immediately beneath a *posten*-box. Suddenly he dropped his pliers, making sure that they fell into the German compound on the other side of the double fence.

He swore with feeling. It was too far to go round by the gate to retrieve the pliers, he declared; instead he would climb the wire. He bridged the gap between the fences with a short plank, and a moment later was picking up his pliers.

Warning the guard to see that none of the prisoners used the ladder while he was away, he murmured that he was going for a cup of coffee. Under his ferret's dungarees he wore civilian clothes, and it was as a civilian that he walked out of the German compound.

At the station we were waiting for the train to start. Our carriage was drawn up immediately opposite the station canteen, and, enviously, we watched one man drink a pot of beer almost in a single swallow, and order again. He drank like a man who had not tasted beer for a long time, like one of us for instance.

"Bloody Grimson," said someone in an awed voice.

With pretended nonchalance we watched for Grimson's next move. Arrogantly he buttonholed the commandant of the train, who had been racing from one end of the platform to the other, giving and contradicting gesticulatory orders, until his face was wet with the sweat of ineffectuality.

The officer smiled painfully; his jack-boots tapped out a nervous rhythm as if he beat time to a hidden orchestra. With a nod of condescension Grimson broke off the conversation and marched towards the guard's van. We were stupefied, and showed it. To our guard, who also had watched the scene on the platform, it was no mystery; he murmured one significant word, "Gestapo".

It was true. Grimson had assigned himself to duty on the train, and, anxious to impress him, the hauptmann was more than ever energetic, until, at about 5 p.m. he gave the order for the train to commence its long journey to the North-East.

For the first hours, until it grew dark, we watched the drab landscape, and talked desultorily. Stalag Luft 3 could have been built almost anywhere in the area. There was the ubiquitous grey sand and the same tenebrous pines. Here and there was a farm, and Toby grew excited as he identified for us the various crops. We argued about the breeds of cattle, and the quality of the herds. We counted the tanks on trains bound for the Russian front, and weighed the total against that of the battle-bruised monsters returning for repairs.

We counted the carriages of ambulance trains, and estimated the numbers of the wounded. Sometimes, when the trains were stationary, we glimpsed pallid faces, or a movement made in agony. Nurses went among the patients, and, at times, we were moved by an expression or an act of tenderness, but, so ingrained was our conviction that brutality was endemic in Germany that this solicitude slightly shocked us.

We did not enjoy the journey. Every elbow seemed to

pivot between neighbouring ribs like the mortice and tenon of a snake's backbone. The windows were wired up, the heat was on, and blandly we were told that it could not be turned off. The guards, stationed a few feet apart along the central corridors of the open carriages, did not like it either. Most were smoking on the sly, and the palms of their hands were shields of yellow.

Women and children waved to us, believing that we were German heroes sent to bolster the fierce post-Stalingrad resistance, but by morning we were in Poland and the people did not wave. Once a Polish prisoner shouted in his own language, and there were quick, smiling responses. Angrily the guards dragged the man from the window.

Poland looked bleak; her melancholy was almost touchable. Peacefully the people worked, but we knew that here were the strongest skeins of resistance in Europe. Wearied of the constant parcelling up and sharing out of their country, hating German and Russian alike, the Poles were fanatical.

Jack Gilbert was a Pole. Probably that was not his own name, but a name adopted in England to which he had made an heroic way after escaping from a concentration camp. Again he was hedged about by German wire, this time at Stalag 8B, and again he found a gap. He went home. Warned that the Germans were coming to search the house, he hid, and from hiding saw his parents murdered. Recaptured, he turned up at Stalag Luft 3, and he had some fearful tales to tell; how, for instance, three Polish girls were raped by German soldiers, then hanged from a tree, and how, a day later, the bodies having disappeared, from the same massive bough dangled the bodies of three German service girls.

I do not want to labour atrocity stories. The organised butchery, the elemental horrors of Dachau and Ravensbruck would have appalled our guards as they did our liberating armies. They occurred because sadists and perverts of every kind rejoiced in a power they could have enjoyed only under the leadership of men of the same ilk.

That the concentration camps existed must have been known to the German people. But if tales of horror were bruited about, they were thought to be untrue, or exaggerated, or vicious Allied propaganda. If there were doubts people put them out of mind. It is not difficult to put from mind the unwitnessed sufferings of strangers.

From the train we saw both the concentration camp and the ordinary prisoner-of-war camp. The outward appearance was the same. A parallelogram, every line running to its appointed vanishing point, a neat wire mesh hung upon evenly spaced posts, and all along the wire neat little knots with neat little points, drab hutments clustered in rows, *posten*-boxes like an essay in cubism. Everywhere symmetry. Not a curve, save the coils of wire between the parallel fences.

The sight of groups of men tramping drearily around the arid square, their indifference to each other palpable, distilled our sympathy. Penned in a prison train though we were, yet we enjoyed a sense of freedom, for a train belonged to the outside, the so nearly forgotten world, and so we belonged to it, too. The train moved, the landscape changed; we saw that people still lived, working and playing as always. We envied them but were grateful for the glimpse of normality.

It was only a glimpse. Polish women worked as navvies along the permanent way, and shovelled coal at the depots. They had arms like oak branches; some worked stripped to the waist. Halted at a station we saw people pushed into cattle trucks, whole families, the children bewildered, whimpering. Because they were Jews they were crushed into the trucks as cattle never were. Many must have died and their bodies remained immovably wedged until the end of the journey. The children had no chance.

Turning to the guard, we saw that he was pale with horror; one word he said, in English: "Bad."

After a second night in the train we crossed the Niemen River at Tilsit, and from the massive bridge gazed down, trying to visualise the scene of 1807 when the Czar of Russia and Napoleon, conferring upon a raft, concluded an infamous pact.

Northwards towards Memel we went, but our destination, Heydekrug, lay a few kilometres short of the seaport. To the east was Lithuania, also in German hands. We marched from the station; the sun was hot, the road dusty, and the way led to prison once more.

Recumbent in long, green grass in the Vorlager we waited for the endless dragooning and searching and counting. We could see that the grass was lush in the main compound, too, but within weeks thousands of boots would destroy every blade of it and reduce the top soil to the grey dust that we knew so well.

None of the listed party had escaped, but Grimson had left the train somewhere in Poland and had made his way to Stettin in the guise of a Polish conscripted worker. A self-appointed espionage agent and saboteur, he mingled with slave labourers to whom he reported the progress of the war against Germany, gathered information, and made contact with the Underground Movement, a liaison which was to have far-reaching effects.

From one Baltic port to another he went, seeking no way home for himself, but discovering how each port was organised. He possessed forged papers, but these were supposedly valid only in the Stettin area. Detained on suspicion at Rostock, he argued so convincingly that the authorities issued him with a rail pass back to Stettin. There he was caught in a net spread for a Russian prisoner who had murdered a German N.C.O.

The Germans were pleased to make this unexpected capture. The Russian, too, had been caught, and for one night shared a cell with Grimson. They spent the night hilariously chasing bed-bugs, and the Russian was disgruntled when the game had to end at dawn, the appointed hour of his execution.

CHAPTER
9

We were led into the camp by a German officer, nearly seventy years of age and sapling straight, though the sap was slow. His face was gaunt, and brown, and creviced, and from it jutted a figurehead of nose upon which the peak of his cap all but rested. His glittering, black eyes, half hidden by the cap, looked in different directions.

"Just take a look at that cross-eyed old bastard," someone remarked.

"Gentlemen, please," protested the officer in English. "You really ought not to be so disrespectful to an old man." His gentle rebuke was more effective than twenty-one days in the cooler. "Cross-eyes" or "Jiminy Cricket" was an ineffectual officer, and did not stay with us for very long. He was just a kindly old gentleman who, doubtless, would rather have been looking after his grandchildren than trying to cope with two thousand intractable prisoners of war. Yet, among us he found some happiness, for he was a clever mathematician, and liked nothing better than to discuss mathematical problems with several of our men whose knowledge surpassed even his own. "They can't be bothered with me in the Mess," he said.

Stalag Luft 6, A Lager, comprised four brick barracks, each divided into nine rooms, a dozen or so wooden huts, two cookhouses, and two latrines. Two compounds adjoining were under construction. A hundred new prisoners, who had come straight from Dulag Luft, were already in the camp. They had expected their tiny community to grow

71

only slowly, and were bewildered when they found themselves absorbed into a large and highly organised society.

Among them were several from my squadron, and in George Kirk, scion of a well-to-do Melbourne family, and, until lately, the rear-gunner of a Lancaster from which he had had to chop himself free before baling out, I found a sturdy friend. As a small boy he had once built a cage for his dog, and his mother reproached him with: "How would you like to be caged like that?"

"Mother, I'd love it."

She wrote now to remind him of the incident.

His refinement of feature, delicate complexion, and fine, very blond hair, still carelessly brushed across in public school style, many a girl would have envied, and his husky brown body was the kind of which Denton Welch loved to write in his journals. "If only he could have acted," sighed Peter Thomas recently, as we reminisced about the Stalag Stage, "he would have been the best 'female' lead we had."

He did dress as a beach girl when the "Flieger Jockey Club" had a gala day, and I escorted him in the fancy dress parade. The races started, and gaily clad jockeys rode all manner of contrived steeds along a squared track, moving to the throw of a dice. There were numerous sideshows, the most popular of which was run by the Scots who, with superb insouciance, invited the rest of the camp to interview their genealogists to determine whether they were fortunate enough to possess a drop of Scottish blood.

Dixie and the Commandant attended the races together and vied with each other in finding names of horses apposite to their respective national points of view, and backing their fancies at the tote. The Commandant enjoyed his day, and at the end of it ordered, and paid for from his private fortune, a bottle of sarsaparilla for every man in the camp. If only he had made it beer he would have ensured lifelong popularity for himself.

I had no cigarettes to bet on the horses for I had given

them all to new boys from 460 Squadron. Most of my cigarette parcels had come from the squadron. By the auction of tinned food from the kits of men posted missing enough money was raised to send a monthly parcel of 500 cigarettes to every captive member of the squadron. Now I could repay that kindness.

Godfrey Loder was not yet able to show his gratitude. He had been convicted of sabotage. Major Tauber, taking a less serious view of the crime of purloining a window strap from the train than his fellow officers, sentenced him to three weeks' solitary. Tauber's rather sympathetic attitude towards us soon led to his transfer elsewhere. Loder was fortunate for already sabotage figured in his record; serving a sentence for smoking on *appell* at Sagan he had wrecked his cell and thrown the pieces through the barred window. At Sagan, also, Rob McKenzie, in spite of an impressive defence by Peter Thomas at the court martial, had been sentenced to six months' solitary for putting sand in the petrol tank of a German lorry.

Another intractable prisoner, Peter Buttigieg, after twice escaping from Barth with T. B. Miller, had been sent back to Sagan, and had travelled with us to Heydekrug. In spite of previous bad luck, Buttigieg made one more attempt to escape. The day we arrived at Heydekrug he tunnelled from a latrine six feet towards the wire. The acknowledged fastest tunneller in the camp, he drove forward at incredible speed, but too many new prisoners crowded into the latrine to see what a tunnel looked like, and the startled Germans came to investigate. Disgusted, Peter gave up, and settled down to write the story of his remarkable life.

A tunnel was begun from our room, D5. The idea belonged to the Australian, Buchanan, and the Canadian, Olsen. Olsen had neither time nor breath left for singing, and to our relief, "You are my sunshine," the interminable duet which he had been wont to sing with Porter, was heard no more. Underwood had brought his mouth-organ and was vigorously improving, but John Valentine, though he scraped indefatigably upon his violin, made no audible progress, and even the men digging underground declared that the noise was unbearable.

When he practised, Valentine was banished to the five-foot-square annexe to the room, where stood the bucket which served as a night latrine. He was requested to go even further away, and, hounded by the staff from the cookhouse, ejected from one of the washroom latrines where, despite rough seating, men found comfortable niches for their philosophising, he found sanctuary at last in a large brick incinerator. Valentine wanted a rest from the cares of room leadership, and Dick was elected to succeed him.

The idea of the tunnel, which was reached by a trap-door cut in the floor, was to drive into the unfinished compound later to be occupied by the Americans. Between the floor and the ground was a space, inaccessible from outside, into which the tunnellers pushed the freshly dug soil until it was packed so tightly that the floorboards were forced into convexity, and the soil had to be carried elsewhere in kitbags. The disposal organisation was not good enough. Major Peschel, the Abwehr officer, and a squad of ferrets, elated at so soon detecting the first major escape effort, turned us out of the barrack while they demolished the tunnel.

To prevent further tunnelling from D Block the Germans dug a ditch between the warning wire and the fence, along the whole length of the compound. When the adjoining compound was occupied both the warning wire and the ditch became meaningless. After months of argument the Commandant agreed to remove the wire, which gave us a few more square yards, the opportunity to talk to and trade with the Americans, and access to the ditch.

The ditch having mysteriously acquired a flow of water, complete with minute fish, our schoolboy instincts found outlet. Anglers, deployed at finely judged intervals, spent patient hours with bent pins attached to pieces of cotton.

They resented the activities of the model boat fraternity, but tolerated them until the advent of Bristow's steamboat, which took bad sportsmanship too far. Launched originally in the fire pool at Sagan, it was a piece of superb craftsmanship, but there was a weakness in the boilers. The boat blew up, and the anglers did not know whether they should be overjoyed at the disappearance of this threat to their peaceful pursuits, or grieved because so many fish had been in the vicinity of the explosion.

"Blackie" Porter's interest in the ditch was more materialistic, for, until he ran out of patience, he was able to supplement the menu by frying the hind legs of frogs which he caught in great numbers.

At Stalag Luft 3 we had handled our own food parcels, cooked our own meals. The new camp had no facilities for cooking in the barracks, and most of the contents of the parcels went to the cookhouse. The monotony of the fare resulting from mass preparation was compensated for in the relief from chores and in other ways, not the least of which was the marked decline in the numbers reporting sick.

Before we left Sagan Dixie Deans knew that there would be no provision for individual cooking at Heydekrug, but he made no move to alter this, having been convinced always, as indeed were the medical officers, that irregular eating habits, particularly that of "woofing" the Red Cross issue then going hungry until the following week, were the primary cause of ill health in the camp.

CHAPTER

10

WATFORD born, Frank Hunt went to New Zealand at the age of ten, and it was as a member of the R.N.Z.A.F. that he was aboard the *Rangitane* when she was sunk by a German raider on 27th November, 1940. Women and children having been landed on a Pacific island, the men were imprisoned in the hold of the raider which, in many guises, and under many flags, continued its predatory way.

Six weeks later the men were transferred to a supply ship, and, a plot to seize the vessel having been aborted by treachery, they sailed round the Horn and sneaked across the Atlantic, reaching a French port eighteen weeks after the *Rangitane* went down.

So it was that Hunt became one of the men whose lot it was to alleviate the boredom of prisoners of war. Profiting by long hours of practice, Hunt's thirty-two-piece camp orchestra, many of whose members were very ordinary players apprehensive of serious music, became an impressive combination. At times he taught them note by note, even placing the fingers of the violinists, his lean, sensitive face betraying no impatience. And hundreds of prisoners who went to recitals because there was little else to do, learned from Hunt the power of music to confer freedom.

The rival bands of Parris and Fender were the popular props of the variety shows, but a camp poll proved that "straight" plays were the most satisfying entertainment, and *Grouse in June*, *Love in a Mist*, *The Ringer*, and *For the Love of Mike* followed quickly; a Canadian cast gave us *Front Page*.

Twelve performances of each show were needed to allow the whole compound to see it. The theatre, again an ordinary wooden hut converted by much hard work and original planning, provided full-time jobs for many, for dress designers and "seamstresses", and all the other makers and menders. The feminine roles, once the bane of producers, were now convincingly played by a small group who were dressed and made up with much cunning. We had become accustomed to them while they, having overcome embarrassment, and learned to deal with "stage-door Johnnies", had gained confidence and style.

Music, debating, literature, the theatre—they were new and exciting worlds to many. Now it was that Alderton's spade work at Sagan was built upon. Arts, Science, Medicine, Law and Professional Studies; these were the faculties. Alderton himself, George Higginbotham and G. J. Springett formed the Education Committee which supervised work and examinations, and a useful educational library was built up from books supplied by the Red Cross Educational Section at Oxford, and by prisoners who had received book parcels.

Fifty-four lecturers, specialising in some forty subjects, instructed over a thousand prisoners in A compound alone. Interests ranged from Metallurgy to Hotel Management, from Local Government to Greek. There were, as well, study groups too small, or too specialised for inclusion in the general scheme.

For some imprisonment was a great opportunity for it brought them into contact with men of an intellectual stature whom in other days they would not have met. They learned, not only in the classroom, but in the day-to-day business of living together, even in the gregarian latrines, where a good free bowel movement seemed to stimulate good free conversation.

Soon after the collapse of the D5 tunnel project another tunnel was commenced, this one from a boiler room, indeed from the very base of a boiler. While the tunnellers worked the fire was cheerfully stoked above them. Jack Catley of D5 had conceived the plan, and with D. V. Smith, also of our room, was allotted a place in the escape queue. The tunnel ran deep, to counter the seismograph detector, and had the usual amenities of electric lighting and air pumps. It was scientifically propped.

Suspecting the existence of a tunnel, the Abwehr made strenuous though unavailing efforts to find it, and the Commandant was inclined to think that they were wasting their time.

"No one is thinking of escape, these days, are they?" he asked Deans as they walked together to the American compound one morning. "You don't know of any schemes afoot?" Half an hour previously Deans had himself inspected the tunnel, and was hard put to answer with conviction that he knew of nothing that he "felt ought not to be there".

To our astonishment the Abwehr brought in a steam-roller which was driven round the camp perimeter. German hopes were not realised, the roof of the underground passage held. Patently, however, the ferrets were sure of their ground, if we were not of ours. The tunnel would have to be driven upward and broken, though it was still short of the wood, in spite of the opposition of Paddy Flynn who was prepared to gamble on the roof holding.

Nearly fifty men were to make the escape attempt. They said taut farewells, and went clandestinely to the wash-room. In the huts we read, talked, played cards, but men kept turning back pages, or stopping in the middle of a sentence, or making nonsensical bids.

A moment before the shot there was a waiting silence, as if we had sensed the drama that was being played out in the darkness. A second shot followed quickly, then there was only the darkness and the stillness, and a dread of knowing what had happened.

The eighth man to leave the tunnel, mistiming his exit,

had been seen by the patrolling sentry. The German had fired warning shots, well clear of the escaping prisoner. Then the uncomfortable queue in the tunnel was ferreted out and crammed into the cooler.

Convinced that they had caught the first man to break the surface, the Germans were jubilant. Nevertheless the counters were soon making a confirmatory round. The Tally-ho "gatekeeper" had counted the captured men as they were escorted through the gate, and word that seven were free went from barrack to barrack. When the counters had done, they found that the number of dummies which, with great glee, they had uncovered, tallied with the number of prisoners arrested. Seven dummies, in various barracks, had been removed, and seven men had contrived to be counted twice. So began a comedy which was destined to have a long run.

The following morning's roll-call confirmed the night's count, but during the day one of the escaped men was re-captured. Immediately another roll-call was held, but once more the grape-vine had functioned, and this time we covered up only six men. The Germans were satisfied, albeit somewhat bewildered by their previous miscounts. The same thing happened on the following day.

When, on the third day, yet another prisoner was dis-covered many miles from the camp, we were confined to barracks, and the task of matching each man to his identity card was begun. Ferrets carried a box with the 450 cards for A Block into room A 1. The plan was to check the fifty men in that room, then move on to the next.

Major Peschel called his men to the door for final instruc-tions, and the box was left unguarded on the table. Promptly the 450 cards were emptied into the stove. In other barracks, too, cards were filched. That ended the security check for the time being.

The Germans resorted to what we called the "sheep count". Massed on the parade ground, we were made to pass in single file between two lines of counters, and assembled again outside the ring of guards, away from the men who had not yet run the gauntlet. The count took a long time, but between their own ineptitude and our chicanery no two counters scored the same—and they averaged forty-five too many.

We had to go through it all again, but, this time, two officers alone counted, holding hands and encircling each prisoner with their arms. It was like the children's game, "Oranges and Lemons", and as we went we chanted "... last man's head, head, head ... OFF!" A man who had been counted went quietly into a hut and opened a window overlooking the parade ground. To distract the attention of the sentries we inserted lighted cigarettes in the barrels of their rifles. Some were angry, but they never liked the English to think that they lacked a sense of humour, and so they laughed and did not see uncounted prisoners climb through the window into the hut and disappear out the other side.

The counting went on into the night with the searchlights illuminating the parade ground, in the centre of which men danced Maori haakas round a searing bonfire. Towards midnight, after eight incredibly patient hours, the Germans gave up.

But for several weeks, even after all the escapers had been rounded up and the numbers made correct, the sheep count was persisted with. We knew that it could have been made foolproof, and that, sooner or later, the Germans would learn our tricks and make it so, but our luck stayed, and to our relief they reverted to the old system.

Meanwhile efforts were being made to reconstitute the files. Duplicates held in Berlin had not been sent for, either because the Commandant was apprehensive about asking for them, or because Berlin did not wish to risk losing the only complete file.

We were marched into the Vorlager and drafted back, one

at a time, into the compound. Those for whom no card existed were shepherded first to clerks, who filled in new cards, then, in turn, to the photographer and the fingerprint man. At the end of it the Germans should have had every man accurately tabbed. Instead, they had five hundred composite cards, for almost every man was recorded under one name, fingerprinted under a second, and photographed as someone else again. As many had switched identities at Stalag 8B two years previously, and were actually army privates masquerading as R.A.F. air-crew N.C.O.s, the whole business was becoming incredibly complicated.

Ken Bowden and Jack Lipton insisted that they should be photographed together. It would be easier for the Germans, they explained, for they were inseparable, and if they escaped would certainly do so together. Impressed by their deadpan reasoning, the Germans agreed. They were also somewhat surprised when several likenesses of King George VI appeared on the film, someone having affixed a postage stamp to the camera lens by means of a little gum borrowed from the reverse of the stamp. The King would have been surprised, and no doubt amused had he known that he was for a time the mystery prisoner of Stalag Luft 6.

It became obvious to our captors that all was not well. The duplicate records were obtained from Berlin, and with Gestapo reinforcements the Abwehr was able to detect most but not all of the composite cards.

A ditch, two or three feet deep, was all that remained of the tunnel. Realising that the steam-roller had panicked the tunnellers, the Germans persevered with it; the monster rumbled round between the warning wire and the fence, about once a week. Invariably it was driven head-long into the ditch where it stuck like a giant burrowing animal.

In stupefaction the crew gazed at the ditch as if they had forgotten that a week before they had faced the same predicament, and the week before that. They stared with bovine reproach at the derisive prisoners and spat contemptuously but somehow without rancour.

Leaving their undignified goliath, they went for assistance, to return with a squad of men armed with shovels and balks of timber. The camp kleptomaniacs edged forward; timber was beyond price. A ramp was contrived and up came the front roller, into the ditch went the giant's haunches.

When its equilibrium was assured the Germans leaned against the wash-house wall to enjoy a cigarette. Eager hands reached for the coveted balks, prisoners dispersed in all directions so that it was impossible for the Germans, belatedly realising what was happening, to see which way the thieves had gone.

Then, one day, Godfrey Loder audaciously ran with a piece of wood which the other miscreants, most of whom had already disappeared, had thought too heavy. A guard chased him. Seeing that the odds were against him, Loder half swung about and dropped the heavy plank so that the end went neatly between the legs of his pursuer. The guard fell, winded.

Warned by telephone from the sentry boxes of the mêlée, the dog-handlers let their hounds into the camp and followed with Tommy-guns.. Men seemed to go through open doors and windows in solid packs. Doors, slammed in the faces of the pursuing animals, shook as frustrated paws slashed at the wood.

Only one dog succeeded in entering a barrack, and Ali Stamford, who had not had time to slam the door, leaped for an upper bunk. The dog was gathering itself for a leap, too, when a well-directed boot, catching it cruelly upon the snout, put it to flight.

"That was comic relief, all right," gasped Toby, "comic for the Jerries, relief for us."

THE capacity of the cooler was limited, and other crimes required to be expiated, so that it was some months before the tunnellers had all completed the three weeks' solitary to which they had been sentenced. Bedboards had been used as props in the construction of the tunnel, every man in the camp having contributed two or three.

To prevent further "sabotage of Reich property" our captors took six bedboards from every man and loaded them on to a lorry. As it went from one barrack to another, a prowling crowd of prisoners stole back as many boards as they could carry. In the middle of the rain-soaked parade ground the vehicle became bogged, and a concerted rush won back a good many more.

The guard, who had been sitting atop the pile protesting ineffectually, decided to take action. Unarmed, he picked up a bedboard and tried to slam the fingers that reached from all directions. Some he hit, but there were plenty more to drag boards from the bottom of the pile, and his balance grew more precarious by the second.

Flourishing a pistol, an officer appeared, and the prisoners fell back a few yards. He ordered everyone to withdraw a distance of two hundred metres. In any direction that boundary lay well without the camp, and there were derisive offers to go if the officer would arrange to open the gate.

A little German with a Tommy-gun, politely asking to be excused, pushed through the crowd to the bogged lorry. With the bedboards as an insecure plinth, he assumed the kind of pose with which statesmen cast in bronze stand gazing omnisciently into the distance. We knew that he was a clerk in the Commandant's office. "If he tries to use that thing," remarked an old kriegy, "we've got a slightly better chance than he has." We remained massed round the lorry up to a distance of about ten feet.

The little German stood self-consciously, and, in a moment, the whole gathering was singing "Why was he born so beautiful?" after which there was applause, and cries of "Speech! Speech!" Once he raised his Tommy-gun, but it was just a rather pathetic reminder to himself that he was, in theory at least, top dog. He continued, with an obstinate blush, at his post, until at last the lorry was extricated and the prisoners drifted away.

The steam-roller made one more appearance—when it desecrated a small strip of watered and sunbaked sand sacred to nine-tenths of the prisoners. That strip was a cricket pitch, and, wittingly or otherwise, the driver took his roller across the holy ground RIGHT IN THE MIDDLE OF AN OVER.

England was playing Australia in the first of a series of three "Test Matches". There was that same shattering excitement in the atmosphere which has characterised every England versus Australia Test ever played.

The parade ground, which did service as a sports area, was long-rectangular in shape, and local rules had to be devised. The pitch was placed near the barracks, and from one end the bowler's run-up was between the buildings. There was thus a full boundary circuit except for that segment behind the wicket at the "Barracks end". The batsman at that end automatically earned one run when the ball hit either of the wooden huts adjacent to the wicket. From the other end two runs were scored from a drive to the huts.

The Australian captain, Johnny Shierlaw, scored a century, batting in a style which delighted the connoisseurs of the game who had been denied such a feast for so long. A tow-headed youngster, shot down while piloting a tor-pedo-bomber based on Malta, Shierlaw had played cricket for Adelaide University. Such was his promise that he might well have been playing for his country today but for his tragic death in the last days of the war.

England's most dangerous bowler was Harris, a clever "seam" bowler who had played for a County second eleven. His efficiency was impaired by a leg injury which had left him with a permanent limp, and caused him much pain. In spite of that he would have troubled many first-class batsmen.

On the Australian side was Raymond, dark, short Queenslander, who had played for his State's "Colts", easily the fastest bowler of either side, and schoolmaster Jack Connelly, a veteran Sydney University cricketer and baseballer, who had been good enough to rate a trial for the New South Wales Sheffield Shield side.

Another fine cricketer in the Australian team was "Jumbo" Falkiner whose family owns great tracts of the Rìverina, that area of New South Wales, bounded by the Murray-Darling-Murrumbidgee river system which produces the finest Australian wool. Educated in England, at Radley, he had played cricket for that school, and hockey for the England schoolboy side against Holland. Returning home just before the war, he joined the R.A.A.F. and was soon back in England, flying Spitfires.

Shot down over France, he baled out of his blazing aircraft, and, badly burned, lost consciousness. His arms were entangled in the shroud lines above his head, his clothes were smouldering, and as he floated through low-flying white cloud, against which the canopy of his parachute was almost invisible, superstitious peasants who saw him believed he was the Christ returning to the world to succour their stricken land.

The story of that first match will often have been told in cricket pavilions. When the players in their white shirts and shoes and slept-on service trousers walked on to the field in that leisurely, almost reluctant way of cricketers, they seemed to bring with them a redolence of a civilised and peaceful world.

Less serene was the end, when it came. England, batting in the second innings, needed ten runs for victory, and to make them had one batsman, McGlashan, and Harris. The Australians knew that if they could get Harris to face the bowling the match was all but won. But McGlashan continued to foil them by taking a single off the last ball of each over. At the barracks end he simply turned the ball against one of the walls; a run was entered, the batsmen changed ends. The margin between the teams dwindled to four.

Connelly ran up to deliver the first ball of what was likely to be the last over, and was determined to get Harris up to the batting end. He bowled one that was fairly wide, turning away from the batsman who, believing that Connelly sought to trap him into hitting it against the wall, so scoring an unwanted single, let it go. The ball bounced against the wall. Only then did it become apparent that the wily Connelly had turned the local rule to his own advantage. By bowling a bye he had compelled the batsmen to change ends.

A bellow of disapproval came from the spectators. "Dirty old Connelly!" "Hang him on the wire!" Then, as Lex Smith made a diving catch to end the game admiration superseded derision. Controversy flared again afterwards, and for days Connelly's action was hotly argued.

Partisanship around the sports field was intense whether a game was between huts or national teams, and it was a brave man who consented to referee. In the American compound the same spirit prevailed, and we saw one referee pursued by hordes of infuriated spectators of a gridiron football game.

A quarrel brewed up between the Americans and ourselves after a boxing match in which John Tracey, our champion, was defeated by the "Bearded Marvel", a tough Philadelphian metal worker. Beards were not permitted in boxing, the British argued, overlooking the pre-fight ballyhoo which had made a feature of the American's hirsute jaw. But insults were cried from a distance for between us was the fence.

Our captors had resisted all our efforts to have the compounds opened up so that we could pass freely from one to another. We were particularly anxious that the gate between A and K Lagers should be opened. These were the two British compounds, A holding two thousand men and K half that number. There seemed little purpose in dividing the British compounds so inflexibly. The case was not quite the same where it concerned the American compound; the Germans wanted to foster discord between prisoners of the allied nations, and that was understandable. Moreover many British prisoners, disapproving of American boisterousness, were glad the Americans had their own compound and wished it further away.

Some Americans were no more kindly disposed towards the British, but, for the most part, they were more tolerant, partly because they were so by nature, and partly because they had lived in England for a time, and had some understanding of English ways, while many of the English kriegies, shot down before the American invasion of Britain, saw the Americans as infiltrators into their homes and thieves of the affections that rightfully were theirs.

The American Man of Confidence, Paules, had been serving in the Royal Canadian Air Force at the time of his capture, but, subsequently, had been transferred on to the more liberal American pay-roll. To control the extraordinary amalgam of humanity of which he found himself leader was an exigent task, indeed. The ubiquitous net of the "draft" had spread over the most unlikely crannies of the vast United States, and into it had fallen some strange characters.

Apart from temperamental differences most of the Americans were very like their British counterparts. They had been clerks in the big cities, salesmen in small town stores, factory workers and farmers. There were students from Princeton and Columbia, cotton planters from Alabama, tobacco growers from Virginia. But among them were some hard cases, dubious operators from the purlieus of Chicago, and one man, at least, who was a gangster by trade. This man was planning to escape.

Most men who escaped, or attempted to escape, accomplished little. Worthy as the effort may have been, it was foredoomed because of insufficient preparation or inadequate equipment. There were men physically too frail, or whose minds were not agile enough, or who had not the unyielding courage and ruthlessness of the born escaper. Some had no real intention of trying to get home; a couple of days of freedom, the right to say "I've been outside" was all they asked, and the price, three weeks in the cooler, they reckoned cheap.

The camp was usually fully behind an escape which had a real chance of success, but some men were antagonistic when inconvenience resulted from an "outside chance" effort (though outside chances sometimes came off, and never did less than cause the Germans trouble), and even sometimes when a good idea failed. The average prisoner, however, hating the confines of the wire, unable to find a way out of it, was encouraged when a man, not one of the gods of escape, but ordinary like himself, hit upon a plan and found courage enough to put it into action. "I could have thought of that," he would say.

Resentment, often a matter of the mood of the moment—classes might be disrupted at a vital time, perhaps—was not always unworthy. It can be argued that service men had no right to be disgruntled because someone else did his duty, but the older men particularly were civilians by instinct, and now that they were non-combatants they reverted as far as possible to a civilian way of life.

At the same time it was an unnatural, a humiliating existence, for they did not belong in a wholly masculine world but desiderated a proper family relationship. Gladly they had halted careers, suffered the breaking up of their homes, the parting from young wives and small children, and had learned to pilot aeroplanes, to work radio sets, to understand the mechanism of machine-guns, to plot courses over dark and angry Europe, and to do these things though the devil himself battered their machines. Now they would never fly again, and they wished to pursue the common-sense course of re-equipping themselves to resume their broken careers.

For some of the very young men the great adventure had staled and they wanted to begin their planned lives. It was not easy. None knew for how long he would have to remain immured. For the married man there was the fear, for ever growing as others suffered what he dreaded, that the young wife he had left, growing assustomed to his absence, and unable to comprehend the mentality induced by his insularity and implicit in his letters, would find comfort from other men whose presence at least was a reality.

"For you the war is over," the Germans had said to each man in the first moments of his captivity, and by many that truism had been accepted. Strangely there were men for whom the barbed wire was a symbol of security. As a prisoner of war, they reasoned, there were no responsibilities. You neither looked for your food nor paid for it. You could read, paint, act, or play the trombone, sleep for long hours and eat when you felt like it. You did not have to go anywhere or get dressed for Sunday. You were never lonely. You did not have to vote. Laws and regulations were not multifarious and complex, but rigid and easy to understand. There were not many of these, some philosophers, some fools, but their contentment was enviable. These advantages, if they were advantages, recked little in the minds of the majority.

No one who has not been a prisoner can comprehend the captive mentality, and of the many prisoners who have attempted to explain it I doubt if any have succeeded unless it be that alchemist of language, Sir Winston Churchill, himself an escaped prisoner of war, who gives it thus: "It is a melancholy state, you are in the power of the enemy. You owe your life to humanity, your daily bread to compassion. You must obey his orders, await his pleasures, possess your soul in patience. The days are very long, the hours crawl like paralysed centipedes. Moreover, the whole atmosphere of prison is odious. Companions quarrel over trifles, and get the least possible pleasure out of each other's company. You feel constant humiliation in being fenced in by railing and wire, watched by armed men, and dogs, webbed about by a tangle of regulations and restrictions. . . ."

One thing only would I add, that companions get not only the least but also the most possible pleasure out of each other's company. True it is that that they quarrel over trifles, are often but not always selfish. It is understandable; quarrels arise from a conflict of interests, petty sometimes, but sometimes signal.

The escaper and his detractors were furthering each his own interests, but was one man's hope of gain justified when there was a certainty of trouble for several thousands?

Paules held that it was not. Deans had explained some of the problems he was likely to meet, and those problems very soon arose. "He had come to appreciate a fact which I had always maintained," writes Deans, "that running a P.O.W. camp would be much simpler if friction with the enemy were reduced." Deans thought that "Hun baiting", much of which was pointless, could be soft-pedalled. He believed in skilled trouble-making but not the constant repetition of inane irritants.

Paules went much further and banned escape. Self-interest apart, it was the duty of a prisoner of war to escape, or to co-operate without reservation with those who were planning to escape. In practice, however, much was involved. The gangster and his friends wanted to escape, and Paules may well have felt that these men who boasted that, as civilians, they had no respect for law and none for life, once loose upon the German countryside, might have embarked upon a mission of pillage and murder, jeopardising the position of all prisoners in German hands.

The qualms of Paules very nearly encompassed his death, for the gangster and his cronies hatched a plot to "bump him off". Frustrated, the conspirators learned that even if some of Paules's ideas were grumbled about, the great majority held him in some respect and affection. After that they lost all appetite for trouble.

The K Lager prisoners under Vic. Clarke who, in spite of illness, ultimately fatal, carried on valiantly, came from Barth, and I was delighted to see T. B. Miller again. Through the wire we exchanged news, but there was surprisingly little to say.

In K Lager a morale graph was posted up each day by Bluey Maher who spent his days conducting a private "Gallup Poll" in order to determine the exact level of morale. In the words of T. B. Miller: "It got so that you used to look at the graph every morning to see how you felt."

Maher was the wireless operator from Doug. Hurditch's crew whose swim for life despite terrible injuries has already been described. After twelve months in hospital he arrived at Heydekrug, his lean face wearing its customary smile, his thin jaw protruding. Too ill to travel, he had missed inclusion in the first party of incapacitated prisoners to be exchanged during July and August of 1943. The repatriates from our numbers had remained at Sagan to await their journey to Barcelona. Now, "Bluey" and others were hoping that another exchange would be made. It was, in fact, in the summer of 1944.

The German prisoners exchanged at Barcelona were now back in their own country, and accounts of ill treatment at the hands of the British appeared in the German press. One of the worse instances seemed to have been the issue of but one razor blade every nine days, and we were cynically amused.

Perhaps the Canadians had issued razor blades more frequently; perhaps, less affected directly by wartime short-ages, they had been able to make the lot of prisoners more comfortable. Because Germans in Canadian camps had been much better treated than those held in England, the High Command was pleased to announce that, in future, Canadian prisoners would receive preferential treatment.

Much hilarious speculation as to the nature of the prefer-ential treatment the Canadians could expect was indulged in, and the Canadians themselves entertained some thoroughly immoral ideas.

"I don't suppose any good will come of it," said Toby, "but it proves that I'm superior to you guys."

The Canadians were told that they were all to move into certain barrack-rooms where they would live together. The present occupants would fill the vacancies left in other huts.

Extra hand-outs the Canadians were willing to accept—and share with their friends—but living as a separate and favoured community they could not stomach. It had the smell of Dr. Goebbels's Department of Propaganda. The Canadians notified the Commandant that they did not want the preferential treatment, and were told that they had no choice; the High Command had ordered it.

The Canadian leaders, Red Gordon and Ivan Quinn, the former nowadays a founder of youth clubs, the latter a hard-working lawyer, had some caustic and rather vulgar com-ments to make to the Commandant who decreed that, as punishment for their rudeness, the privileges would be denied the Canadians at Stalag Luft 6.

Dixie Deans having given vigorous support to the Can-adians, the amicable relationship which had existed between him and the Commandant since they were introduced at Sagan by the admirable Von Lindeiner, languished, and when Deans, tired and unwell, was admitted to sick-bay by Dr. Pollock, he was ordered to return to the compound. On the score of illness he delegated his responsibilities to Hancock, who proved unco-operative to the Germans, and the Commandant made his peace.

Friction between the Oberst and the Camp Leader might have ceased after the sick-bay incident, but because he felt it necessary to establish the principle that he or any other prisoner could be admitted to the sick-bay for observation, or as a precaution, if the Medical Officer thought fit, Deans brought the matter up with the Protecting Power when, shortly afterwards, the Swiss made one of their periodical inspections. Deans could not afford to allow the Germans to override the decision of the M.O. That way lay danger, indeed.

The Swiss upheld him, no doubt discounting the Commandant's ingenuous explanation that, because of his respect and admiration for the Camp Leader, he had not wished him to run any risk of succumbing to infectious diseases by remaining in the sick-bay. Afterwards the Commandant was noticeably less cordial to Deans.

Quite incidentally, Dr. Pollock made use of volunteers from sickbay inmates to help his research into the question of whether prison life affected fertility in the male. A Canadian, "Blackie", after investigation, shouted jubilantly across the wire to Red Gordon: "It's O.K. Red. It's O.K. They've got tails on 'em."

"GROW up, for Christ's sake!" Dick's moustache prickled like a wind-swept thorn bush. More prisoners had arrived; another double-decker bunk had to be squeezed into each hut, and men were measuring alleyways between bunks to a quarter of an inch, protesting any diminution. Always it was the same argument until, with the room strength sixty-four, it was not possible to put more bunks in the huts, and some hundreds of new prisoners found themselves living in tents where they slept, backside to belly, on three-tiered platforms.

"My job is hard enough," Dick shouted to the room, "without having to pander to the whims of a lot of silly kids."

Most of us were guilty of occasional childishness, and when I saw that I was listed for an extra pumping shift in the wash-house I went to Dick accusingly.

"You're taking it out on me for some reason."

"Someone had to do an extra shift."

"I've done extra turns before."

"I know. So has Toby. So have I. For God's sake, Cal! You know damn well that if I put on half the others they'd start binding, I thought you and Toby wouldn't mind doing an extra shift to save me getting mixed up in another row. Now you have to go and start one."

The men under the showers got a remarkable volume of water as I worked with my mind made up to die of over-exertion so that Dick should be sorry.

I had worked off my temper, and was beginning to see the

joke, but at lunch-time we quarrelled again. Picking up my bowl of mashed potato and salmon, I launched the contents at Dick. The food clung to his hair and moustache, and, for an instant, I saw him blinking salmon from his eyes.

My first inclination was to laugh and forget the whole thing, but somehow it did not seem my place to laugh. Dick probably would have laughed, too, but I did not wait to see. I flung myself out of the barrack and into a sulk which endured—and was endured—for five days. In that time I ate not a morsel of food, but, apart from meal-times, we carried on as near to normally as we could. Sometimes Dick remonstrated angrily, or Toby reasoned with me. I was never quite sure what Toby was thinking, and I feared his scorn. Dick, I guessed, had exhorted him to be patient.

The contretemps ended when it dawned on me at last that they were anxious and alarmed and I gave in. It seems a trivial enough incident in retrospect. At the time it was crucial, and yet I knew from the moment of my capitulation that the whole business was finished. No apology was asked, though it was happily given. We none of us knew when, and in what way, we might make demands upon the understanding and the tolerance of others.

And yet, sometimes we were cruelly intolerant. When, for once, the room numbers were to be reduced and no one would volunteer for transfer, or risk separation from friends by drawing lots, the stalemate was invidiously resolved by having a secret ballot to discover the two least popular men.

Not surprisingly, the two to go, if not the latest to join us, were newcomers. One was a youngster who did have a rather unfortunate manner, although he was able to settle happily enough in the room to which he was moved. A little more patience on our part would have enabled him to forget the shyness which was the true villain in him.

The other was Alfredo Freed, a stout, swarthy Uruguayan with long sideboards and a tenuous moustache, one of a number of South Americans who, because of an adventurous disposition, or upon ideological grounds, had volunteered for service with the R.A.F. Freed was a camp lecturer in Spanish, genial, obliging, and philosophical. He went without resentment, and there was an immediate reaction of regret. Men who did not wish anyone gone had put down Alfredo's name for no other reason than that he was a foreigner whose temperament they did not quite understand.

Colourful Freed had gone, and it was a pity, for he had added a spice of the unconventional to a good but orthodox stew.

Each barrack-room had an atmosphere, almost a personality of its own. There were studious rooms, tidy rooms, dull rooms, lazy rooms and noisy ones. Some were charged with animosities, and some bespoke comradeship and optimism. The way a room was laid out was often a clue to the characters of its occupants; something had always to be sacrificed for something gained. The clue lay in what had been sacrificed, and to what end. Was privacy desired, or space? Was light wanted or the convenience of clothes lines across the room? Was everyone out for his own good or was there consideration for neighbours?

The men of D5 were solid, clean-living citizens, the patrons of the theatre rather than the performers, the audience of the debate rather than the protagonists. Among us were students and sportsmen and bridge players, a few of the stoical but none of the brilliant brand of escapers. We were the ruck of camp life as we are now labelled "the man in the street". Not one of us had ever appeared on the Stalag stage. Only Toby could have been called a musician, and he, as he put it himself, was "too 'ornery to play". I was the only artist and one of four writers.

In a corner lay Al Wright, a Lancashireman, who had once held the welter-weight boxing title of Wales. When baling out he had hit his leg on the tailplane of the aircraft;

now, inexplicably, the limb was withering away, and he could not move from his bunk.

He had blond, wavy hair that ran in flawless grooves and ridges across his head, and, incongruously, the unshaped nose, the puffy brows that one associates with his craft. And from the corner, where this man lay in solitary witness of his own decay, radiated a cheerful warmth like that of a coal fire in a Lancashire parlour. Eventually Al was moved to the sick-bay, put into iron "trousers", and subsequently repatriated.

Vincent Ross was the least selfish man I have ever known. Shy as a leprechaun, a dreamer, Paddy would sometimes stand as still as water in a glass for an hour, perhaps in the middle of the compound, perhaps even at the urinal, and I began to worry lest he became like another man in the camp who, no matter what the weather, for the whole of every day stood quite motionless, gazing through the wire, obsessed with none knew what vision of liberty.

His was a harmless form of melancholia, Paddy was only dreaming. It seemed a pity to interrupt his reverie but whenever I saw him I would greet him loudly. A little startled, he would look up, a light of the affection which he had for all humanity would return to his soft Irish eyes, and his smile was almost an apology.

If there were not many as altruistic as Paddy, as generous as Buchanan or Jake Watson, or as courageous as Al Wright, for the most part the men of D5 were quiet, reliable men with a capacity for friendship, and a mode of life evolved that was compounded of security and peaceful ways.

This was the stuff of suburbia, the stuff of most of the rooms. D9 was as different as Chelsea is from Harrow. Here lived many of the actors and the intellectuals, the eccentrics, the humorists, and some of the leaders. Others were scattered throughout the compound, but nowhere had they collected as in D9. Of all the rooms it was the liveliest, the most stimulating to visit. To the Gestapo D9 was the epitome of the "mad dogs and Englishmen" tradition.

We were not usually warned in advance of searches to be carried out by camp security men; to a degree both sides enjoyed the perpetual game of hide-and-seek, although, as Tally-ho grew in power and more was at stake, the contest became ruthless and bitter. The Gestapo was not in the game at all, and we were quietly warned by the Germans of the impending raid for it was aimed at the camp staff as much as it was at us, to expose any instances of bribery by the prisoners or commerce with them.

It was a bleak October morning when the Gestapo arrived. From the windows we saw them turn into the road between C and D barracks, a hundred strong. Many were in black, jack-booted, felt-hatted, some wore green breeches and black coats, some ordinary lounge suits. At close quarters they seemed to divide roughly into two categories, the bullocky, brutish type with a certain native cunning but little intelligence, and the weasels, sharp-witted and pitiless.

We were ordered, breakfastless, from the barracks. Those who had the courage to protest I admired; most of us tried to slink out without catching the eye of any of them. The room leaders, to Dick's relief, were not permitted to remain.

Herding us on to the parade ground the usually inoffensive guards were scowling and threatening. We had tried to make ourselves inconspicuous by silence, they tried to achieve the same end by being as arrogant and noisy as they could.

The morning wind was chill as we stripped naked, to be searched by the black-coated workers. When I was half undressed I pretended to be dressing again as if I had been searched. A few casually sauntered to join those who had been "done", and escaped the indignity altogether. Buchanan tried this ruse, but was too big a man to go unnoticed, and a Gestapo man, bigger even than he, began to manhandle him. Buck's slow anger was roused. Clubbing his fist, he was about to strike his tormentor, heedless of the consequences, which might have been terrible, when we grabbed his arm and somehow hustled him away.

The Gestapo man had patently wanted Buck to hit him. Thwarted, he seemed to forget why he had singled out the big Australian in the first place, and contented himself with menacing imprecations, making no attempt to go after him. Those who had not been searched hastily formed queues behind the other searchers, and the bellicose one had difficulty in finding customers.

Much of the damage which confronted us when we returned to the room, some hours later, was the result of deliberate wrecking. It went beyond the indifferent tossing away of articles to get at something beneath them. Many of our ordinary possessions had been looted. Sack upon bulging sack stood outside the doors and nearby, complacently, were grouped the marauders, so accustomed to inspiring fear that they did not think any prisoner would dare to tamper with the sacks. Our guards knew better and turned away, grinning, as they saw sacks disappearing while intrepid kriegies distracted the attention of the Gestapo, one by obsequiously asking for autographs.

Gestapo property, torches, and the like, also had been filched, but perhaps the Gestapo feared loss of face, for there was no complaint. Their bewilderment in D9 was described gleefully by some of the Germans who were less well disposed towards this claque of their countrymen and of mercenaries and sadists recruited from occupied Europe, than they were towards us.

Booby-traps, laid by Ken Bowden and his friends, worked one after another, and the Gestapo men were staggered when they found a tin, containing dissected frogs and mice in formalin, labelled "Food—Don't touch". But they were finally routed by the wall clock. Its motive power was a gramophone spring which had worn out on one side and was now working satisfactorily on the other. The hands went anti-clockwise, and the figures had been reversed. An anti-clockwise clock summed up kriegy life, but it was all the Gestapo needed to convince them that D9 was the hut where the camp lunatics were housed.

"Toby's got flat feet." The sufferer made the announcement to the barrack immediately upon his return from sick parade. "Anyone else in this barrack got flat feet?" he demanded.

"I've got a bum as flat as a punt from spine bashing," a plaintive voice put in, but no one admitted to flat feet, and Toby, beginning a ritual of knees-bending exercises, sighed with mock satisfaction, and descanted on the theme of his uniqueness.

Dick and I were pleased that Toby had nothing more serious. At Sagan, and again at Heydekrug, he had been admitted to sick-bay with eczema, and we had missed him. So far, neither Dick nor I had had to sojourn in the Vorlager, either in the sick-bay or in the cooler (Toby had also done one spell of solitary), though both of us were frequent dental paraders.

A German dentist had been on the staff when first we had come to Heydekrug. The surgery was primitive, just a kitchen chair, with a bucket beside it, and a drill operated by pedals like an old-fashioned sewing-machine. If the pedaller, a fellow kriegy, relaxed his concentration the drill went slower and slower until it seemed that a rasp was in use on one's tooth.

A dental mechanic was required, and Charlie Dare, who had followed that calling in New Zealand, volunteered. He was invited to try his hand with the drill, and with the German watching, he bored vaguely at someone's tooth.

"You do it well," said the dentist. "Carry on." That

was the last we saw of him, and Dare found himself the dentist for a camp of five thousand men. The Medical Officers helped, but were really too busy to add dentistry to their day's commitments. The New Zealander began to study the theory of dentistry, in the evenings, and, learning from his mistakes, Dare became a proficient dentist. Eventually Captain Harris, a qualified man, was posted to the camp, and there was more than enough work for them both.

Local anaesthetic had to be used sparingly, and none could be afforded the two dozen Russians who begged our dentists to extract decayed teeth. Their wailing sounded in the Vorlager, melancholy as the winds of Siberia, but once the ordeal was over they formed themselves into a guard of honour, and a Colonel of the Red Air Force addressed words of gratitude to Charlie Dare.

The few Russians at Heydekrug were employed outside the camp, and we rarely saw them. I doubt if they looked upon us as allies, for the Germans were making propaganda of the Russian agitation for a second front.

We ourselves had expected the invasion in the spring of 1943. The tide had turned in Africa, the Nazis had suffered appallingly at Stalingrad; the Dieppe raid, surely, had been a measuring punch. New prisoners talked of immense troop concentrations in the south of England, of unusual activity in the ports, of prohibited areas, of great road convoys.

But spring passed, and the summer. Autumn was the time, our strategists said. A good foothold gained, the troops would dig in for the winter while our bombers denigrated the concentrating Germans, and while the Russians rolled forward, as invariably they did during the winter months. When the spring came again there would be a devastating push by our troops, and we should be home by the middle of 1944.

Disconsolately we saw the coming of the winter snows. Our only hope now was "Nobby" Clarke, a saturnine-looking man, craggy-featured and melancholy, who claimed to be a spiritualist and logician. He was in demand for evening lectures in the rooms. Recent conversations with informed spirits, he told us, enabled him to give December 22nd as the date of the invasion. As a logician, however, he had discovered that the spirits had erred by a trifle; the correct date was December 23rd.

Some thought him a leg-puller, most believed that he was completely round the bend. No one paused to reflect that he had not long been a prisoner. The Repatriation Board diagnosed acute melancholia, and home he went. Reports received later indicated that Nobby shed his melancholia as easily as a snake sloughs its skin the moment he was safely aboard the Red Cross ship.

If there was a moment of disillusionment when the dates given by the redoubtable Nobby passed barren of great event, it was forgotten in the preparations for Christmas. The cookhouse offered to bake our cakes, and the Germans announced that any illicit brews found hidden would be confiscated, implying that barrels left in the open would not be "seen".

The best brews had been made months before, the barrels sealed with tar melted from the roof-paper and buried, but every room was sour with the smell of fermenting raisins, prunes, barley or potatoes. The search was performed with that hilarious pretence with which one looks for objects hidden by a child. The guards investigated the most unlikely places and went away expressing satisfaction. They returned "in an unofficial capacity" to taste the brew. Having indulged in a number of other rooms, the Germans retired from the compound, as merry a band of prison guards as ever one would see.

Until now, alcohol found on the premises had been poured away. The latitude on this occasion was inexplicable, but it is unlikely that the Commandant was aware of it for he issued to every man a bottle of sarsaparilla masquerading as beer. In seasonable humour, the Commandant also handed to Dixie Deans a large parcel, and a letter he had received with it.

DEAR HERR COMMANDANT, [it ran in German]

We are sending you this parcel of Christmas crackers in the hope that you will, with the assistance of the British Man of Confidence, distribute them to British P.O.W.s under your protection so that some of them at least will enjoy a truly English Christmas.

You will understand, no doubt, that owing to the shortage of paper and other materials resulting from the war we are unable to make up individual parcels, and, as in any case we do not know the names of many of the prisoners, we are convinced that the distribution of these few crackers that we have been able to get together can be made only through your good offices, and those of the Man of Confidence.

We take this opportunity to express the hope that the war will end before next Christmas, so that all prisoners of war, British and German, may spend the festival of goodwill at home with their families.

We wish you and your staff a happy Christmas.

(Signed) HENRY J. HARDING
Secretary
Lancashire Penny Fund.

Thanking the Commandant, who was impressed by the letter, Deans revealed nothing of his own bewilderment. That there was more here than met the eye he was sure, and when the crackers were pulled what did meet the eye was rather remarkable. German money, maps, and information calculated to assist escapers spilled on to the table.

By early evening of Christmas Day we had converted one corner of the room into a bar, and Harry Thomson into a barmaid. "Tange" Turnbull visited each room in turn with his make-up box to put the finishing touches to the various barmaids. He was aghast at the size of the bust we had given Harry, and reduced it by two-thirds. Tange was allowed the first cup of our brew, and was far from polite. It was a muddy olive colour and deceptively innocent-looking.

In other huts the brews were equally innocuous in appearance, though some had a sparkle that ours lacked. The "Red Line" system, now a permanent feature, enabled us to go from hut to hut to drink the health of friends. Rarely has an area of such insignificant dimensions contained so many drunks. In A Lager alone there were between fifteen hundred and two thousand drunks, the majority of whom had become intoxicated fortuitously, underestimating the potency of the brews which, for a time, had no effect at all, then were suddenly paralysing.

In the middle of a conversation with a Scottish namesake of mine, jovial, little Willie Younger, I felt my limbs stiffening. Somehow I reached the door and sat on the step while Willie, unaware that I had left him, went on talking to himself for ten minutes. Violently ill, I wanted only to retire to my bunk, but my legs would not move. Toby, who had sensibly eschewed the "rotgut", anxiously warned me not to wander near the wire and get shot. If ever I moved again it would be to bed, I wanted to tell him, but could not.

At last I was able to totter indoors, and to get up on to my bunk. Solicitously Paddy Ross, another abstainer, inquired if he might help me, but I waved him away. While, having removed one sock, I was gathering strength to attack the other, I became aware of a hullabaloo at my elbow, and with some satisfaction, saw a prostrate Dick hoisted on to his bunk.

In the morning I was the first man awake in D5, and sheepishly made my way to the wash-house for a cold shower. Self-righteously, I decided to "put the whole thing down to experience".

One thing troubled me. I remembered with some horror having kissed one of the "barmaids", even enjoyed the almost forgotten taste of lipstick, and I was afraid that some unsuspected proclivities had been awakened in me. Although it was some consolation to know that many others had succumbed to the lure of painted lips, and were seemingly easy in their consciences, it was a long time before I forgot my shame.

The prevalence or otherwise of homosexuality in prison camps is a subject which appears to interest a good many people. I am often asked direct questions; more often it is a circuitous probing. When I tell inquirers that I knew of no case of homosexuality, and that I never even heard a rumour of one in a community where rumour flourished like fungi, I see, all too often, an expression of smug scepticism. There were probably homosexuals among us; they may even have had the opportunity they wanted, but it must be remembered that you could not turn the page of a book without someone seeing you do it, and at any moment of the night, in every room, half a dozen cigarettes burned restlessly.

Prison camp life compelled the abandonment of many inhibitions, but the observance of the moral code was more rather than less rigid. Stealing, for instance, was a more despicable crime than in ordinary life because it meant stealing from comrades, and because there being nothing to stop him from stealing, no kind of police force, every man was, in a sense, upon his honour.

In the camp community doubtless there were as many degrees of intolerance or understanding of homosexuality as exist in present-day society, and there was some vulgar horseplay, but there could have been no divergence of opinion about any erotic exhibitionism.

In the New Year the winter became more bitter, every day the temperatures were well below freezing, and Dick's diary records snow-drifts as late as the 28th March.

The winter brought, too, an epidemic of influenza; the sick-bay was soon crowded and in every barrack room half a dozen or more men were confined to bed, dependent for nursing upon their friends. I went down with it early in February, and the misery of it enabled me to camouflage that which had come upon me from another source.

On February 3rd there was an issue of mail, and in my hands I held a letter which, even before I opened it, I knew was the dreaded "Mespot". Nancy had broken off our engagement. An older man would have expected it, would probably have released the girl long before, but I had never allowed myself to believe that it could happen, though her letters had been troubled and less frequent. Yet here it was, in words of kindly finality not so different from those which countless other men perforce had read.

Dick alone I told of the calamity. In the cold air of the night we strode up and down the roadway outside A Block, and because we were both young, and to the young a shattered romance never seems the commonplace tragedy that it is, even the stars seemed drear, the darkness steeped in melancholy. Silently, we walked in the snow.

CHAPTER
14

A NEW interest was Dick's prescription for my melancholy, and he pronounced for skating. I had helped to build the ice-rink, digging, levelling, carrying water, as we had done at Sagan. Men had swarmed over the site like ants, in purposeful chaos. Apart from that I had scarcely moved from the barrack for months. Dick and Toby emphasised the need for exercise, and, one on either side, propelled me round the rink. My début as a skater surprised others of my friends. "I thought you'd gone home," remarked Wallace Betts.

After my first lesson I collected my books and hurried to a classroom for Mike Custance's lecture on Jeremy Bentham. A bullet crashed through the wooden walls. We heard the rattle of a machine-gun, like dice shaken in a box, and hurried outside. Someone had ventured near the warning wire, and the *posten* in the corner box opened fire. The kriegy ran, found himself on the ice-rink, travelling at about twenty miles per hour in a sitting position. The trigger-happy *posten* directed his fire on to the crowded rink. Bullets ricochetted off the ice, and soon almost every skate was pointing skywards while the wearers glissaded on their backs.

When the firing stopped a number of kriegies found that bullets had gone through the slack of their clothing, but not a man had suffered a weal from the lethal jumping-jacks. Skating was resumed; we returned to the classroom. "Benevolent paternalism," continued Custance from the point where he had left off.

The brilliant Custance had taken a first tripos in History at Oxford and become a civil servant. He had talked himself out of an important wartime job to join the R.A.F. and he was one of the first Mosquito pilots to be taken prisoner. (The first was Chrysler, a young Canadian, who spent his first few hours on German soil throwing the wreckage of his aircraft into the Rhine, on the banks of which he had crashed.)

Custance was soon a force in the intellectual life of the camp. He was an authority on music, had a rare appreciation of the arts and literature. A beautifully composed lecture on "The Art of Criticism" was one of the highlights of my years in Germany.

The classrooms were a welcome refuge when, because of a search begun while we were on the parade ground, we were unable to get into our barracks, and were condemned otherwise to a bad-tempered and breakfastless tramping round the compound.

On January 25th, 1944, Major Peschel let his searchers loose in the barracks, and spleen was abroad in the compound. Dixie Deans was not directly affected by the search, but his humour accorded with the prevailing mood, perhaps was attributable to it, and he joined in the restless prowling. Noticing Major Peschel near one of the rooms in A Block, he was prompted to bait that unpredictable officer. "I am surprised, Major Peschel, that you should choose this, of all days, for a search. I thought that you at least, would respect a sacred day."

Major Peschel pleaded ignorance. "It is Burns Day," Deans went on reverently, "a day when all Scots honour their great national poet. It also happens to be my birthday."

"Certainly there would have been no search if I had known," said Peschel contritely. "It would not be practicable to abandon it now, but perhaps there is some way in which I can make amends?"

"Get me out of this place," said Deans.

"I shall see what can be done."

Deans thought no more about it, but, an hour later, a German officer came to his room. "Major Peschel's compliments, Sergeant Deans. I'm to take you for a walk."

"I'd like some of my friends to come with me." Deans felt that the most should be made of this unwonted magnanimity. So it was that he, Mogg, and one or two others went walking in the woods, and the camp applauded.

Although the Germans were now rigidly enforcing the ban on intoxicating liquor, the Christmas dispensation having proved too much of a good thing, the celebrating Scots had succeeded in concealing some very potent brews. Innocently Deans accepted a mug of liquid dynamite just before he went on the stage in the evening, and he made a speech which was received with clamorous Scottish approval, but of which, subsequently, he had no recollection at all.

More barrels lay beneath the floorboards of many huts, ready to celebrate the Invasion, and search for them was intensified. A barrel of Invasion brew, which had been three months buried beneath D5, the Germans discovered with a steel probe. Dick, exercising his right as room leader, was present, and invited the searchers to sample the brew. They liked it and had some more, unaware that it took a few minutes to act and was then anaesthetising. When they had entered their Nirvana, Dick hailed Jake Watson from a window. They poured the drink into every receptacle they could find, and handed it out to all who wanted it.

This was the moment chosen by Major Peschel to see how energetically his men were conducting the search, and he indulged in one of those foaming orgies of temper to which German officers were prone. The men were galvanised sufficiently to shamble to the gate, and Major Peschel himself took the barrel and poured away what remained of the contents.

Discovery of the brew created a diversion for which Buchanan was thankful. For Buck had an escape plan, and already he had hidden various articles which would facilitate his getaway. Quigley and Carpenter also were in the plan, one of those simple ideas which, often, are more successful than elaborate schemes.

An engineer among the prisoners had proposed to the Germans that the waste water from the wash-rooms should be collected in a great cistern, and used to flush the latrines. Plans which he produced were studied by German engineers, and the project was agreed to. Already work had begun on one of the two washroom-latrine buildings. For the convenience of their labourers, the Germans had put a gate in the main fence at the rear of the building, and run a temporary fence round it. The enclosure very quickly had become a typical builder's yard, with honeycomb stacks of sewage pipes, and planks in casual piles slanted against the brick wall. There did not appear to be any additional guards.

The new fence was slackly strung, and Buchanan's plan was to divert attention from himself and his companions while they bellyslid under the wire. Beneath their great-coats they wore workers' overalls. Once in the builder's yard they would hide overnight, and, in the morning, make a plausible departure.

Each evening, for a week, twice the usual number "bashed the circuit". The three would-be escapers waited, the men who were to signal the propitious moment waited, the prisoners who walked and scuffled, kicked balls and flew model aircraft waited, and the sentries waited, lolling in their boxes with such elaborate unconcern that it was obvious they had guessed, and the plan was abandoned.

Buchanan was disappointed, but two days later came another opportunity. Because more beds were being moved into the barracks the tallboy lockers had to go. These, incidentally were the most useful pieces of furniture with which we were ever provided. There was just room in a locker for a man to stand, and Buchanan, Quigley, and Carpenter, having first bribed the driver of the horse-drawn wagon moving the furniture, shut themselves in lockers and went undetected through the main gate. Then, moved by treachery, penitence or panic, the driver signalled to a German officer, a young dandy wounded at Anzio, and the escapers were no longer escapers.

Solitary confinement for three weeks was the awarded sentence, but, perhaps to make a good impression, the new Commandant, declaring his admiration for the attempt "made in a brave and sporting manner, without damage to Reich property", reduced the term to one week. Buchanan's attempt had been "brave and sporting"; it belonged to escape tradition. It was part of the game played to recognised, almost to agreed rules. The Commandant could afford to be admiring and magnanimous. He had caught his men, and the incident seemed to show that the British prisoners still conformed to the old order. These were sinister days in Germany, and everywhere there were sinister men. To a man of the old school, as the Commandant was, it must have been a relief to find that he had nothing more diabolical to deal with than three men concealing themselves in cupboards.

And, no doubt, his relief was little attentuated when he heard the story of Jim Wilkie's escape, a story as charming as the shy twenty-year-old veteran himself.

Wilkie, who was in combine with Doug. Hurditch and Alistair Benn, had captained the Manchester in which Toby had made his fateful last flight. He had made an unsuccessful escape bid at Sagan when, briefed by Allan Morris, he had attached himself to a German shower-party.

Now he was ready to try again. For patient months he had cultivated the friendship of one of the dogs which prowled the compound at night, feeding it titbits through the window while its handler, in some discreet corner, enjoyed a cigarette. Sure of the dog's affection, Wilkie jumped from the window, and having altered his R.A.F. uniform sufficiently to pass a cursory inspection at night, walked out of the camp with the dog on a leash. He needed no password or paper; possession of the dog was credential enough.

But it was the Alsation that encompassed his downfall. Loving his new master he refused to leave him. All Wilkie's pleas were in vain. The dog which had been his guarantee now became an innocent tale-bearer. He was caught and brought back to the camp with the Alsation, weary and in disgrace, limping along still in treasonable attendance.

CHAPTER
15

O F the events of the spring of 1944, culminating in
triumph and in tragedy, so frequently and so unfortunately concomitants, ninety-nine per cent of the
camp knew very little. Rumour abounded as always, and
because, up to a point, some co-operation was required of the
camp, a certain amount of information was vouchsafed, from
all of which we concluded that a fantastic story was in the
making.

We read, kicked footballs, went to the theatre and the
debates, played trumpets, bartered with the Americans, and
attended the Saturday morning auction sales at which we
sold things we did not want and bought other things we did
not want, all in the search for entertainment.

The *Daily Recco*, which had changed hands to become a sort
of kriegy *New Statesman*, attracted a large audience and was
watched closely by the Germans for it went as near as it
dared to the line beyond which its extinction was inevitable.
Indeed, we were sometimes surprised that certain comments
went apparently unremarked, but the Germans may have
hoped that a careless inclusion would furnish proof of the
existence of the secret radio, so far only suspected.

Twice while the canary was concealed in a gramophone in
Dixie's room it was almost discovered. When the Gestapo
searched the room Deans had the machine playing; the
Gestapo switched it off, examined the record then put it on
again. On another occasion Deans had but a few seconds'
warning of the approach of a German officer when the set
actually was being operated. He and Dr. Pollock managed

to get a record going, and were executing Indian war-dances with great zest when the officer entered.

Behind the façade of normality men were organising conspiracy. They were men who had never accepted prison-camp standards as the norm, men of imagination and guts, ruthless, restless men, tirelessly planning and acting, blackmailing, coercing, corrupting and proselytising. At far-off Sagan, our friends, the officers, were outwitting the security system of Stalag Luft 3, driving through their great tunnel projects, and we were soon to be told of the tragic aftermath of their efforts. They succeeded in making the security system ineffectual, but the men at Heydekrug went further, for they infiltrated into the system, corroding loyalty, evoking treachery, employing Germans as couriers and spies.

This is not an escape book, but some account of the strange events of these months is essential to it. I can tell but a fragment of the story. Only those who participated in it could give the whole of it, and the man who was the centre-piece of the pattern, whose story it is more than any other's, the audacious, fanatical George Grimson, must be presumed to have died.

From the outset, Grimson and the men like him had been determined to escape. Grimson's own first attempt was farcical for he did no more than kick the backside of a guard, then run. It was a long way to the classical escape from Sagan of 1943. And it was that Sagan adventure which is the true starting-point of the Heydekrug happenings. On his journey through Poland, as was said earlier, Grimson made contact with members of the Polish Underground, and, although he did not actually go to Danzig, word of him was passed to the organisation there, and he was told how to communicate with its members.

That knowledge, and the knowledge gleaned from his reconnaissance of the Baltic, was more important than personal escape, and he did not attempt to board a Swedish ship. If he could establish a secure escape route, not he alone but others could also use it.

So began the conspiracy, the campaign to inveigle Germans into accepting bribes, a lever then for blackmail, and the seeking out of men from the invaded territories of Europe who had thrown in their lot with the Nazis, but whose loyalty to the cause they had espoused was dubious. Some had grievances, others regretted their lack of scruple or of courage in going over to the enemy. Grievance was exacerbated, conscience exploited.

But the downfall of most was cupidity. They were the victims of the paradox of prisoners having what their captors lacked—cigarettes and chocolate. These things they wanted for themselves, or for wives and children, or to purchase the favours of the local girls, and to obtain these things they sometimes went to extraordinary lengths. One German N.C.O. actually purveyed pornographic photographs which he had taken of his wife.

Indiscriminate bartering with the Germans was forbidden. Tally-ho had a near-monopoly and prices were kept down. Collections of cigarettes were made periodically for the escape fund. But there seemed to be nothing to show for the cigarettes collected; nothing happened. It was true that men like Allan Morris were to be seen earnestly conversing with various Germans, but were they making good use of the purchasing power bestowed upon them by the camp? There was no supervision of spending; the ordinary prisoner had no say in the disposal of the cigarettes he had contributed.

A grumbling resentment began to grow; to many it seemed that Tally-ho was no more than a group who talked cloak-and-dagger language and accomplished nothing.

Grumblers were a menace. Intent upon airing their grievances, they were not always aware of the composition of their audience. A few Germans were on the Tally-ho pay-roll, the others remained our enemies. They included men whose wits were not to be despised, men who held high places in the Nazi hierarchy, though they were often of lowly rank in the Wehrmacht forces. Heinz was one of these, a corporal in the Luftwaffe, a colonel in the party. Even the Commandant went in fear of such men. The pallid Heinz had once worked in a welfare organisation in Glasgow, and had even been engaged to the sister of one of the prisoners.

It only needed a careless word from one prisoner to betray to the loyal Germans that there were traitors among them, and the whole precarious structure of the conspiracy would collapse. How was the grumbling to be silenced, the innuendo, the half-spoken criticism stifled? What was to be done about men who went about professing knowledge of dark doings, claiming attention by half-promising revelations?

The answer was to show the man who genuinely felt that he was entitled to know how his "money" was being spent, that he had no cause for complaint. Convince him, and not only was his resentment eliminated, but the exhibitionist was deprived of his audience. The prize—the silence of the camp—was a big one, and to win it Tally-ho took a shattering risk. Room leaders were invited to attend at the library where, set out for their inspection, were the purchases of Tally-ho. On the tables were complete German uniforms, every kind of pass, ration card and identification paper a German soldier would possess, not forged but genuine, valuable cameras and photographic equipment, tools, radio parts—for transmitters as well as receivers—and civilian clothing. They had purchased, too, knowledge, knowledge of the whole way of wartime life in Germany. Regulations governing the movements of foreign workers, the habits of servicemen on leave, the canteens and clubs which provided accommodation for men in transit, the rationing system, travel vouchers—Tally-ho was well informed on all of these points. They even had up-to-date information of passwords required at certain places.

The room leaders moved in wondering silence from table to table. A shoulder crashed upon the door. "Wass ist das? Wass ist dast?" The words enfiladed like shrapnel. Uniformed Germans invaded the room. Shocked stillness, transient, unendurable!

At first it seemed that Germans were crowding into the room in great numbers—panic's exaggerated impression, this. There were but two, a hauptmann and a gefreiter, captain and corporal. And then, with sickening relief, came recognition. Morris and Grimson! Dramatically they had pointed the motive for the exhibition, reminded the room leaders that this was more than a remarkable museum, here was the paraphernalia of escape. And cogent was the argument that security was dependent upon discreet tongues and upon vigilance unceasing.

No German could have entered the library as Morris and Grimson had done, without warning, for Tally-ho had chosen a time when most of the Germans were at their mess tables, and any who happened to enter the camp were always pin-pointed on the map in "Control". The lesson was no less effective for that. The room leaders returned to their barracks; a still-trembling Dick called for silence, and with look-outs posted, briefly described what he had seen. Throughout the camp the voices of the grumblers were ligatured.

Sometime in February, Grimson left the camp in German uniform, presenting correct papers, and giving the password to the sentries. He travelled to Danzig where he booked in at an hotel, sharing a room with a German officer. Linking up with the Underground Movement, he organised a courier system, using Germans on the Tally-ho pay-roll, himself travelled widely through North-Eastern Germany, and when his mission was more than ordinarily vital, returned to the precincts of the camp, and indeed walked past the fence.

He arranged for delicacies to be sent in to several men

dying of consumption in the sick-bay, and Red Cross food and cigarettes, with which he was able to purchase the services of people useful to him, regularly were dispatched to him. Finally, discarding his erstwhile role, somehow he persuaded the German authorities to employ him as a boat-man in Danzig harbour, thus assuring his escaping com-rades of a means of reaching a suitable Swedish ship.

Flockhart, Lewis and Callender left the camp at intervals up to the middle of March. All were properly equipped, all went quite casually through the main gate of the camp. Their absence, as was that of Grimson, was covered up. The outside roll-calls were faked in a number of ways, sometimes by clever adjustments to the sick list, sometimes by taking advantage of the "hollow square" formation, either with the cognisance of disloyal Germans or by dis-tracting the attention of the loyal unwary, to transfer men who had been counted across the "joins" of the square to sections which had not been counted. Men slipped through concealed trap-doors to be counted twice at the nightly lights-out check.

The trap-door system was only narrowly saved when a German officer made a fluke discovery of a trap during a room search. When he turned to the room leader for an explanation he was met with an audacious wink and, as the room leader psychologist had intended, at once assumed that the trap was used by homosexuals to visit friends during the night. He closed the door, exclaimed upon its cunning, and incredibly made no report of it.

Jack Gilbert, the Pole, and Townsend-Coles were next to go, Townsend-Coles on April 4th. And then, on the 19th, using the plan which Buchanan had been unable to carry through, Nat Leaman, having spent the night in the wash-house, in the morning mingled with the workmen and made his bid to get away.

He was caught, recognised perhaps by a German who knew him, or else his Jewish origin was suspected. He was caught, in civilian clothes, and on his person things were found that the authorities had never dreamed prisoners of war ever could have obtained; he was, as Dixie puts it, "absolutely loaded". He was caught, and the Germans knew that they had stumbled upon something pretty big.

We assembled for the ordinary morning *appell*, and Hancock walked quickly round the ranks. "The balloon's going up," he warned. Roll-call lasted until 10 a.m. when we were dismissed.

The Germans were in an ugly temper. At 10.30 a.m. another parade was called, but it took the Germans a threatening thirty minutes to winkle us all out of the barracks. The delaying tactics infuriated the guards and their officers. This time it was a "sheep count", and it dragged far into the afternoon. Enmity inflamed, prisoners and guards snarled at each other and several rifle butts were provoked into aggressive swings.

The parade ended at last, then, at 5 p.m. another special assembly was called, and we went more promptly for there had been appreciable strengthening of the guard corps. Reinforcements, numbering hundreds, had been brought in from outside. Armed with machine-guns and sub-machine-guns, and having had no experience of handling prisoners, having acquired none of the peculiar tolerance exercised by the regular camp staff, they were not, we thought, a safe risk. Too, there was an unusual atmosphere, a sinister miasma transcending the normal cloud which hung over us after an escape bid. The average prisoner, to whom so little was known, began to glimpse horrid shapes moving nebulously in the surrounding darkness.

When we were all gathered in the customary ranks, when the sentries had taken up their positions, the old hands casually watchful, the outside soldiery tensely crouched, so that we felt encircled rather than guarded, the Adjutant, Major Heinrich, stalked solemnly to the centre of the parade ground. Behind him the camp interpreter marched, with knees thrust high, and halted and turned with clashing heels. Then came Dixie, marching formally, but undemonstratively, marching out of step with the Germans, deliberately dissociating himself from them.

From his attitude we knew that the Germans had done something rather unpleasant and were trying to cover it with this display of pomp, this ceremony of self-justification, with the reinforcement of guards in case we were not deceived; we knew that the occasion marked something that was ordinarily revolting, that we could forget the trimmings.

There was a cynical silence, then Major Heinrich began to read from a document. He read in a sombre monotone. I understood none of it, and yet all of it. Major Heinrich finished and, in a piping, stilted voice, the interpreter read the official translation. Over seventy prisoners had escaped from Stalag Luft 3 at Sagan. Fifty had been shot dead "while resisting arrest, or attempting a further escape after being recaptured".

"Dead-eye Dicks, every shot a bull's-eye," I heard Toby mutter in his most ironical tones as he picked on the very point that Group Captain Massey made to the Commandant at Sagan.

It could only have been murder. A few boos sounded, breaking a silence which would have been more effective unbroken. Why had we been told? Why had the Germans taken such elaborate precautions against possible disturbances when their simplest course would have been to tell us nothing? Were they justifying themselves to us, or was this intimidation? Nat Leaman had been caught. To the average prisoner there was no particular significance in this, and yet, there were those shapes in the darkness, those strange shadows of things we had not seen. Was it because they had caught Nat Leaman that the Germans chose this day to tell us that they had murdered our friends.

Shapes in the darkness! Strange shadows!

In Danzig the body of a member of the Polish Underground had been picked up from the gutter. In his pocket was a note which meant little to the German Intelligence, and which in no way referred to the camp. It was doubtful if the man was connected with Grimson or the other escapers. But the documents found on Leaman showed that Germans were involved in the prisoner conspiracy, and no line of inquiry was too flimsy for investigation. Yet it could only have been a hunch that led German Intelligence to discover that a name mentioned in the note was the same as that of the camp photographer, a Pole. Even this may have been part of the strange sequence of coincidence which was now in train; the note may have referred to another of the same name. The Germans, assuming that it was the photographer, concluded—and they were right—that he was a member of the Resistance, and in league with the British prisoners. He was arrested and thrown into the "cooler".

More watchful now, the security men intercepted a German named Monckhart, Grimson's most dependable courier, and before he could get rid of it, seized the note he was carrying. The name "Dixie" was mentioned, other than which nothing is known of the note's contents. Monckhart was arrested, taken away, and presumably put to death, in what manner one can only conjecture. Torture, not death, was the photographer's dread, and he tried to hang himself with his braces. He was cut down and revived.

Apparently Dixie's name had not been mentioned in any dangerous connotation for no action was taken against him. He was thus free to deal with certain problems, the first of which was the saving of Leaman's neck.

As an escaping prisoner Leaman was entitled to wear civilian clothes, but he did not have his identity disc, having staked everything on the documents he carried to get him out of a tight corner, and the Germans were determined to treat him as a spy.

A privilege of the camp leader was to bath in one of the

boilers in a disused kitchen which some enterprising prisoners had, with German permission, converted into a laundry, and Deans was able to arrange for Leaman to have a bath at the same time in an adjoining boiler. Soaking in the warm water, they discussed Leaman's plight, and Deans was able to provide him with a uniform and his identity disc. This manoeuvre frustrated the German plan to pretend that they had no knowledge of Leaman as a prisoner of war.

The Camp Leader was unable to do the same thing for Townsend-Coles, who, some time between the 19th and the 24th of April, had been recaptured, and brought back to the camp in civilian clothes. A letter posted to the Protecting Power was returned to Deans next day. He was told that the espionage agent held in the cooler, as far as the Germans knew, was not connected with the camp. On the 5th May, Townsend-Coles was taken away, and has never since been heard of.

A message was smuggled into the compound from the camp photographer who had been left with no means of taking his life, and, one presumes, was closely guarded. The Pole said that he had no great objection to dying, but that he had no wish to die in the way that the Gestapo would devise for him. In the process of dying he was afraid that he would divulge a lot of things he would prefer to keep to himself. These concerned not only the camp conspiracy, but the Polish Underground Movement.

He pleaded that on these grounds, if humanitarian grounds alone were insufficient, he should be provided with the means of destroying himself. Here was a neat problem in ethics, indeed. It can only be said that the man died of poison, self-administered.

Jack Gilbert and Flockhart succeeded in getting back to England. Lewis was shot dead in Danzig, and Callender, too, was liquidated. Of Grimson, the key man of the conspiracy, in the view of many the greatest escaper of the war, the man whose hatred of totalitarian creeds was so fanatical that he forced himself to feats of incredible audacity and courage, though he was ill at the thought of his own plans, of him there has been no trace. For long, men who knew him well, like Morris and Deans, Aynsley and Larry Slattery, thought of him as indestructible, and nourished a tiny hope that one day he would reappear, having completed some mission to which he had dedicated himself. But all this happened more than ten years ago. There can be no doubt, now, that in the end Grimson, too, died.

CHAPTER
16

IT was little wonder that the perfunctory dislike which had existed between prisoners and captors, the outcome as much of formal enmity as of incompatibility of temperament and ideology, now hardened into bitter animosity. To some of the Germans who had hopefully pigeon-holed themselves in their safe billets, far from the Russian front, almost untouched by the fever of war, the ruthlessness of the R.A.F. prisoners had come as a surprise, and many of them must have realised how near they themselves had sailed to the wind of treason.

But, more than this, there had been murder done against recaptured prisoners, while the intrigues of the prisoners had impelled a German to commit suicide, and although few of the facts were known to the rank and file of either side enough had leaked out to create a new and unpleasant atmosphere, and, emphasising the change of temper, on the night of April 29th, an American was shot dead in deplorable circumstances. With a compatriot, this man, having paraded sick earlier in the day, had managed to stay hidden in the Vorlager until nightfall. The two had then set out to cut through the main fence. They never reached it. A ranging searchlight, suddenly purposeful, made a swift traverse, and the little piece of darkness sheltering them was shattered. Now, the warm waves of darkness which lapped the white conical cell in which they were imprisoned and alone, were infinitely far from them.

The sentry in the tower, refraining from using his gun

as he had a right to do, ordered them to raise their hands over their heads, while he summoned authority.

Into the beam of light stalked a German feldwebel. Deliberately he placed his pistol against the ribs of one of the surrendered Americans, and pulled the trigger.

Incredibly the other was spared to tell the tale of the murder of his companion. No doctor was allowed to view the body which, wrapped in a blanket, the next day was buried in a shallow grave in the woods by four friends of the dead man. No wreath was there from the Luftwaffe on this occasion, no firing party, no coffin, no flag, no honour, no Christian blessing.

No matter how the Germans might protest that the shooting had been an attempt to prevent escape, and therefore justified, we knew that they did not believe it themselves. For when there was nothing on the German conscience our dead were not buried unhonoured and unsung, but with full military honours. A protest to the Commandant was answered by a warning that a similar fate was likely to be the lot of anyone else who attempted to escape. He who had reduced a sentence in one case, now condoned the summary execution, without trial or inquiry, of a man who had committed an almost identical offence, and who had been spared by the one man entitled to fire upon him. But perhaps the Commandant had been held responsible for all that had taken place.

On the 30th April the American compound signalled a silence of three minutes to honour their dead member. Officially we were not to observe this rite, but as the volatile Americans gradually desisted from all noise and all activity, until there was a strange stillness, as when the sound of a liner's engine at sea ceases, the very air about us seemed supercharged with emotion, and grief, almost tangible, reached us with such impact that our life too was brought to a standstill, and we mourned.

And on the 30th, too, Allan Morris, Jack Potter, Snowden,

"Wee Willie Wood" and several others were taken from the compound and locked in the cooler. These were the men the Germans believed to be the brains of Tally-ho. Their selection showed that they were guessing. Only Morris had been a leader, and, with his record, the Germans could hardly have failed to include him in any such purge. Of the others some had played minor roles, and one or two had had nothing to do with the organisation.

Anxiety was felt for the proscribed few, for there had been so much killing of late that inevitably we feared the worst when, in darkness, men were roused from their beds and taken away. Had not the Nazi régime itself grown strong by liquidating at night potential adversaries! In the event the men went to a camp near Sagan, but it was some time before we knew where they were.

Sanction of visits for sporting events between the compounds suggested that the Commandant was trying to make amends for recent unpleasantnesses—"flushing the sewer" as Toby put it—but it was not long before his tolerance was again under strain. An American having neglected to salute him, the Commandant reminded the camp that failure to salute an officer of the Detaining Power was an offence under the Geneva Convention, the tenets of which we were constantly drawing to his attention, and warned that any such omissions in future would be punished.

Six Americans, sun-bathing in the nude just inside the wire, had taken heed of the warning, and brought their caps with them. When the Commandant, with his wife, walked along the footpath on the other side of the fence, the Americans rose unself-consciously to their feet, donned their caps, and saluted carefully in unison. The mild aftermath was a new regulation which laid down the minimum dress allowed outside barracks, and which was translated by Hancock, on parade, as "John Thomas must be covered".

The American who left his barrack at five minutes before 6. a.m. on May 26th, was adequately clad. He wore pyjama trousers, and his towel was slung round his shoulders. In slippers that did not fit very well he shuffled towards the wash-room.

The night before a violent storm had broken windows, and lifted roofs, although the tents in which some hundreds of prisoners lived had stayed up, but now it was a mellow-gold morning; even in a prison camp, it was good to be alive. Whistling guards went round a little earlier than usual, unbarring the barrack doors. Not before 6 a.m. were the prisoners supposed to be abroad; the sentry in the corner box looked at his watch, picked up his rifle, and sent a bullet crashing into the guts of the unsuspecting American.

His friends, running to him, assumed with bitterness that they were safe, for the clock hands had moved that fraction which legalised exit from the barracks. Before the squirming, cursing man could be moved to the sick-bay, there were formalities to be complied with, and the guards were strangely unhurried, heedless of the man's agony, or else afraid that his survival would mean the indictment of their friend.

Blood transfusions failed to save the boy's life, and he writhed, sweat-browed and bitter-tongued, from this world, leaving not only friends who mourned, but five thousand men who were angry, and perhaps a little afraid. The day following was a day of silence in the camp, a silence of protest rather than of respect, and, in the course of the day, into the woods went a little procession of Americans with the body of their friend in a blanket, and as the other murdered American had been furtively buried, so now was he.

A German court of inquiry, as expected, pronounced that the man had been shot while attempting to escape. One wonders how the youthful sentry justified his action to himself. Yet his conscience may have been armoured by knowledge of tragedy. Disaster was visited upon so many German homes in those days, and who can tell what horror may have confronted him on a recent leave. They were, in any case, the days of the "nerve war".

When was the invasion to come, and where would the blow be struck? The Atlantic Wall was impregnable, the Germans said. They boasted of this so often, that it seemed to us that they must inspire suspicion rather than confidence among the civilian population.

For the Gestapo-ridden people of Europe, too, nerves were strained. Every day Nazi news bulletins contained reports of "terrorists" liquidated, particularly in France.

Perhaps the tag "terrorist" was to be attached to us, also, for a proclamation was posted in which all prisoners in possession of arms and ammunition were warned to surrender them at once. This seemed egregiously silly. But to a few men in the camp the proclamation was not the joke it was to the rest of us, for they, at the risk of their lives, and for the protection of ours should it be necessary, did have in their possession guns and bullets.

"I DREAMED about lots of little invasion barges swarming like spring leaves on an elm," said Toby, waking on the morning of June 6th. The hut laughed. "Invasion day, today, as sure as God made little toadstools," he went on, then took his towel and trotted from the hut.

"There. What did I tell you?" he said smugly a little later when Jimmy Poynter hurried wobbly-kneed into the barrack. "What did Mrs. Tobias's bright little boy say?" He babbled on. We looked at Poynter, waited for him to speak, knew what he had to say, but first must hear it.

He was very pale; his eyes seemed to have grown larger and rounder, the blue of them to have deepened, the expression to have been lost. Between his lips his tongue was gripped tightly as if it were being steadied, held back, so that when the time came for it to move it would be unrash, controlled.

"Fellows, it's on."

Toby was still crowing to himself; otherwise there was silence. I felt as if someone had rubbed his knuckles down my spine.

"It's in the *Daily Recco*. I've just seen it," Poynter insisted, for none dared to believe him. We all went to see, to get the proof we demanded, though the electricity of excitement was firing the camp. Some went unashamedly running, others of us sauntered, hands thrust into pockets, affecting—what?—dignity, indifference, nonchalance perhaps?

From the rear of a boiling crowd we could see the *Daily Recco's* banner headline, in red:

INVASION.

During last night the enemy began his long prepared offensive against Western Europe which has been awaited by us.

Accompanied by heavy air attacks upon our coastal defences, he dropped airborne troops on the North-West French coast between Le Havre and Cherbourg, and, under cover of strong naval forces, set troops ashore at several points along the coast. In the area of action bitter fighting is in progress.

"Well, it's true, all right," Dick said to me, and we pretended that, for the first time, we were convinced. In front of us Jimmy Poynter stood gazing silently, as if he had been assailed by doubt. Toby was still chattering about spring leaves, and toadstools, and all kinds of foolish things.

Maps began to appear on the barrack walls, reminiscent of briefing-room maps, with coloured pins and arbitrary lines of wool, erratic blue and scarlet boundaries of the fronts, taut between pins so that one was convinced not a man could be on the wrong side of his line. The wall maps had to be much less informative than we should have liked, and the coloured wool often could not be moved forward though we knew there had been Allied gains.

Rome had fallen on June 2nd; we had hardly noted it, though until then the struggle in Italy had been the kernel of the news bulletins. Its import was lost in the great tide of optimism which the invasion began. But within a few days flying bombs were falling in London, and men who had believed that their homes and families nowadays were in little peril, were disillusioned.

For twelve months at Heydekrug we had lived a strangely normal life. The once endemic frustration, engendered by deprivation of the drug of flying, time had diminished. Far from the battle-fronts, seldom hearing even distant aircraft, insular within the matted trellises of wire and the impenetrable palisade of conifers, we had existed, informed of the war's changing patterns, but too far from them to have any sense of their reality, waiting for the one great event which could affect us, waiting, in continuous suspense, so that suspense became the inspiration of our existence, the drive without which there could have been only lethargy and decay.

Hope lay in the continuance of suspense, security in the arrival of food, mail, cigarettes, books! Books were our link with humanity, with the order of established and familiar things, with the sane side of this perennially schizophrenic world. They were, too, an escape. This last aspect, perhaps, was in the minds of Australian stationers who, when compiling "Games parcels" really hit below the belt. They sent dozens of little cardboard boxes, with celluloid tops, containing little metal mice which, by patient tilting and shaking could be so persuaded to enter appropriate mouse-holes.

In the course of that life, which we accepted as the norm, came changes, came events, sickness and death; men acquired knowledge and learned to appreciate the arts; they forgot the crafts of war; there was a daily outpouring of verse and story, of painting, of musical composition, of practical invention, the constant taking and giving, absorbing, exuding of the ordinary cycle. Now there was no pressure, nothing to drive us forward.

Another way of life had to be established, and this could not be done at disrupted Heydekrug which now was soulless.

The new circumstances had left the Germans more than ordinarily irritable, and, finding pinned on the wall of a latrine in the American compound photographs of Hitler and Goering, which had been stolen from the counters' hut, they closed up the recently completed theatre in that compound. Our own theatre-going now came to an end, but in a very different way.

Until the early hours of June 13th, the cry of "Fire" had never been heard in the camp. Roused from sleep we heard feet scudding past the window. "All out. Fire. Fire." Terror first, the swelling nausea of terror. Then incredulity—who would dare leave his barrack at this time of night?

It was a still night; voices suddenly stirring across the compound seemed to be borne upon the stillness, seemed not to destroy it. From the scrummage of words only the insistent "Theatre. Fire. All out" could be distinguished.

Barred doors. Pyjama-clad figures fill the windows, and one at a time leap to the ground, emerging from the crush like pips squeezed from an orange. "Buckets. Buckets." We bring buckets. Someone's laundry, in soak, is poured over the floor. Along the length of the nine-roomed barracks men in pyjamas and slippers are leaping, pausing, running.

Flames we see gushing upward, jousting with each other, an angry ballet of leaping, cavorting, red dancers. The wooden-built, tarred paper-roofed theatre flares into a copper-coated sky. But it is not of the theatre that we think now, it is of the nearby hut which houses the library, Dixie's office and sleeping quarters, and the store of nine million cigarettes, a quantity which had staggered the Gestapo.

But there was no breeze; the flames and the hurrying smoke spat and spurted straight up. To the consternation of the guards in the *posten*-boxes, who did not know whether to fire at us or not, we formed bucket chains from the washhouse. German firemen stood gazing at the fire, trailing hoses that had a dry-cleaned and pressed look about them.

All hands to the pumps. The buckets were filled, went from hand to hand. On the roof of the hut end-on to the burning theatre Ken Bowden and Jack Lipton stood precariously but carefree as ever. To them were passed the buckets, and they hurled the water, across the intervening fifteen feet, on to the flames which instantly vapourised it. More practically they kept dousing the end of the hut upon which they were mounted. At times they threw with, it seemed, wild inaccuracy, cheerfully apologising to the various German officers and N.C.O.s upon whom the water descended. The twice soused Heinz must have entertained some doubts.

Suddenly the forgotten fire-hoses grew fat and water spouted from the nozzles. One jet hit a stout German officer between the eyebrows, and he fell flat on his back, gaped at by the man who held the hose and who, even now, did not think to direct the water elsewhere.

The flames, dark-flushed after the orgy, nosed along the ground, inquisitive and predatory, but there was little left for them to feed upon. Slowly they died.

Gone was the theatre, built with skilful hands, employed with thoughtful purpose, with imagination, with unselfishness, in the cause of ameliorating unhappiness and boredom.

Next morning, in the ashes was recognisable only one thing, a gramophone record, by some freak surviving, a record of "I don't want to set the world on fire", sung by Vera Lynn.

Strange and melancholy was the burnt, blank patch, the charred wood, the ashes. And though many said that the fire was the best show the theatre ever turned on, and perhaps it was, it is not the fire, not the drab burntness that we remember. Neat rows of seats made from Red Cross boxes, with eager prisoners leaning forward in them, the simple square proscenium, the atmosphere of first nights, Frank Hunt's orchestra tuning up with the feast about to begin, the joyous cheering of success, the aisles packed as Peter Thomas, Mike Adams, Jack Connelly, Cyril Aynsley, Mike Custance, Alex Kerr, Dicky Beck, Mike Featherstone and so many others evoked the best in the art of debate.

There was that moving Watchnight service when, in the darkened theatre become chapel, a single light burned in the shape of the Cross, while the choir sang softly, and one could single out the sweet, over-assured voices of the Welsh, and there was Shakespeare day when five former Oxford men and Cyril Aynsley each spoke on some aspect of the Bard's life and work.

Show business! How well Mr. W. Macqueen Pope would have written of the show business of the prison camp, recalling the delightful cameo of Lascelles's police sergeant in *The Ringer*, the tireless Peter Thomas in *The Rotters*, *Grouse in June*, and so many more, the courageous performances of the "leading ladies", Junior Booth, Roy Dotrice, Howard Squires and Alex Lewis among them, the versatile Bob Martin, Paddy Sheppard, the funny men, Snowball Morton, Bunny Austin, Ken Bowden and Jack Lipton, the bands of Fender and Parris, Tange Turnbull dancing, partnered by Ron Damman . . .

The list grows too long perhaps. There were more shows, more men who will be remembered—and some who probably are forgotten, who worked behind the scenes which John Murrell painted for every show.

Backstage, where the electricians and the tailors worked, in a cupboard relocked by the Germans every time it was used, the amplifying set presented by the Swedish Y.M.C.A. had been kept. The cause of the fire was generally believed to have been an electrical fault, some thought brought about by a model aircraft fouling a wire. Only a handful of prisoners knew that earlier that night the theatre had been broken into, the cupboard forced open, and equipment which it was imperative to have to keep the radio working, removed. And, to prevent the crime being discovered—for its motive was palpable—an ingenious time-bomb was set by its maker, Bristow. The theatre, which would soon have played its last show, in any case, was destroyed, but the voice of the canary was assured.

Dominion Day on July 1st offered a break in the monotony, for the Canadians from K Lager were allowed to visit our compound. For a time I was able to talk to T. B. Miller, then, with a casual farewell, he returned to his own compound. The next time I saw him was nine years later, when hearing by chance that he was in London, and, indeed, had been for four years, I knocked at the door of his Notting Hill flat. He was then writing a thesis for a London Ph.D., and now teaches in Canada.

A strange and evanescent tranquillity settled upon the camp. The days were long, soporific, with sunshine pouring down like melted butter, soaking the limp canvas of the tents, and crinkling the tarred paper on the barrack roofs like overcooked crisps. An epidemic of fleas provoked a campaign of spring cleaning, a patient picking over of blankets.

In the evenings we watched the unsurpassable sunsets, or fished in the ditch, or flew model aircraft. On the circuit the stream of promenaders was thick and knotted. Then, as the darkness became purple-fat, and plummy, we were herded towards the barracks, and grouped ourselves near the steps until the barring of the doors.

Toby showed us a cigarette-lighter for which he had just paid a lot of cigarettes. Again and again he flicked it, too engrossed by the little spurt of flame to hear our warning hiss as a German approached. Only when the forbidden lighter was quietly taken from his hand did he look up. Quite still he stood, in his eyes that tragic sense of loss one sees in a small boy deprived of some wondrous but prohibited possession.

Now the German flicked the lighter, as if to discover the magic it had for Toby. He shrugged, hesitated, then with a word of warning handed it back.

And then the nights, the cloistered, sleepless nights when the turgid air was heavy in the lungs, and the thin light was absorbed by the ceaselessly spooling smoke. Even when the black-outs were opened there was little movement of air in the barrack, and cigarettes glowed like fireflies.

On his bunk Blackie Porter sat steadily sewing a label on the rucksack he had cut from old kitbags. When he paraded his handiwork we saw that the rucksack was addressed: "c/o Mr. J. Stalin, Moscow."

Russia was thrusting powerfully at her weary adversary. We realised suddenly that the war, which had seemed so far from us, was rolling towards us. Rumour fattened and thrived. We were to move. No, too late, the Russians were but twenty miles away. The civilian population was rioting in Heydekrug. Bristow was in radio contact with the Russians. Was any of it true? We did not know. If the Germans intended to move us they had not much time. Surely the Russians would bomb the bridge at Tilsit to prevent our evacuation; those who suggested that the Russians probably did not care one kopek about whether or not they liberated six thousand allied airmen were scoffed at.

Day succeeded day. The German population of Heydekrug was being evacuated, ran the rumour; there were not enough trains to take us as well. In spite of this optimistic estimate of the situation, more and more men were making rucksacks. "Pouchy" Davies demonstrated how he would carry his possessions rolled up in a blanket in the way of an Australian swagman, and others decided to follow his example. Some had not attempted to contrive any sort of pack and were galvanised into sudden action when, on July 13th, the move was officially announced. The Americans were to move first, some time during the night.

They had little time, and not wishing anything to fall gratuitously into German hands, they transferred their surplus possessions into our compound by the simple expedient of throwing them over the wire. Unfortunately they did not warn us of their intention, and their first fusillade, mainly of tinned foods, struck down several unsuspecting British airmen.

For the rest of the day there was an incessant barrage of tins, books, clothing, sports equipment, and even cigarettes.

Ironical that after the strenuous haggling between the compounds, the cigarettes should now be thrown over the wire in their unwanted thousands. The scorched earth policy in our compound began, heart-breakingly, with the library of eight hundred classical gramophone records received from the Red Cross only three months previously.

Now was the time of levelling up. The rich were no longer rich for they could keep only what they could carry, and the poor were no longer poor for they could choose whatever they wanted from the abandoned goods of the others.

The Americans went from the camp, noisily, in the early evening.

When they marched back into their compound a couple of hours later the camp frothed with excitement. It could mean only one thing—the Russians had struck deeper; the Germans had been thwarted. But, like froth, the excitement staled and collapsed, became a sour scum of emotion. At 3 a.m. the Americans were on the way again, catcalling and caterwauling, jeering and shrieking.

The Americans never massed without the herd noise. If at times it sounded inane, it was always zestful, always exuberant.

Until the night one would have believed that the Memel Peninsular was a still and silent land. We became aware of the stirrings of the day, of the rustlings, and tinklings, and pipings only as they were muted. Then the silence could be listened to.

Now the air was charged with sound, and yet one was aware of that underlying, that containing silence as one is conscious of the spaciousness of great railway trucks as much as of the coal that perhaps spills from them.

For a long time the noise of the march came to us, almost as if it had shape, rising and receding, altering in pitch, in volume, but never seeming far off. And then, quite suddenly, the uncanny sound entity was no longer there.

Friends were they who had gone, noisy neighbours with unfamiliar ways who had engendered scorn, or dislike, or amused tolerance. Friends now. And missed. Their compound, derelict, flanked ours, left us vulnerable. Always they had been distant from us; the fence between the compounds as well had been the Atlantic. Across it goods had been bartered, news had passed, insults had been exchanged, compliments traded. The leaders had met to cement cracks in the common policy, and the rank and file had, perforce, to come into line, though at soapbox corners there had been grumblings, and glowerings, and the rumblings of isolationism, and the other bogeys of dead days.

K Lager went too, and the barracks in our compound began to empty. After three days only D Block remained. We ate until we were ill. Some of the gardens were intact, as if their proud owners could not bear to destroy them. The vegetables stood in their lush rows. As many as possible we used, and, only at the last, destroyed the plots.

In miniature the destruction in the compound, necessary because we had to deprive our captors of booty, reflected, epitomised the waste of war. Until it is a personal thing, until your ship sinks beneath you, or your home is blown up around you, or your aircraft is tumbled from the sky, or your best friend dies, you think of destruction as a terrible abstract.

Amid the wreckage of one hut I found the beautiful little library which had belonged to Mike Adams intact on the shelves above his bunk, and went quietly away thinking of the books, with their brave reds, and greens, and blues, as some kind of monument, a memorial, but to what?

We were staying as long as we could in the camp, hoping that the Russians would pounce suddenly and free us, hoping that the Red Air Force bombers would destroy the bridge at Tilsit. Ron Kennett fastened himself to our combine apron-strings, and asked if the arrangement could be permanent. A little reluctantly we accepted the young Canadian.

The last morning came, and, outside the barrack, we lay back upon our kits, slid our arms into the straps, and got unsteadily to our feet. Pouchy Davies, his swag riding comfortably, watched grinning.

In the Vorlager were Red Cross food parcels. German guards watched hungrily as we ripped open the boxes, selected the things, mainly meat, tea and chocolate, which would be most useful to us, and stuffed them into our kits and our pockets. Some, to whom we gave tins, thanked us warmly and were jeered by their comrades, who pointed out that they could take what they wanted. Suddenly the German in the sentry-box began to shout at his compatriots. They should be ashamed, he cried bitterly, ashamed to accept charity from the murderers of their wives and children, ashamed of scavenging through the rubbish left by the *luftgangsters*.

Several of the soldiers called back defiantly; others threw down the things they had picked up, but sheepishly, as they moved further from the protestant in the *posten*-box, again changed their minds and shoved tins into their knapsacks and pockets.

Toby had a brainwave and went to fetch the laundry cart. We piled our kit into it. Within seconds a dozen men threw their kitbags on top of ours, then hurried away. "March! March!" We looked at each other, then literally put our shoulders to the wheel. In his sentry-box the guard wept with anger and with mortification.

18

WITH the exception of three men who remained in the camp, hidden in an unfinished tunnel, Toby, Dick, our new combine partner, Ron Kennett, and I were the last prisoners to leave the Vorlager. Ahead of us was the long column of marching men, and a horse-drawn cart loaded with office equipment. At our backs, in a row, marched six guards, each with a scowling hound on the leash. We heaved the laundry cart with its tottering load of cuckoo kits at a good speed.

We left a derelict camp. It had been spanking new when we had come with the grass, springing green, setting off the clean red brick of the barracks. Now the earth was grey-powdered, littered with torn cardboard, ripped clothing, trampled cigarettes. There were trails of powdered milk, and patches of jam-glutinated soil. The gardens had been kicked to pieces, the plants lying like a decimated army. From the electric-light poles streamed toilet paper banners, the ultimate expression of contempt.

Hostile Germans lined the road. A kriegy tossed a bar of soap to an attractive girl who, scornfully, let it lie. The "gift" was not meant as a gesture of arrogance, but she could not be blamed for interpreting it as one. Yet, cynically, one remembered that for soap and chocolate a girl at Sagan had done a strip tease act in her room in the adjacent German compound, that Alex Kerr had received a note from a woman censor promising better delivery of mail in return for gifts of soap or chocolate.

A group of women, weeping—because the Russians were

near?—picked up stones and threw them viciously. Then there were no more people, just the road by the side of which greatcoats, blankets, and tins of food lay, already discarded by men who had set out with more hope in their hearts than strength in their backs.

Somewhere in the throng ahead men strolled with no burden, trusting to the generosity of four fools with a cart that went uneasily, the wheels rolling in drunken spasms, threatening to buckle each time they encountered a stone. Occasionally one of the bags rolled on to the road, and, though we were tempted not to see it, somehow we always did.

The load on the horse-drawn wagon became insecure, and oddments fell off. I retrieved them. A record file tumbled, scattering papers. I had seconds to collect them. As I bent to pick up the last sheet, a dog misjudged the distance by no more than an inch, and the snap of its teeth was terrifying.

Exhausted, we sat near the station, watched by the towns-people, not with curiosity alone, but with envy; no train had been laid on to take them out of reach of the triumphant hordes from Russia. We were ordered to line up, with our kits. A German officer was detailing men to act as a baggage-party and, perhaps because we were sitting on a porter's truck, his eye fell upon us.

Bag after bag we stacked in the trucks, hundreds upon hundreds of kitbags, back-breaking work made no easier by: "Careful with that one—it's got a picture with glass in it." "Put mine next to Paul Robinson's. His is there some-where." "If you don't think mine will hold together, run the rope round it again, will you."

Once rid of their kits the prisoners were drafted into lots of sixty. Toby, who had sneaked away when the officer first approached, realised that we were now likely to be separated, and appealed to be allowed to join us. To Toby's diffident but infectious smile the German responded at once, and his refusal was most jovial. Soon we saw a disconsolate face peering at us from behind barbed wire.

We were to travel in cattle trucks, French rolling-stock, labelled "40 Hommes, 8 Chevaux". They were closed vehicles having small, high ventilators, and, on either side, centrally placed sliding doors. Partitions of wood and interlaced barbed wire divided each truck into three, thirty prisoners being crammed into a cage at either end, leaving an area from doorway to doorway, roughly a quarter of the whole space, for occupation by six guards. From this central alleyway a door led into each cage.

With all the other prisoners in their cages we enjoyed a curious sense of freedom, and to prolong it worked slowly. Standing on a pile of kit I could see beyond the station, and, joyfully, I observed horse-drawn wagons, loaded with Red Cross parcels, coming from Stalag Luft 6.

But the wagons turned away from the station. Never had we known the Germans to steal a single parcel; now they were looting some thirty thousand. We had not doubted that the parcels would be removed, but after our captors had sworn there was no transport, the haste with which they removed our property to their own use was disillusioning.

Our party of ten was now escorted to a cattle truck, and, as if to reward our labours, we had the same room as was occupied by thirty men in other trucks.

It was several hours before we moved from Heydekrug station. Under a hot sun the trucks seemed to shrink, and the prisoners were soon plagued by thirst. To requests for water the guards shook their heads, not because they were callous, but because no provision for watering had been made, and it was not their business to organise these things.

Half the population of Heydekrug seemed to be on the platform. Touched by the appeals for water, a woman bade her small son fetch some. He handed a brimming bucket into one of the trucks and, rewarded with a bar of chocolate, needed no bidding to fetch a second bucket. Within seconds, all the small boys of the village were scampering home for buckets of water. Some of the trucks, guarded by ill-disposed Germans, were not allowed to have any, but most of the prisoners were well served.

Not until the broad Niemen flowed beneath us did we cease to hope that the Red Air Force would destroy the bridge. We imagined that within a few hours the Russian thrust would penetrate to the Memel-Tilsit area, but it was not until a week later that the district was occupied.

Thirty-six hours we spent in the train. Frequently we were shunted into sidings to make way for troop trains travelling to the east, and to allow the passage to westward of hospital trains, and trains carrying maimed tanks to the repair shops, and battle-fatigued men to find what refreshment they could in their home towns where life was dominated by fear of the bomber fleets of the night. The men on their way to the front had that taut nonchalance endemic among men nerving themselves to battle. There were few young-middle-aged men among them. Germany was dipping deep into her treasury of man-power, and these reinforcements comprised striplings who had stepped from Hitler Youth briefs into field-grey uniforms, and men whose faces were minted of experience.

Once, a trainload of Russian prisoners went slowly by and we hailed them as brothers, but there was no response. British or German, it mattered little to them. We subscribed to some alien and despised ideology, even as the Germans.

Through Insterburg we went, and Allenstein, and Deutsch Eylau, and again we saw the concentration camps with their shambling men. Dick noted in his diary that the Germans were "obviously draining Poland of land wealth". There was little stock in the fields, and German axes were pillaging the woods.

A railway bridge of immense length stretched across the superb Vistula, and beyond it, deep in Poland, lay Thorn. It was dusk. The guards formed up on the platform, the cages disgorged. We, the baggage-party, now had to unload the kit, and men milled about the truck, anxious to claim their belongings. The office equipment was to be carried by motor-lorry, and with cigarettes we purchased permission to travel with it. Our own kit we put to one side, and we singled out Buck's, Toby's and those of several others who would help the less robust on their way.

The prisoners formed column for the march, watched by some pretty Polish girls. The officer in charge raised a clenched fist, then jerked it down. This, the recognised signal to start, was the movement of a train-driver tugging the whistle cord, and the men moved off emitting train noises. The girls laughed and a guard threatened them with a rifle butt.

It was some time before the lorry arrived, and we were worried. Precarious is the bargain made on the basis of bribery, and it was not unlikely that, in the end, we should be compelled to walk. What should we do then with the kits for which we had accepted responsibility? But the truck came, and ensconced upon a pile of kit we started for the camp, situated some six kilometres away.

We had an impression of tall, gaunt buildings and white faces in dark windows. A few lounging figures outside a poky theatre, more outside a brothel, were the only signs of life. Then the cobbled streets of Thorn were left behind, and we smelled the countryside, rainwashed and fragrant.

Stalag 357, built in and around an old sand quarry, was an army camp, and for the first time we passed from Luftwaffe control. The three thousand five hundred army prisoners received the R.A.F. contingent, three thousand strong, with no great enthusiasm. Our arrival virtually halved their Red Cross food, and the prospect of more supplies was doubtful.

There were eight connected Hofs, or small compounds, and the complete circuit was two miles. To us, bashing the circuit was like a ramble in the country. We were housed in airy wooden huts, twenty-four men to each, but there were no facilities for cooking, and for the first few days no palliasses. The cookhouse, which provided only a midday soup, and hot water for tea three times daily, was half a mile away through ankle-deep sand. The absence of a potato ration was keenly felt. However, Red Cross parcels were issued complete, the tins unpunctured.

Some army men resented the inclusion of the R.A.F. in the first week's parcel issue, for many still had tins brought from Heydekrug, and, in the months to come, the army never quite forgave us for settling upon them without bringing our store of parcels. But no real friction existed between the two services; indeed, there were numerous pairings off, and conversation on the circuit was livelier than it had been for a long time. The stories which had staled were refurbished for the new audience.

After lunch, one day, I was sitting moodily in the hut when a debonair company sergeant-major in Australian uniform inquired for me. It was Neilson Whyte with whom I had gone to school in the little country town of Kerang in Northern Victoria. Whyte had been captured in the North African campaign early on when a Rommel tank nosed to the edge of a foxhole and practically poked its gun in his belly. He had been held in Italy until the Germans moved as many prisoners as they could into their own camps when the Italians began to crumble.

We had to adapt ourselves to a strange environment, for army methods had never been ours. For one thing we had never been conscious of rank. Even in England the army had never understood a system that allowed a wing commander to fly as a rear-gunner under the captaincy of a sergeant pilot.

At Stalag 357 the Camp Leader was a regimental sergeant-major, and the room leaders were senior men. No idea of electing a leader had occurred to the army men— quite understandably, since in all officers' camps throughout

Germany the senior British officer was automatically leader. Deans remained the R.A.F. Man of Confidence, but in the camp took second place to R.S.M. Turner.

The soldiers when they addressed or referred to someone they did not know well used rank, something we never did, and it did introduce a note of courtesy into camp life, a formality which was not unbecoming. Even the Australian soldiers, reputedly not very amenable to military niceties, were punctilious in this.

Paradoxically there seemed to be a greater sodality among the R.A.F. This may have stemmed in part from the closer confinement to which we had been accustomed, and in part to a more rigid policy of non-fraternisation with the Germans, the prohibition of bartering in competition with one another. Most of all it could be attributed to the common loyalty to Dixie Deans, for it was this which brought unity to the pattern composed of so many highly individual personalities.

Within the camp we had greater freedom than we had enjoyed previously in German hands, although there was a punctilio on parade which the Luftwaffe had not insisted upon. The huts were not locked at night, and kriegies took their blankets and slept outside, relying on information received that the dogs were harmless.

Discipline was sharpened, however, soon after the advent of the R.A.F. An airman was shot dead at point-blank range by guards one night. Whether he was trying to escape, or merely wandering abroad was not known. After that the barracks were locked at dark. Sleeping outside had been discontinued already, the canine troops having proved less sympathetic than had been supposed; the Heydekrug dogs had been added to the force.

A small consignment of Red Cross parcels arrived and the men who unloaded them at the station claimed that they saw Hitler go through Thorn in a special train. The following day we read of the attempted assassination of Hitler at his woodland H.Q. near Rastenburg, East Prussia—the 20th

July plot. "Heaven has held its protective hand over you," cried Mussolini who arrived to confer with Hitler two hours later, and the German press, with photographs of the two examining the wrecked room, thought his words inspired. We heard nothing then of the horrifying fate of the conspirators, but a curious aftermath of the incident was the introduction into the German forces of the Nazi salute in place of the orthodox military one. Dixie resisted an attempt to compel us to use the outstretched hand, and it was agreed eventually that we should salute in our own way, and that the Germans should respond with their gesture of loyalty to the Führer.

There being no cooking facilities, an ingenious machine, the "Blower" was much in vogue. The principle was that of a blacksmith's forge. On a wooden base, about two feet in length, was mounted a wheel, cut from wood, and grooved to take a belt which was connected to a spindle. The wheel turned, and the spindle rotated a fan, forcing air through a vent into a clay-lined tin containing wood chips which, burning fiercely, would boil a dixie in a minute. In the camp were probably a thousand blowers, and, as tea was brewed half a dozen times daily, wood was in demand. We were adept at removing rafters and beams which had been considered essential in the construction of the utility buildings, but which we proved were not—though not a hut in the camp could have remained standing in a very high wind. Even the thickness of the floorboards was reduced by half.

A small, isolated latrine, probably used by workmen building the camp, which would have been described in Chic Sale's memorable *The Specialist* as a two-holer, was removed altogether. An unfortunate trombonist on his way to band practice, blithely trying a trill or two on the way, failed to notice that where there had been a building none was now, and stepped into the hideous pit which had lain beneath it, taking his trombone with him.

Every Sunday there was a band recital, and in Poland, as

elsewhere, a Sunday afternoon walk appeared to be an in-grained habit. A main road from Thorn running past the camp, what more natural than that the local populace should saunter outside the wire to watch the human zoo, and to listen to its noises? To us the traffic was entertainment, and so we stood near the wire to watch the movement outside, and the promenaders stood and gazed reciprocally in. Occasionally a woman would flick a note through the wire and walk quickly on. We heard that before our arrival a girl who tried to throw a message to a Polish soldier was shot dead. Some of the Poles among us had relatives in the passing crowds.

On August 3rd the Poles, in handcuffs, were led from the camp, convinced that they were going to execution squads. Vigorously Deans protested against this segregation and transfer of ordinary members of the R.A.F. He persisted in agitating for their return, and eventually was informed that the men were incarcerated at Muhlberg. A guarded note from the Polish leader, Sergeant S. Ablamowicz, was handed to him.

A sudden thunderstorm one Sunday afternoon sent prisoners racing for soap and towels. The rain fell soft and warm, and the cult of nudism found favour in an instant. To take a shower normally demanded great hardihood, for the camp's water came from deep wells and was bitterly cold; every drop had to be pumped. One stood beneath a wooden sluice-box, removed the stopcock, and endured for brief seconds a fierce gout of water which pierced the flesh like refrigerated needles. The queue kept moving rapidly.

But the rain plumped tranquilly upon our bodies, the soap lathered richly. Past the fence went a lorry crowded with girls who squealed at the sight of so much masculine naked-ness.

On the opposite side of the road from the camp was waste-land, sand-dunes and gorse. It was used for manœuvres by the German army, used to train the old men of the Reich in modern combat. In the wallets of many of them doubtless were the black-edged photographs of their sons, issued by the grateful Reich to the next-of-kin of those who had died. We watched the veterans crouch behind bushes, and rise with knots in their backs, and crawl on bellies which between the wars had grown soft and flabby. In spite of that they seemed somehow more like children playing at soldiers than grown men in serious training.

All day long the crash of mortar fire reverberated, rocking the billets. Flights of F.W. 190s continuously patrolled the Vistula, air sentinels of the bridge. Sometimes, in a spirit of mischief they "beat up" the camp. In the sky were strange vapour trails, vertical, white pencil lines which shot upward at fantastic speed, and, occasionally, at the tip, we caught a gleam. We were uneasy.

Every day in the German news appeared the phrase, "Retribution fire continued on England". The B.B.C. was guarded. Men were receiving news of the deaths of relatives. These were the days of the V1. What did the vapour trails signify? Patently, some kind of rocket was being fired, and we were to discover, in time, that we had witnessed final trials of the V2.

For the first few days at Thorn the existence of the "canary" was kept a secret. Was it safe to reveal to the unknown quantity that we had the precious radio receiver? Were there among the three thousand five hundred army prisoners men of doubtful loyalty? After conferring with the senior army N.C.O.s the R.A.F. men decided to take the risk. Again the canary sang, the shorthand writers took down the news, and the reader corps, including now some of the army men, made its rounds.

Army journalists produced a wall-newspaper, *Time and Tide*, which was more elaborate than anything we had attempted. It ran to nine sheets of articles, short stories, and news columns, all beautifully hand-lettered, and original cartoons in colour. It seemed incredible that each day so much work went into the production of a newspaper of which there was but a single copy.

Other enterprising men lent colour to the life. These were the proprietors of the swopshops, the barrow boys of the camp. Set up on a purely commercial basis, the swopshops possessed an entertainment quality that was unique. Working mainly on commission, both vendor and purchaser being charged, the swopshop men bought and sold food, clothing, blowers, boots, soap, razor blades, watches, musical instruments, books, every kind of prisoner-possession. Even medal ribbons cut from toothbrush handles could be purchased by the vain, or the old regulars who felt undressed without them.

Most of the proprietors had German contacts from whom they obtained civilian bread, lighter fuel and other items for which there was an assured sale. Only on the purchase of this stock did they outlay their own capital. But they earned their money, for they worked long hours, and because of their skill and experience, they were able to dispose of goods which the average prisoner would not have succeeded in selling.

To the hard-up kriegy they afforded a means of ameliorating poverty without advertisement or loss of pride, for, too often, his own efforts would bring not a price but charity. If he decided to sell a blanket, and risk the war running on to the winter, in order to enjoy a smoke, he could do so, paying for the service rendered him in the selling, and he knew that his alone had been the sacrifice.

Many did not believe that we should have another winter in captivity. The Russians were rolling on at such speed that we could not think the Germans capable of holding out much longer. Would they, in their headlong retreat, burden themselves with prisoners of war? What point was there in retaining us? These were the questions that we had asked ourselves at Heydekrug, and the answer then had been the transfer of A Lager to Thorn, of K Lager and the

Americans elsewhere. News of the journey of the other two Lagers already had filtered through to us.

They had not travelled across the bridge at Tilsit, which we had believed to be the only exit from the area, but to the port of Memel, where they had embarked upon the *Insterburg*, a bleak hulk into the hold of which all four thousand of them were crammed so that the engorged ship rolled sluggishly. For two days and three nights they lay in the stinking bowels of the *Insterburg*, and were given neither food nor water.

Landing at Sweinemunde, another Baltic port, they were loaded into trains in which they spent another day and a night before reaching Tychow in East Pomerania. The camp lay four kilometres from the station. In the station yard they were lined up and counted after which they were handcuffed in pairs. The guards, young submarine trainees of about eighteen or nineteen, were strangely accoutred; they wore running shorts, singlets and shoes, and carried rifles and bayonets. To these young men red-faced Hauptmann Pickard made an inflammatory speech.

Remarking the excitement of the boy guards, the prisoners acknowledged that there was trouble ahead, but they could do nothing, and were too weary to think much about it. The Luftwaffe guards who had accompanied them from Heydekrug marched to positions to the side of the road. They were armed with machine-guns.

The march began, and, aware of the tension, the kriegies were careful not to provoke the Germans, but, bowed beneath their packs, trailing in comatose misery, stumbling over cobblestones, they marched, a shambling, weary band. Boots, boots, boots. A melancholy pattern of sound. Inexorability begotten of numbness, of desperation. The monotony of the sound was as silence.

A pistol cracked—Hauptmann Pickard's. Into the untidy ranks went the guards with bayonets prickling like steel cactus, forcing the marchers to break into a run, the infamous "run up the road". As they ran the prisoners tried to loosen shoulder straps, to untie knotted cords, to prise their cumbersome packs from their backs. Handcuffed as they were it was almost impossible, and German bayonets slashed the straps, piercing clothing and flesh. The packs fell to the ground.

Now the feet sounded like the fierce spatter of hailstones on an iron roof, a cacophony of despair, of rhythmless clattering that had no end. The bayonets, skilfully measured to an inch of flesh, described coruscating arcs then flashed at a tangent to jab, and jab, and jab.

Men surpassed exhaustion so that movement became almost effortless, a demand upon nervous resources which can be made only at moments most critical. Pickard and his officers, riding bicycles, fired off their pistols. "That's for Hamburg, that's for Essen, that's for Berlin," they chanted with each shot.

The athletic young guards were tireless, lunging with their bayonets in rhythm with each step, sometimes striking with the rifle butts. Still the worst was to come, for now the guard dogs were set loose, and flung themselves into the prisoner stampede.

At the end of it the prisoners were herded into kennels sixteen feet by eight feet, and only four feet high, ten men to each kennel. They had nothing but the clothes they wore, some, torn by dogs, slashed by bayonets, practically useless. T. B. Miller for weeks had to use a handkerchief for a towel, even had to share it. One American airman had sixty-four bayonet wounds.

Ultimately, some of the men from Tychow joined us at Fallingbostel near Hanover, after a fifty-three-days' march. Miller, unfortunately, marched to another camp.

It was to Fallingbostel that we were now transferred while the Russians wavered just outside Warsaw, which they appeared likely to overrun at any moment. Deceived, the Poles revolted in the city. But the Russians did not move into Warsaw until the Germans had smashed the insurrection and taken fearful reprisals.

On the 8th August, only three weeks after our arrival, we quitted Thorn. Except that it accustomed us to living in an army atmosphere, our stay contributed little to the shape of those years.

The thing which moved me most profoundly in those three weeks, though few gave much heed to it, was a notice pinned up by the Germans, which read: "At 9 a.m. this morning Flying Officer Adams was executed at Thorn Fortress." Often I have wondered who was Flying Officer Adams, and why was he executed.

CHAPTER
19

THE Germans have miscalculated. According to their records three men more than entered the camp are leaving it. We wait, it seems interminably, in alternating sunshine and rain, our packs heavy upon our backs, the road steaming beneath our feet. A few paces forward. Halt. We are counted again. A few more steps. Intense German faces peer along the ranks; earnest fingers check off every man with solemn emphasis. Ein, zwei, drei, vier, funf . . .

In a small compound Italians, once allies of the Germans, watch interestedly, perhaps enviously. They must be wondering what is to happen to them. The Germans have turned upon them; they can expect little sympathy from the Russians. There are a few Russian prisoners, too, among them a buxom girl in an ill-fitting uniform. She is sewing a patch on a pair of trousers.

Ein, zwei, drei, vier, funf . . . They have forgotten the three men who stayed in the tunnel at Heydekrug, and walked from that camp free men, only to be caught in Lithuania, transported to Thorn, and lodged in the cooler. They are with us again, but their names have not been added to the list. We could tell them, but "let the bastards work it out for themselves. . . ."

"March!" The muddle could be sorted out another time—preferably by someone else. Although the day was oppressive and our packs weighed like the consciences of the damned, it was good to be in the open, upon a country road, with the fields rolling away on either side and trees lacing over our heads. Twice we rested, not unshouldering our packs but using them as back rests. Lying there, smoking, and listening to the sounds of summer, we could have forgotten war but for the blasting of the mortars, and the white pencil lines streaking upward to an invisible apex, reaching into skies that no projectile from the earth ever before had penetrated, and that most pathetic of wartime sights, the sad, slow stream of refugees, an unending cortège moving to some unknown, far-away destination. The burial was done. Hope was interred in the lively fields sprawling in the sun, and monumented by farmhouses, desolate in in desertion, from whose chimneys smoke wisped uncertainly.

Ageless the scene and immutable, the simulacrum of a past era, and the indictment of our own. A woodcut illustration in a history book suddenly had taken on colour, dimension, movement, as if we had gazed for too long upon it. Were these the same melancholy oxen, the same carts with the clumsily stacked bedding lapping the wheels, the upturned chairs, the motley utensils of the kitchen; were these the women, shawled in grief, the same bland babies, the same men ponderously smoking short-stemmed pipes, stolid and incurious, that had journeyed upon this amorphous pilgrimage since first the statesmen of Europe had put scissors to Poland's map?

Strangely akin to these people were we who were also the unwanted backwash of the battle, suffered to live because humanity, though enfeebled, yet was not dead. Only as hostages had we any value.

In Thorn we waited a long time before we were commanded to climb into cattle trucks the floors of which still had a covering of straw and manure. While we waited we watched the town, and the town watched us. Upon the adjacent corner a group of blonde Polish girls of quite startling beauty conversed with sham earnestness, turning towards us, pointing beyond us, but watching us. Whatever temptations may have surrounded them in their day-to-day lives, there being no men but the German garrison, now they could be as coquettish as they wished without their patriotism being suspect.

Amused, the guards did not hinder them but addressed crude witticisms to us, to which, alas, some prisoners who spoke German replied in the same coin.

It was a strange journey to Fallingbostel. For the second time in a month the Germans had been compelled to move us ahead of their own retreat. Optimism suddenly enthralled the prisoner ranks, and the journey became in our minds the prelude to liberation. Who would want to escape now, to venture into hurt, embittered Germany, the Germany whose lamp-posts were, all too often, gallows trees for allied airmen, when soon we would be free. Conversely, the guards were resigned to defeat, and because of this and the knowledge that we were unlikely to escape, they were lax as they never had been on past journeyings. Sometimes, when the train started after we had been allowed to alight for necessary reasons, prisoners actually had to run after it; once even, when the guards of one truck failed to get aboard in time, they handed up their rifles to the prisoners and were themselves helped to mount. When two kriegies were left in a walled outhouse near the railway, their absence unremarked, they could have stayed there; instead, they came running out, not even observing the time-honoured principle of "adjusting their dress before leaving", and the train was stopped for them. No one blamed them. So gladly men would have faced the perils of escape had they known that many more dreary months of imprisonment were ahead.

After leaving Thorn the first stop was a potato patch by the permanent way, and we were invited to ameliorate any physical discomforts we might have been enduring. At the edge of the patch stood a farmer who was probably calculating the damage that would be caused by these hundreds of prisoners. If his downcast slouch was any criterion the assessment was ruinous.

At Bromberg, the train having halted, we in our truck

persuaded the guards to let us alight, and Dick and I were talking to some French prisoners working on the tracks when the officer-in-charge of the train stamped up, ordered us back, mouthed invective at the guards and sent them in disgrace to the rear of the train. The corporal in charge he placed under arrest. Six more guards marched to our truck.

In the next truck a kriegy, finding the tin of tea he had brought was undrinkable, put his arm through the cage and hurled the liquid into space. The irate officer, numb with fury and astonishment, stood with tea dripping down his immaculate uniform, with tea leaves clinging to his moustache and splattering his cheeks. Admirably he recognised that it was an accident and turned away. Storming at the guards he had been a puffed-up little man close to hysteria. Now he marched towards the rear of the train with unexpected dignity.

On the platform at Stargard were massed hundreds of girls in the dark uniforms of the Hitler Mädchen. "Strength through joy" was the motto of young Germany, and these girls looked both strong and joyous; many were pretty—until they saw us. Then the transformation was startling. Their faces were flushed and contorted; they hissed and spat; their bodies writhed as they tried to communicate their loathing of us. Natural enough to hold the enemy in contempt, but this exhibition bespoke more than patriotic antipathy. The doctrine of evil which since their babyhood had been inculcated in them transcended the natural graces of youth, of femininity.

Unhappy the night. We lay like crabs in a crate, each man pinioned by his neighbours, the whole locked and flailing mass contained by the walls and the barbed-wire mesh. Beneath us the boards ground into pelvises, but any attempt to move brought cries of protest from those who found themselves in a fortuitous half-nelson or an inadvertent Indian deathlock. Draught spikes protruded from the gaps between the boards, tactile to the flesh. Above us swung Pouchy Davies, roughly hammocked in a blanket, giving us a little more room—until the moment when the hammock broke.

In sunshine we by-passed Stettin; beyond it lay the grey shimmer of the sea, gently swelling as if it breathed in its sun-warmed sleep. German little-ships swarmed in the harbour, torpid like smoked bees, strangely unsinister, unbelligerent. Four of us at a time were allowed to sit in the guards' corridor, benevolence having once more been purchased. In all, three sets of sentries were relieved of duty in our truck. Finally an oberfeldwebel was put in charge of us, a little man of middle years, urbane and friendly, in a quiet way proud of his silver-tasselled dirk and of his Afrika Corps service ribbon. He accepted a cigarette.

"You are sure you can spare it?" The words conveyed that he was neither taking a bribe nor believed that we offered one.

He too allowed us to take turns in the guards' section of the truck, and, on the second night, even allowed two prisoners from each cage to sleep there, to make conditions a little more pleasant. It was a privilege not bought but dictated by humane principle, and it was good to feel that here was a man for whom we had respect.

While there was some satisfaction to be had in tempting the enemy into defection, yet to procure a man's humiliation, to compel his disloyalty is to vitiate one's own standards. So nearly defenceless as we were, bribery, since we had the means of it, was our most effective weapon; the employment of it at times was unavoidable—it had been so at Heydekrug; and yet something of our own integrity was lost.

At the time it was a nebulous disquiet, and, I suppose, moralising is easier in retrospect.

If we had been nourishing any feeling of good-fellowship it was dispelled by an incident in the late afternoon. Dysentery was rife among us, and fairly frequent halts were necessary. Sweat was gleaming on many brows when the train came to a standstill. This, we were told, would be the last opportunity to leave the trucks for some time.

We found that we had stopped in the centre of a village the main street of which was contiguous to the railway line, and, almost as if there had been forewarning, the populace was gathered. We were allowed only on the street side of the track, and the watching villagers, mostly women, jeered with remorseless vulgarity. Remarkably, most of the prisoners succeeded in achieving a genuine and touching dignity.

Soltau was reached during the night, and for long hours we remained in the siding. The bomber stream chose nearby Hanover for its target that night, and we could see the suddenly flushed sky, and hear the bass rumble of the bombs. One of the guards groaned as if he had been hit, and in the blackness of the truck we sensed a dividing, a reiteration of national loyalties, the reinfusion of enmity. The hostility of the villagers, their urge to demean us, seemed no longer unprovoked. Were we not terrorfliegers, luft-gangsters, impotent now but the forerunners of the nightly hordes encompassing the ruin of the Fatherland? In us these people had seen the unseen destroyers, and if they could not hang us at least they could humiliate us.

In the morning we arrived at Fallingbostel. Through a barrage of stones we marched, in parties of two hundred, over the cobbles of the narrow street, and again into the country, not now the broad, aching plains of Poland, but the closer-knit terrain of Hanover. More familiar was this rural pattern of Western Europe, and the people, though they hated us, were less remote. Now, too, we were in our own theatre of war, and in Normandy the Germans were retreating.

We were avid for news; for two days the "canary" had been muffled. Somewhere among the marching prisoners was Bristow, and in his kit was the model racing car he had built, with its engine to scale, perfect in every detail. Always the German searchers handled it with reverence, which was fortunate since it housed the radio receiver.

It was a six-kilometre march. Just past the half-way mark we rested outside the barracks of an S.S. Panzer regiment. The young devotees of the Death's Head emblem, immaculate as sinister black swans in their proudly worn uniforms, gathered to stare at us with that maddening admixture of complacency and sympathy which the man still in a tournament reserves for those who have been knocked out.

Dispatch riders swept down the road and swung into the barracks, man-handling their motor-cycles with contemptuous assurance into near-horizontal turns, palpably eager to impress the shabby ranks of enemy prisoners. One overdid it and lay bemused for a moment before picking up his wheel-spinning machine. We jeered, the young Germans became threatening, and, hastily, the officer in charge of us gave the order to march. Tony "Hank" Hunter was bayonet-prodded by a guard and had to be wheeled to the camp on a stretcher carried on a handcart.

We passed a large prison camp, Stalag 11B, and poker-faced French prisoners stood on the other side of the wire watching. Our own camp was labelled 355, but we retained the Thorn number, 357. As we marched into the delouser earlier parties shouted advice about the methods of the German searchers.

While our clothes baked we had a hot shower operated by a squat Russian who, because of his enormous down-ended moustache, immediately became "Joe". He would not talk. At a later date he did vouchsafe that he was a Ukrainian farmer, had never been in the forces, but had been taken prisoner by the overrunning invaders, none the less.

I had a tussle with the searchers when they discovered a copy of Richard Hillary's *The Last Enemy*. Recognising the word, "enemy", they imagined that the book disparaged the Germans, or, alternatively, glorified the British.

In sign language I tried to explain that the word symbolised death, but I could not get them to understand that the sleep I meant was permanent. Another German, overhearing the argument, read the quotation from which Hillary took the title, and handed the book back.

The search completed, we assembled for a pep talk by a German officer. Dixie contrived to warn us that the officer's grip of the English language was somewhat insecure, but that he had not liked the laughter with which earlier parties had received his blunders. Ordinarily we accepted mistakes when Germans spoke only halting English, as they accepted our attempts to communicate in their tongue. But this man had not only a comic delivery, but a reckless confidence in his ability. Typed regulations posted in the huts appeared also to have been his doing. Under the heading "Air Raids" we were informed that "should a high explosive bomb fall into any billet prisoners therein must evacuate with immediate effect".

CHAPTER

20

Of the men in D5 at Heydekrug only eight of us now remained together. The quarters were not good. Long, low barracks of grey brick built by forced Italian labour. Floors below ground-level, windows small and square and but four in number, just above it. Seventy-two men to each room. A small night latrine fitted with a concrete trough and a minute flushing system. Damp, rough stone floors.

For each eight men there was a long trestle table and two forms, and the eight of us formed one section. We were two combines of four, in the one Toby, Dick, Ron Kennett and myself, and in the other the three Australians, Buck Buchanan, Alan Scanlan and Pouchy Davies who had never been separated since they ditched their Manchester in the North Sea, and the French Canadian, Junior Gauthier. But when there was food to cook we cooked together, and the "stooge" work was performed, one from each combine, on a weekly rota.

Our bread ration was one-seventh of a loaf per man each day. Buck used to cut three or four slices from each one-seventh; Toby, with his jealously guarded, craftsman-sharpened knife, obtained seven wafers from each of our rations. Throughout the camp some method involving chance was employed to ensure that there was no favouring one rather than another in the apportioning of food. When belts were tight—and mine was drawn in four inches in the next few months—it was easy to become obsessed with the idea that one was ill-used. Allocation by chance forestalled

163

this. We recognised our own frailty; no man was offered temptation, and none a premise for doubt.

The area of the camp probably exceeded that of Thorn. The largest compound was C compound comprising six barracks, with wash-rooms at one end, and three latrines. The latrines, sixty yards from the barracks, were divided into two sections, and were walled only two-thirds of the way to the roof. As time went on the walls diminished, bricks being appropriated for a variety of purposes, and as the draughts became fiercer Ron Mogg composed verses, unfortunately not fit for publication, exhorting prisoners to desist from this vandalism.

Recalling *The Specialist* once more, each section could have been described as a 48-holer. The holes were crudely hewn in two splintery rows of 24 in a long wooden platform, so that when there was a full house—there was usually a queue—there were 24 pairs sitting back to back.

Beyond the latrines was the parade ground, and, on the other side of the fence which skirted it, the inevitable belt of conifers. Adjoining C compound, on one side was R compound, and on the other the very small D compound which was never used, a promise to allow us to convert one of the two barracks into a theatre being not fulfilled.

These three compounds all opened on to a large central area known as the main compound on the far side of which were situated two more compounds, A and B. In the main compound a number of wooden huts housed our domestic administration, the library, and, at a later date, more prisoners. There, too, were the four cookhouses, a fuel store, and sundry other buildings used for the most part by the Germans themselves.

The rest of this enormous compound was "open country", too rough for playing pitches, but invaluable for less active recreation. It is likely that R compound was intended originally to accommodate German personnel, for the barracks were of wooden construction, smaller, roomier, and better lighted. It was occupied by the Army prisoners. The army also had B Lager, and the R.A.F. were put into C Lager.

For the first few weeks we were locked in our respective compounds; there was still a lot of timber lying about, and the Germans knew that the kriegies regarded timber as legitimate booty. Our first excursion into the open country of the camp arose from the still unsolved puzzle of the three superfluous prisoners. To save trouble Dixie had given the answer to the German authorities, but they refused to be convinced that they had made so simple an error. They wanted a full-scale count.

Seldom were the eight thousand or so prisoners massed together on one parade. A sobering sight it was, for here was so much man-power squandered, here were so many men upon whose shoulders Death's hand had rested for an instant, to be brushed away by the humanity of their enemies, so many shabby, insignificant, unaggressive-looking little men, objects of the contempt of their foes, and of the pity, that pity which has often an element of contempt, of their people at home, yet having a dignity of their own, having the will to fight frustration and boredom, having, most of them, the admiration of their fellow prisoners.

Tragedy they shared amongst them, tragedy magnified, often-times by their being helpless to do anything about it. Families were wiped out by German "retribution fire" on London, homes, businesses were lost, friends and brothers were dying in the fighting that was without end, or rotting in the undreamed-of purgatory of the Japanese prison camps. There were the defections of wives, increasing in number as the sterile years broke down resistance, and weakened the power of memories—which in so many cases were pitifully few. Anxiety was the backcloth against which most of the men played out their prisoner lives.

Peter Thomas believes that the ever-growing number of divorces appreciably lowered the morale of the camp.

In his three and a half years as a prisoner he assisted, on an average, four men a week to prepare affidavits, which Deans was empowered to swear, for cases brought against their wives, usually so that the wives who pointed out that theirs had been a hasty wartime marriage (though not a minute of it regretted) could enter into another hasty wartime marriage.

Men brooded, and pitied themselves, but in the darkness, or, wrapped about with blankets, silently upon their bunks. Few there were whose miseries impinged, except indirectly, upon their friends. Laughter came not cheaply, not easily, but it did come and was for ever sought.

In the ensuing months much of the comedy stemmed from the fight for firewood, stemmed from the multitude of shortages that compassed our existence, although in the end the comedy paled like a third act unsustained. But, if we were ready to laugh at ourselves, we laughed with more enjoyment when, by audacity or by ingenious ruse, the Germans were outwitted.

When we made our way to the waste ground for what we knew would be a prolonged counting session, the sight of timber not in use at once put us in good humour. Because normally we had not access to this part of the camp, there were no guards in the corner boxes; the ground was rough, the grass flourished to the height of our knees. In such conditions eight thousand men could camouflage much mischief. Stacked against the fence were the cage frames from the cattle trucks, ready for use again or for dismantling.

Dismantling we thought the better of these alternatives, and soon the wire was wrenched away, the frames broken apart. Other oddments of timber also were appropriated, and seventy-two ambitious men of one hut hauled away an electric-light pole which, presumably, had been one too many when the camp was built. While they were counted the pole lay in the long grass between the ranks, and when, six hours later, the Germans acknowledged that the three extra men were indeed the Heydekrug escapers, and were so pleased to have the rolls in order again that they superintended our return to the compounds with something less than their customary thoroughness, the pole was borne by the seventy-two kriegies, marching in tight formation, safely to their hut. Other squads helped to screen them, and created light-hearted diversions to engage the interest of the guards.

Eventually all the timber lying about the camp was collected by Russian prisoners and stacked in D compound. Once this was done the rest of the camp was thrown open to us, but, as a precaution against bold prisoners entering D compound by dint of picking the lock, a guard was stationed at the gate. A new lock might have proved more effectual. Skilful questions drew from him the naïve belief that he was there to prevent us from escaping; it had not been explained to him that his prime responsibility was the timber.

We were able to convince him that it was ours by right, certain imaginary clauses of the Geneva Convention being glibly quoted, and suggested that he permit us to enter the compound in parties of six. The sentry allowed in six prisoners whom, after he had carefully relocked the gate, he conducted to the timber heap. Would it not be a good idea, they put it to him, if they were to pass the timber through the fence to their friends. In this way only one party of six men would be required.

The sentry not only concurred but helped in the work. The timber was passed to eager hands, and the stack was diminishing rapidly. This was the position when the feldwebel who had posted the sentry appeared to assure himself that all was well. First to see him were the kriegies. Politely they thanked the guard and departed with as much timber as they could carry.

The feldwebel, a short, stocky man with a temper that frothed suddenly like milk rising to the boil, began to pursue first one prisoner and then another. His vacillation robbed him of any victim, but the sentry received such a verbal thrashing that I found myself quailing, although I was on the other side of the fence.

In the ceaseless foraging for wood we were again to disturb the complacency of the feldwebel. Jauntily he patrolled the camp, his thumbs thrust into his belt against the amplitude of his belly, his short legs strutting as if he wanted to feel the power that was in them. He examined the locks of a wooden shed into which we had forced an entry several times to requisition crosscut saws, hammers and other tools. The locks were secure, so impressive that, by contrast, the shed looked flimsy.

When the feldwebel had gone a prisoner jabbed an experimental boot at one of the walls, and, encouraged by the movement of a board, kicked and kicked again. Nails screeched. It was enough. The building was simply wrenched and kicked to pieces. Within five minutes there was no sign that it had ever existed, save for the guilty procession of wood carriers making a way to C compound.

Appearing from behind the cookhouse the feldwebel found himself walking among prisoners whose arms were full of timber. The disappearance of the shed was obviously a shock to him, and, as the kriegies began to run, he bellowed imprecations which sundered all barriers of language. Grasping his pistol he fired a fusillade of shots, simply as a means of self-expression, and the prisoners, to whom guns were anathema, though often enough they provoked their use, became anxious to find shelter.

Such uninhibited tumbling and contortionism there was in those moments, and we who were mere observers of the scene, and comparatively safe, watched with delight the antics of these involuntary clowns. The act had a perfect climax; one kriegy, flinging away his bundle of wood, executed what seemed to be a nearly perfect swallow dive through the wide open window of the cookhouse. Unexpectedly, water gushed through the window, and it was seen that the man had gone head first into a boiler of, fortunately, cold water.

Against this cold douche of comedy even the feldwebel's incandescent anger was not proof, and the episode ended amicably enough, although in consequence of it we were once more, for a week, confined to compound.

When the between-compound gates were again opened to us, the only timber left to pilfer was that which had been used by the garden-loving Italians who had built the camp to make trellises, ornamental gateways and rustic seats for their skilfully laid-out rock garden. Never before had we enjoyed such a perfect little oasis in our barren environs, but it was sacrificed to the insatiable blowers, wantonly, and unjustifiably in the opinion of many. Once the woodwork was gone, the trellis fences, the seats, there was no protection for the garden, and little incentive to retain it. The plants were neglected, the rocks scattered by careless boots.

To improve our circumstances Dick took a job in the cook-house, temporarily. Such commerce as he was able to engage in was to the advantage not of the four of us alone, but of all eight. The work brought him into contact with German guards and Russian workers from whom, in exchange for cigarettes, he obtained a small quantity of firewood and some spring onions.

Some of the Russians appeared to enjoy unusual privileges. They were birds of prey with, somewhere, nests that they were lining comfortably with feathers plucked from us timid chickens. A different type from the Mongol-featured Russians who predominated, these men suffered none of the indignities of their compatriots. Nor did they seem to have anything to do with them.

Shortly after our arrival at Fallingbostel I saw a party of Russian prisoners dragging a heavy handcart. Their guards carried whips, and from time to time a lash fell across a sweating back, or curled into the crevices between ribs.

Little malice was in the blows, and the Russians themselves were not greatly concerned. Then the party came level with our tin dump near the fence.

Dropping the handcart, the Russians fell upon their knees before the dump, as if the mound of old tins housed a god. Their crab-fingers and cat-licking tongues winkled out every smear of food, and I remembered the cheerful apology of T. B. Miller's "Every little bit of nutriment counts".

With an easy grace the guards leaned back and flayed their charges with their whips. Their action, behind which was nothing more than the cold inspiration of habitual duty, was the more frightening for its lack of passion or conviction. Hard fell the lashes across the thin flesh, so that one expected to see splits appear where it pressed upon the bones. And yet, at first, as they licked and scraped and fossicked, the Russians ignored the blows, and when, slowly, they did retreat, one sensed that they were driven by weight rather than by pain.

Although from new prisoners and from reading we had kept ourselves informed of progress in military aviation, it was not until August 16th, when we saw a large-scale daylight raid for the first time, that we appreciated the significance of the change. Never had we seen anything like the vast echelons of bombers, with sun-reflecting wings, that went with sonorous dignity from horizon to horizon, nor seen the angry shoals of fighters whose minnow-dartings prickled the whole blue sky with silver.

Fortresses and Liberators, a thousand of them, boomed overhead, the engine sound coming with a trochaic flow and ebb, bombers, bombers, bombers, and they were protected by nearly their number of Lightnings and Thunderbolts which left the sky whorled with tenuous white vapour that lingered awhile like insubstantial deposits of foam on the seashore.

But for all their pivoting and quick flurries of flight, the little craft could do nothing to repel the flak from anti-aircraft guns, and, at intervals, black smoke, shot through with scarlet and violet and gold, bunched upon one of the bombers, curling like tangles of seaweed. Sometimes there would be a cluster of white dots, parachutes, gently, gently falling, swinging, falling in silent loneliness. For twenty minutes, perhaps, men hovered, swayed, descended, twenty minutes when there was no reality save the unattainable earth, and the strange device of silk and cord in which it was difficult to have faith.

Often we watched in vain for those tiny eruptions of silk in the far-off sky, and wondered what had held the men fast in their disintegrating craft. And sometimes, too, when the main stream of planes had gone on homeward, a "lame duck", fighting for altitude, would lurch overhead, with perhaps a brace of Lightnings in company, but often quite, quite alone.

When the air-raid sirens sounded the compounds were sealed, and we were supposed to go into the barracks. Angry scenes occurred frequently as prisoners defied orders to return to their rooms, giving way only when shooting was imminent. It was wise to stay with a group, and to stay near the door. If one were visiting another compound it was advisable to stay there. Any attempt to return to one's own compound usually was intercepted, and a spell in the cooler followed.

Junior Gauthier sauntered across the big main compound after the sirens had sounded, but the guards must have been susceptible to his Gallic-Canadian smile for each time he was halted he was allowed to go on.

Buck, his homely brown face gathered into a frown, demanded: "Where the hell have you been, Junior?" with all the venom of a parent whose anxiety for a missing child has given way to relief when the miscreant has appeared unharmed. But Junior only grinned, and Buck relented.

From under his jacket Junior took a small painting on three-ply wood. This was for me; he had traded some pencil sketches of mine for the painting, executed by a Frenchman who resided in the Vorlager. It was the first oil painting I ever owned. True, it was no more than a nostalgic representation of a valley in the Auvergnes, with a square church, neatly spired, in a setting of sombre green. But the moment when I hung it on the wall at the foot of my bed was one of the most joyful of my life.

For many hours I gazed at the picture, thankful for its nuances of tone, its subtleties of form and design, the never-ending discoveries that were in it, when I lay a victim of the summer sickness of prison camps, gastro-enteritis.

The main latrines were primitive, and the flies fell upon us in their black obscenity. Because of the heat we lay stripped, and the creatures oozed over the flesh, refusing to be brushed away. Every twenty or thirty minutes I made the weary trek to the latrine, each time becoming weaker and more despondent. I ate nothing except spoonfuls of powdered milk which did have a binding effect if the attack was a mild one, but which was ineffectual on this occasion until the disease had began to loosen its grip. There were cases worse than mine; Wallace Betts almost died. An army man did die, and was followed to the grave by a dozen scruffy old Germans who looked as if they had been put into uniform especially to represent the Reich on this occasion. A few minutes later we heard a ragged rifle volley, the last shot sounding some seconds after the echoes of the others had died away.

Twenty-three days after they had been marched from Thorn the Polish prisoners rejoined us at Fallingbostel. Excited as children to be with their friends again, and relieved that once more they enjoyed the comparative safety of being but a few among thousands, they hailed Dixie Deans as their saviour, and refused to accept his disclaimer that his efforts had influenced German policy in any way.

Their coming was unexpected, typical somehow of the

day-to-day existence which now we led. Nothing seemed stable any more, nothing was planned or known about in advance; we lived from incident to incident, and the moment was invariably lost before it was recognised as a break in the monotony. You saw a crowd, someone shouting names, and ran to see what was happening, to find that mail had been issued but that there was none for you. Not now the announcement in the morning that mail had arrived, and the ephemera of anticipation until it was given out in the evening.

A few cigarette parcels came in those first weeks. I had several, sent in comradeship by the men of 460 Squadron, reformed a dozen times since my day, sent in penitence by Nancy, and sent in sympathy by Margaret, my pen-friend.

Whenever I received cigarettes I ran over to B compound with a hundred or so for Dick Carlyle and Dick Richardson, South African Army N.C.O.s. to whom I had been introduced by Neilson Whyte. Carlyle had been night editor of a Durban newspaper. If he had not been a newspaperman he could have earned a living playing the part in films. Tall, and built like a front-row Rugger forward, he had fine features, eyebrows like black scimitars, and hair of gun-metal grey.

Richardson, his friend, was a dark, alert man with small wary eyes, an artist. Often, from B Compound, and sometimes from R compound, where Whyte lived, I had to scamper when the sirens went. So continuous were they now that some latitude had to be given to allow us to get back to our compounds.

In spite of the Allies' mastery of the air I had a hunch that we would be spending another winter in Germany. I needed winter clothes. For six hundred precious cigarettes I bought a blanket; two sets of underwear I acquired for the price of seventy cigarettes per garment. Yet the prevailing mood of the camp was optimism, and this was bolstered by first-hand news of the invasion battles brought by new prisoners.

Captured at Caen the men had spent twenty-six grim days in the train, and, strafed by their own aircraft, had lost forty-nine men on the way. They said that the war would end by December, at the latest. A sceptical Canadian climbed over the wire one night when there was thick fog, making his move quickly and confidently as if he had had a special weather report.

His effort was commendable for we had been warned that there were now "Security Zones" where anyone found wandering would be shot at sight, but we had not been told where the boundaries were. Escape, the warning notices informed us in letters six inches high, was "no longer a sport". However, after a few days of freedom, the Canadian, who had not long been a prisoner, was returned to the camp and sentenced to the usual spell of solitary confinement.

Nat Leaman was taken to Hanover under escort to be tried by a German military court for his attempted escape at Heydekrug, there being concomitant charges which were more serious. Peter Thomas appeared for the defence. Anticipating a "mock" trial of the worst kind he was gratified when the German officers behaved with complete fairness and took the view that Leaman had committed no crime except the admirable one of attempting to escape. Nor did the court reveal tendentiousness in dealing with a Jew. Not all Germans were uncivilised, Thomas reflected. Leaman was sentenced to three weeks' solitary confinement, the same as he would have received had he been punished summarily, and must have been thankful for the bath he had taken in the laundry boiler at Heydekrug.

If his fare in the cells was meagre, that of the camp itself was little better. Tins brought from Heydekrug were long since empty, and, except for one issue of half a parcel per man on September 8th, there were no Red Cross parcels.

The German-issued rations were bread, potatoes, and soup made from dried vegetable.

The army, who less than ever appreciated having to share with us, laid claim vociferously to a quantity of clothing which arrived at the camp. Dixie, somewhat dubious of the claim, nevertheless made no protest. There was no point in aiding the Germans in their various efforts to divide us into warring factions. These efforts were at this time directed mainly at the Irish who were exhorted to join the Free British Brigade by the tragically misguided zealot, Amery, whose life was claimed by the bitter, retributive society of the early post-war days.

Differences between the army and R.A.F. prisoners also were aggravated by the Germans, not deliberately altogether, but simply because being army men with no liking for their own airmen, they were prejudiced in favour of their own kind. A soldier, even a British soldier was an honest tradesman, and, as easily, the battle might have gone the other way. The R.A.F. men, on the other hand, were treacherous demoniacs charitably allowed to live. As if to emphasise this point of view, three Thunderbolts flew over the camp at fifty feet, and one of them had a playful shot at a *posten*-box. Then, at night, bombs fell so close to the camp that we thought we had been mistaken for a German town, and some kriegies dived under the beds, but the pin-point-bombing Mosquitoes were demolishing the S.S. Regiment barracks down the road.

Our optimism was unenduring. It died in the remorseless, endless fall and splatter of the rain, and the turgid, moiling cloud that stayed in the skies like a grey scum. Outside the barracks the mud was churned by twenty thousand restless boots. Inside it was so dark that sometimes it was impossible to read the title-page of a book, and to get light for reading I would go over to R compound and share Neilson Whyte's bunk with him and Norman Hennessy. In these well-windowed, wooden huts the atmosphere was altogether different, and although there was present a noisy bunch of Australian soldiers with a cheerful disrespect for higher education, our powers of concentration were by now so well developed that we were seldom distracted.

Whyte and Hennessy were both studying for the Church, Neil for the Presbyterian ministry, Norman to take Holy Orders in the Church of England. Splendid men both, they had an enviable faith and no trace of bigotry. Together they studied Theology and Hebrew and I read International Trade and Industrial Organisation while the rain splashed outside.

CHAPTER
21

WHILE we crouched in the half-dark barracks, waiting for the rain to stop, summer with impatience had gone its way. We went outside only to go to the latrines, or to collect rations, or for *appell*. The rations, soup or millet, both gritty, were hardly worth collecting. Occasionally a little Red Cross food arrived. Pilfering from the Red Cross trucks crossing Germany was rife; previously it had been unknown.

Buck volunteered to cut brushwood outside the camp, realising that he might be able to plunder the Commandant's cabbage patch on the way back. It was a risky forage, but, day after day, he defeated the vigilance of the guards to bring in a cabbage concealed in his stack of brushwood.

Roll-calls were enlivened by the presence of a new counter, a little corporal with a twitch, who could count only in fives. If one file happened to be incomplete the little German was perplexed. Sometimes he counted it as a file of five and chanced the result, or he begged us to tell him how many we were.

Invariably he was the last of the counters to report. One afternoon the officer in charge of *appell* began to bellow sarcastically, and the little man twitched and twitched until his teeth hammered together. Up and down our lines he darted, panicky as a newly-caged bird, glancing fearfully over his shoulder, then imploring us to tell him how many please, how many, how many? We relented at last. With relief he entered the figure in his book, and, mustering what dignity he could, marched towards the centre. As he went the kriegies whistled in unison a tune to which there were rude lyrics both in German and in English. Doubtless he knew the German.

"Double, man, double!" It must have been something like that, for the corporal spurted to a trot. As he approached the officer he gathered himself to throw what was to have been the most impressive Nazi salute of all time. In a way, I suppose, it was. Trying to salute and stop in one movement, he went flat on his belly, his arm rigidly outstretched, his fingers almost touching the jack-boot of his superior, flat in the mud, with the downpouring rain soaking into his back.

From above the clouds came the roar of American engines, and leaflets fell into the camp. Defying German guns, prisoners raced to pick them up. Death was the penalty for having leaflets, the Germans warned, death for civilians, death for prisoners. They searched the camp, and those leaflets which had not been put away for souvenirs, they found pasted on the walls.

As if punitively the Gestapo swarmed in, but not before we had received a warning from guards who did not count their action as treachery. We were marched to the delouser for personal search, and I hated being compelled to go naked into the rough hands of those men. The Gestapo objected, at first, to the presence of the room leaders in the barracks while the search went on. We won our point, but little was gained, for with methodical malice they wrecked the barracks, even tore up clothing. It was fortunate for me that Bill Bowhill was present. On the wall over my bed were my uncharitable caricatures of the Nazi leaders.

"Are you going to leave them there?" Toby had asked, wonderingly before we left the room, and I had replied: "They can do what they like about it," and regretted the braggadocio the instant it was too late to withdraw.

Relating afterwards what had happened, with some embellishment, perhaps, Bowhill declared that the searchers, urious, had wanted to ferret out the culprit and have him punished, but had not been able to decide whether the firing squad or a nearby concentration camp best fitted the crime. Bowhill bravely intervened. The artist admired the German leaders—though he was not quite in accord with their viewpoint—he asseverated, and it was for this reason that he had made the drawings. Unfortunately, being little experienced, he had allowed distortion to creep in. A similarly unhappy result had attended his effort to capture Bowhill's own likeness, and to prove the point, he produced my caricature of himself. Placated, the Germans declared that nevertheless such irreverences could not be allowed to survive, and they ripped the caricatures to pieces.

During the search Dixie Deans patrolled the camp. One hothead could provoke an incident of much gravity, and Deans wanted to prevent any ugly scenes if it were possible. Indeed, he did smooth away a number of difficulties, and did not hesitate to protest against the methods of the secret police when it was warranted.

One objection angered a weasely fellow who flew at Deans, got his hands round his throat, and, with his feet actually off the ground, clung there, digging in vicious fingers. One of the camp officers, seeing what was happening, turned his back, sympathetic, but afraid to interfere. Wisely Deans did not strike the Gestapo man, and finally succeeded in shaking him off. He decided to report the incident at once.

At the gate the guards stood aside, and Deans stalked into the Commandant's office. The Oberst shrugged; they were in this together, the gesture implied. On his way back to the compound Deans saw a man lying by the roadway, victim of an epileptic fit. It was the officer who had refused to help him. This, Deans thought wryly, was a grim jest of Fate, but he nevertheless routed out some German soldiers and sent them to the aid of their superior.

When we were dressing in the delouser Joe, the Ukrainian farmer with the R.A.F. moustache, appeared. He shook his head gravely when we asked him when he was going to give us a shower. There had been no showers since October 1st, and we were having to make do with a cold water hose in a six-foot-square wooden shed outside the barrack door.

And so there was little work for Joe. If he minded he did not show it. Did his expression soften at all, I wondered, when he stood at the tap controlling the water which splashed on to the grimy backs of fifty Polish women captured during the Warsaw rising. After being deloused at our camp they were marched elsewhere, to a camp where their sturdiness fell away from them, where their plump buttocks hollowed, and their breasts drooped thinly.

Some of our men lined the fence to watch through the wide windows those women shower, allying themselves thus with their captors in making a public spectacle of feminine indignity. On parade, Dixie Deans, angrier than most of us had seen him, gave the prisoner peeping-Toms the whiplash of his tongue. Strangely, an incident almost identical in Don Bevan's *Stalag 17* was dismissed contemptuously by one critic who did not believe that American prisoners could sink so low.

Until now women had provided the prime conversational topic. They were spoken of by foul mouths and reverent ones, and, sometimes, the same mouth was foul and reverent by turns. Now one could move around the barracks and hear women discussed only for their prowess in the kitchen.

Lascivious talk, never more than an unpleasant if incessant background furnished by a minority, ceased first. The morale of the camp, fundamentally, was affected neither by its existence nor by its disappearance. But indubitably something was lost when we forgot the women who belonged to our lives. Something was lost because we had been planning, not our own advantage alone, but the happiness of another. Now prevailed an every-man-for-himselfness. Life took on a quality of rawness. There was no violence, except in isolated instances, but there was an atmosphere of violence such as surrounds a crowd that awaits a revolution. And it was in part because in this men's world the influence of women finally was excluded.

Other factors contributed to the doubtful morale. There was no inspiration in our army leadership. Deans willingly had accepted that leadership; his great moment was yet to come. Arnhem had failed. At first we had not recognised the significance of Arnhem, then we came to see that it had been intended to cut months off the war. Weary men with red bérets were marched into the camp, and lodged in the last unoccupied wooden huts and in tents, accepting without bitterness that their latrines were but trenches uncovered to the rain, without even a crossbar upon which to rest their haunches. They were the men of Arnhem, who did not know yet that they had been acclaimed heroes, and thought of themselves only as men who had failed.

For them the heroes were the crews of the slow Sterling bombers who, to succour the beleaguered airborne troops, flew boldly and low, and fell, many of them, in flames to the earth.

Arnhem had failed, and our impression was that supplies of Red Cross parcels had not been sent to Geneva because Arnhem had been intended to wind up the war. Arnhem had failed, and the summer had passed us by. And still it was raining.

The ooze lay in slimy unquiescence, trembling with the fall of a foot, sliding back slowly into the boot-bruised cavities. A cartoon drawn by the indefatigable Anderson shows two prisoners deep in mud, their shoulders hunched to the rain, on their way to a meeting of the Farmers' Club. Says one to the other: "This rain will do the crops a world of good." The gag might have been out of season but it earned its laugh.

We were shut in from 5 p.m. to 8 a.m.; the room was fireless, and the little light that seeped over the mud wastes and between the grey shafts of rain was interrupted and dispersed by lines of clothing laundered in cold water, scrubbed with nail-brushes to an even beige, hung to dry though there was little chance of its ever doing so. There were no Red Cross parcels, and no cabbages remained in the Commandant's garden.

"They've got it in for us to beat hell," said Toby. "The next thing will be that they'll add another hour to every day. If they do I'm going to complain."

Dick thought that worth putting in his diary and when he had done so he said: "I reckon I'm glad though that I'm not a prisoner of the Japs."

We agreed that prison misery was a relative thing; deprivation of liberty was the fundamental factor. In the Isle of Man I had seen internees comfortably settled in requisitioned boarding-houses, but looking as if they endured the ultimate of misery. And at the other end of the scale were the prisoners of the Japanese, and the inmates of the German hell-camps. We did not realise then how much further humans can be pushed after they have decided that they can bear no more. We ourselves had not reached the nadir of our P.O.W. existence.

Enough parcels found a sporadic way to the camp for an issue of one third per man, and Dick and Toby skilfully played a stock exchange game in Foodacco, to which a proportion of the food found its way, and made a little extra. Foodacco always had been the R.A.F. exchange mart; now the firm had been allotted a good-sized brick building which was to have been a cookhouse but was never finished, and the system quite suddenly became popular with the army prisoners as well. It was also a matter of interest to economists after the war.

Toby and Dick happily would spend the whole morning watching the chalking up, expunging, chalking up of prices on the big blackboard, buying as soon as prices fell, and selling to the credit of our account when the price climbed again. By the end of the day's operations they might have profited by a mere five points, or they might have earned the price of a meat roll—say one hundred and ten points.

But soon the stock was exhausted once more, and we reverted to the unsatisfying round of swede soup at midday, and a brace of potatoes in the evening. Bitterly we complained to the Red Cross representative who visited the camp on November 12th, and he, shrugging sympathetically, told us that the K Lager men, now at Tychow, were worse off than we.

The snow, first of the winter, settled precariously upon the slush, thawed and was itself churned to slush; the rain came again. For forty-one of fifty days it had rained, and the mud appalled. Toby began grim mutterings about a "watery grave" and "darkest Germany". We lived, rain-curtained and mud-carpeted, in clothes that were never quite dry, in boots that were always a little damp. Trails of running green slime coursed down the inside walls, and water, condensing on the ceiling, or leaking through, spattered on our bunks. The soup was water except for a few pieces of frost-decayed vegetable, and we slept in beds that were secretly, shamefully wet, sometimes, because overworked bladders could not be controlled.

But life could not be for ever dreary. Toby and Ron each received a personal parcel from home, and there was a little food in them. In Toby's were apple-rings, fragile and insubstantial as smoke-rings, but, soaked in water, they became fat and firm and appetising. And there was cinnamon in a neat little tin to go on them, and chocolate that lay as still as could be in the mouth and slowly melted on the tongue while we dared not even speak lest we hastened the melting.

The little extra food from Toby's parcel came at a good time for me; the examinations for the special Oxford University diploma for which I had been working were but a week away. As much as I could I was reading in Neil Whyte's room, but there were many days when I had to be in the gloom of C6.2 with a text-book borrowed for perhaps an hour, and then I would read until strain compelled tears from my eyes. At the end of an hour, or a morning or a day, I would hand the book to some other student and another book was made available to me.

The examinations began on my birthday, the 27th November. But earlier, unexpectedly, we had hot showers, the first for two months. We stood in the shallow trough, twenty-four of us sharing eight showers, feeling the water slashing the body with hot strokes so that the warmth penetrated to the cold core of us, glimpsing soap-jacketed torsos through the swirling nebula of steam, and having friendly hands scrubbing sweet-smelling suds into the opening pores of the back.

Aloof by the tap stood Ukrainian Joe, his Russian cap pulled deep over his eyes, the broad sweep of his moustache denying him a mouth. He stood with his trousered legs thrust into jack-boots set squarely on the concrete, and the legs seemed short and powerful beneath the straight, floppy tunic that reached to the chunky thighs. His hand was on the tap, and we watched for the first sign of movement, and wondered if he knew how much we longed for the warmth of the water to go on, and on. Aloof on his little concrete pedestal he was at once a peasant and a god administering some strange rite to us, the members of his sect, who were naked and wore plumes of lather on our heads.

And then the hand began to move, and quickly we

sluiced the last scum of soap from us and stood, with thin, pink flesh ridged and hollowed on gawky bones, overcome by anticlimax. Selfconsciously we elbowed our way to the dressing-room. Joe's little black eyes followed us expressionlessly.

Once we were outside again we were elated, and warm, and untouchable under our greatcoats. We wore our towels turbanwise, and the rain thudded upon them softly, though it beat viciously at our faces. But those faces were cheerful, now, and I went to the examinations with more optimism than I had thought possible.

We sat in the unheated library, at tables which had stood outside for weeks, and the rain that had soaked into the wood rose slowly and damped the foolscap upon which we struggled to make legible marks. The rule forbidding pens had not been relaxed, and so we had to write in pencil. The temperature was near freezing, but the cold was dank and insidious, with none of the invigoration of a frosty air. The creeping, gangrenous cold in our feet became unbearable, and we removed our wet boots and socks, and sat with naked feet tucked under us. Muffled in balaclavas, and greatcoats and mittens, we rose from time to time to stamp and slap and punch, fractionally increasing the blood's flow, then slumped and huddled like half-empty sacks in a barn, as strange a group of candidates as ever sat to an Oxford examination paper.

But it was the papers themselves which, in this setting, seemed incongruous. Crisp they had come from lean envelopes heavy with seals which even the German censors had left intact. Between their sealing in Oxford and their opening by the envigilator at Fallingbostel no eye had beheld those papers, which now were spread upon our tables.

For four days the examinations went on, four days of a bleak purgatory brought upon us by a war which, in our answers, we ignored in favour of theories of peaceful international trade. We wrote desperately on the damp paper, wondering if anyone would ever be able to decipher anything that we had written, compelling our minds to analyse the questions, each a sterile poem deceptive in its academic simplicity, and to yield up knowledge and original thinking which they did cantankerously and with ill grace.

The diploma which ultimately I received from the University has impressed no one, but to me it is proof that I had guts enough to keep working when it would have been much easier to let it all go.

Men triumphed in many ways. Some, like Larry Slattery or Neil Thompson, triumphed, if for no other reason because they were cheerful, unembittered men after five years and more as prisoners. The achievements of Dixie Deans none matched.

There were men with an inherent capacity for leadership who failed as prison camp leaders. Deans had an almost unique combination of qualities which were early recognised by his fellows at Stalag Luft 1, Barth, and they elected him Camp Leader. Their decision was confirmed by R.A.F. men from Lamsdorff and other camps when they were all transferred to Sagan.

He was admired by the Americans, respected by the Germans, and loved by those whose loyalty he commanded. Discipline he kept effortlessly, though he had no authority by rank conferred. Morale was excellent; he inspired a sense of security, hated injustice, and would fight for our well-being until he collapsed. In his dealings with the Detaining Power he was tactful and shrewd, avoided familiarity, and never used his position to his own advantage.

The Geneva Convention he knew as a priest knows his Bible, and he insisted upon its observance by us, and, as far as was possible, by the Germans. Rank did not awe him; he was as much at ease with a Nazi general as with a

Cockney sergeant. A natural psychologist, he had been at pains to understand the German temperament, and was not often puzzled by the sometimes devious reasoning of German officers. With their point of view he was not infrequently in sympathy, and he spoke their language both figuratively and in fact.

He was a first-class administrator and handled with aplomb the multifarious dealings with the Air Ministry in England, the Swiss "Protecting Power" authorities, the Red Cross, and visiting dignitaries from enemy or neutral countries.

He had, I think, great faith in his capacity for the work, and drove himself with complete disregard of his health. Yet there was in him neither ambition nor lack of humility. He does not acknowledge the immensity of his achievement.

It would be wrong to regard him as some paragon. He was never that. Had he been so he could never have earned the affection that was his; he was and is too human a person not to have a normal quota of weakness, but such is his make-up that he was the man the hour brought forth, as in the infinitely greater field of war rule Churchill would seem to have been predestined to lead.

When we were transferred to Thorn where the army was already firmly, though not long established, Deans withdrew into quiet liaison work as R.A.F. Man of Confidence, and gave to Regimental Sergeant-Major Turner his full loyalty. He had no desire to usurp Turner, who was in Deans's own estimation a "good chap and a very capable administrator".

Although among army prisoners authority was customarily vested in the senior N.C.O. class, Turner was not, curiously enough, the senior R.S.M. He had been deputed by the senior R.S.M. at Lamsdorff, one of those characters of the British army whose fame endures for longer than that of most generals, to take command of the contingent transferred from Lamsdorff to Thorn. With such powerful backing the army men had never thought to question Turner's authority.

While a most efficient R.S.M., Turner had not had the experience of Deans, nor had he the same command of German. Most important he did not have Deans's understanding of the German mind, that sensitiveness which enabled the airman to tread the very precarious path between antagonising our captors and yielding too much to them.

Even in his subordinate capacity Deans's talents were obvious to the soldier prisoners. In one army room during an inspection Turner asked for a badly leaking roof to be mended, but was put off by German excuses. Deans, however, declared that this was not good enough, and exacted a promise that the work would be done that same day, and it was. Moreover the R.A.F.'s more flexible, more democratic form of government appealed to the army men, most of whom were not regulars. In their own leadership they found little inspiration.

Their dissatisfaction led to a meeting of room leaders being called to discuss the situation. Turner invited Captain Bonham-Carter, one of the medical officers, to take the chair. In a conscientious bid for camp unity Bonham-Carter, unwisely perhaps, elected to disregard the conventions of the chair and the limitations of a medical officer's authority, and promised, in his "capacity of Senior British Officer", to give Turner his full support. Deans, embarrassed by the whole business, yet resented this excess, and pointed out that, under the Convention, a medical officer had no such status.

The meeting decided that an election be held to determine the camp leadership. Deans was not anxious to have the job, but was willing to accept the responsibility if he was wanted. There was a brief, hectic election campaign, which provided plenty of entertainment. For Peter Thomas it was the first experience of political electioneering. The whole camp voted. Foolishly the army put up two candidates but it did not matter; almost unanimously Deans was elected, a most remarkable tribute considering inter-service rivalry. To Deans we were all kriegies and there was born a solidarity which had been lacking.

In the difficult days ahead the camp was to be thankful for its decision, for it was then that his achievements ran far beyond duty's call.

CHAPTER

22

Toby, Dick and Ron had all done their stint, and I
knew it was my turn. Toby put a muddy Red Cross
box in my hands. "Of you go—and don't squib it."

"I know, I know," I returned defensively. He was wrong
to think that because I lacked courage I lacked scruple.
He should have known that I would never have eaten the
swede peelings that he and Ron and Dick, each in their
turn, had brought back, were I not going to take my turn.
Then I knew that he was speaking roughly to me because he
had himself hated the task. A mistake I often made in those
days was not to look deep enough for Toby's motives.

I hurried across the main compound to the cookhouse,
near B compound, where perhaps a hundred men waited
tensely. More here than yesterday. Two men appeared in
the doorway of the cookhouse, paused, then walked towards
us apprehensively. They carried a large box with sliding
handles, like a sedan chair sawn off half-way down. The
container was filled with frostbitten peelings, but there was
not nearly enough to fill all those cardboard boxes. The
men made an ugly, urgent movement towards the carriers,
R.A.F. men, who kept on going though they knew well that
their load would never reach the rubbish tip.

The crowd flexed, then sprang in concert. Sick with fear
of failure, I moved, too, found myself on my knees, clutching,
scrabbling. My fingers encountered a piece of rotten swede,
and thankfully I put it in my box. Before I could prevent it,
a hand, bone tight with avarice, clawed it from me.

Toby would be scathing, Dick reproachful, Ron would jeer. I could see only clutching hands and predatory faces. My box yet was empty. I wanted to weep. Then someone knocked over the wooden container, and a shower of peelings, which had been mud-packed to the bottom, suddenly flew in my direction. Quickly I shovelled them into my little box, then ran.

We filled a small keg with water, ice-cold from the near-frozen pipes, we cut away the impossibly bad pieces of peel, and the rest we scrubbed with nail-brushes to a dirty gamboge. Hands became thick and almost impotent with coldness, and the stale, sour stench of the decayed vegetable was heavy in the room. We boiled the diced peeling until at last it was pulpy enough to eat.

When we had eaten I said: "Well, we've all had a turn; I don't know how you feel about it, but I'm out of it. I won't go through that again."

"O.K.," said Toby. "Actually I've rather had it myself. We'd better think up something else."

He collected dandelions and grasses which he transmuted into violent-looking soups. He did not offer to share these, believing that he was an eccentric; Dick and I followed his example only once, then recognised his claim.

Hearing that one of the men who carried the waste was fed up with the job, Dick went quietly to the cookhouse and hired out his labour for the privilege of first choice of the swede peelings. Sometimes, in addition to his box of peelings, he was allowed to carry away a swede too tainted for the boiler but having portions that were reclaimable. Twice a day he went off to his work, wearing a long Polish coat which he had been given to replace his own stolen greatcoat, and sabots which he had learned to wear to combat the slush, and a hand-knitted hat shaped in a Muscovite style.

He hated the task, but he brought home food. Every day the cold ritual of brushing and scrubbing was performed, and for our several hours' work we were able to add to our dixies of anaemic soup two tablespoons of diced swede. All eight of us shared the "gash"; in this way was Buck rewarded for his generosity with the Commandant's cabbages. If there had been more calories in the cabbages, the swede came at a time rather more critical.

Buck had not yet completed his work for the good of the many. Twice a week two men from each room were escorted into the forest, where they gathered fuel. What they could carry on their backs was the room's entire supply for the week. Our strongest men volunteered for this assignment, and to reward them, and to give them strength, they received a double ration of soup. They would come into the huts quite, quite exhausted, toting on their backs incredible loads, or perhaps others would meet them at the gate and carry the loads for them. Buchanan regularly went into the woods.

Several times, too, Toby, small, chunky, strong as a cheetah, volunteered, and returned shouldering a load that determination alone could account for. Bad-tempered, and white with fatigue, he wore easily the faintly smug expression of the genuine martyr. Later, chuckling, he would claim to be the original poor man whom good King Wenceslas had seen gathering winter fuel in the deep, and crisp, and even snow.

There were occasions when our men returned empty-handed. The Germans had agreed to the parties collecting wood in the forest on condition that there was no trading outside the camp. It was a fair enough rule in its way, but, in applying it, the guards discriminated against the R.A.F. Invariably the army parties went unmolested while the R.A.F. men were detained to be searched for bribe cigarettes, and often kept until it was too late to go into the woods at all.

When we had nothing in the room to burn Buck led a party of us into the darkness to dig up a post from the fence between our compound and the main compound. Timing the swing of the searchlights, alert for the unexpected traverse, listening for the warning from our look-out that dogs or patrolling guards were approaching, we dug and heaved. Buck, groaning with effort, used his shoulder as a battering-ram to loosen the post. We left the wire hanging slack.

In the room we went to work with a crosscut saw, with a hatchet, kitchen knives, razor blades. It was not long before the Germans came to look for the post. By then it was stacked in faggots against the wall. On the floor were chips and sawdust. The guards had been told to look for a twelve-foot post; they took no notice of the chips, or the sawdust, or the fresh pile of faggots, and went on to the next hut.

Sedulously pushing their aim to divide us, the Germans even doctored news bulletins with smooth allegations that the allied ground and air forces were at loggerheads, and deliberately withholding support from each other. The propaganda might have succeeded had we not enjoyed the daily B.C.C. news bulletins; as it was the news sheet issued to us provided the readers of the B.B.C. reports with excellent cover should they be caught at their work.

Much of the German news was a rehash of the bulletins to the German people, and the formula for glossing over bad news we soon learned. Whenever the Reich armies retreated the news would read: "The focal point of the fighting shifted from Flosskossosolavitz (or some similar name) to Askanavakanawicz (or some similar name)." These would be the names of tiny villages few would bother to look up on a map, and fewer find if they did. A perfectly true statement implied that nothing important had happened, but the villages were probably fifty miles apart, with between them several important towns.

Or a name, Thorn for example, would occur in the news for the first time. "Heavy fighting took place near the town of Thorn." Next day there was "further fighting in the Thorn area. Russian attacks in great strength were contained". Another day passed, then "Fierce fighting is still going on in the outskirts of the town of Thorn."

After that the word "town" would be dropped, "fortress" or "citadel" substituted; the word "garrison" crept in. The town was surrounded. Finally it would be admitted that the fortress had succumbed, but the last-ditch heroism of the German troops was acclaimed.

There came a day—it was December 15th—when the German bulletin told not of defeat proudly met, but of sudden and fierce counter-attack. Ardennes. Was it the last shot in the locker, or did this devastating push foreshadow a revitalised Germany? The answer did not come until the 26th, when German armoured columns were halted near the Meuse.

And so came Christmas, and we knew that this was the last Christmas of our imprisonment. Each Christmas past we had reckoned to be our last. This time there could be no doubt. Yet it was not a happy time; there was disappointment and frustration because of Ardennes, because of malnutrition, and darkness, and dankness, and the bitterness that had grown among us. Goodwill was a procrustean burden, and men were reluctant to abandon grudges borne for unkindnesses remembered or imagined.

Our mood was aggravated by the generosity of our neighbouring camp, 11B, which, having been longer established, still had a store of food parcels, and gave us 2,500, enough for four men to share a parcel. Toby and Ron shared a whole tin of corned beef, Dick and I a tin of spam. We had potatoes and swedes, and, afterwards, plum-duff made from potatoes, which had been grated, then squeezed in muslin so that we were left with a sticky, pink suet, and prunes.

When it was all over we had thundering bellyaches, and

took to our bunks. From all the barracks men went track-lessly through the snow, which was still falling slowly, lush and squashy like over-ripe fruit from a ghostly tree, to the latrines which soon gave off a thick aroma, a rich foulness that held the soul of Christmas puddings, and was strangely not unpleasant.

One man had bartered cigarettes for some dehydrated vegetable, and, with sublime ignorance, ate it dry, then drank several cups of tea. Probably he thought he had the the same bellyache as everyone else, but it was not the same. He literally burst, and died.

With the Ardennes offensive halted, though the Germans had not yet withdrawn, we celebrated New Year with more gusto. The lights were on until midnight. At the turn of the year I was sitting in the latrine and growing anxious lest I were shot at on my return journey to the barrack. At five minutes past midnight I crept outside and saw on the horizon what appeared to be a fireworks display, but the streams of colour must have been tracer seeking to enmesh our bombers.

On New Year's Day we ate the remainder of the Christmas hand-out, and it was my bath day. The fuel we had enabled us to keep the stove going for a short time in the evening, and hot water enough was available to allow each man a keg of it once in nine days. There was not room in the keg, which measured twelve inches in height and eight in diameter, for even one foot to stand flat.

One stripped, then, balancing on the toes with the heel hard against the side of the keg, tried to sluice one's body in such a way that the water spilled back, for the same water had to serve for laundry. The clothes we tried to dry by wrapping them around the hot iron chimney pipe, where usually they scorched without seeming to dry at all. Discussion in the invariable queue for the chimney tended to be acrimonious, for the drying process was a long one.

In everything we did we thought more of our own welfare, and less and less frequently stood aside for anyone else. Hardship, such as it was, brought out the worst in many of us, aggravated our faults, or exaggerated our attributes until they became vices, and sharpened our awareness of faults in others. Some men, however, and often they were men whom in ordinary days we had respected little, met the challenge of adversity with unsuspected moral strength.

The challenge became more trenchant. To reach the parade ground on January 14th, we had to pass through a lane of machine-gunners, and when we had formed our usual hollow square, the guards closed in, and the dogs and machine-gun nests were stationed around us. One prisoner, arriving late, doffed his homespun hat to a group of machine-gunners and asked if anything unusual was afoot.

A German officer marched on to the parade ground, and ceremoniously unrolled a lengthy proclamation. In a fulsome preamble allegations were made of cruelty to German prisoners in a British camp in Egypt. We could see what was coming. "The High Command has decided, therefore, that reprisals shall be taken against prisoners of war detained in Stalag 357, Fallingbostel."

Followed a list of the reprisals, a drastic edict. Our tables and benches were to go, and we were also to lose our palliasses and half of our bedboards. All sporting materials were to be confiscated, and the library closed. The D compound hut which had been promised for a theatre, would be used to store the confiscated palliasses. The officer concluded: "I want to emphasise that this order has not originated in the Kommandantur of this camp, but is a decree of the High Command. I know that you will accept these measures with typical British stoicism."

There were three cheers for the officers and another for the High Command, and we heard cheers from R and B compounds. At this the Germans seemed to be nonplussed, and they forgot to count us. We went quietly from the *appell*.

Already the bailiffs were in. Tables and forms were carried out to motor-lorries lined up outside the barracks. Then came the palliasses and bedboards. We had penetrated the guard lines, and were massed around the lorries. The diehards tried to seize palliasses, but most of them made only perfunctory attempts, realising that the Germans were in an ugly mood, and that it would take little to trigger off tragedy. The redoubtable Buck did get a palliasse and slid it on to the roof where, for some time, it went unnoticed, but finally was taken.

Promptly Buck reported sick, and persuaded the doctors to give him a chit which certified that on medical grounds he should have a palliasse. The edict had exempted the sick from the reprisal, and the medical officers gave as many chits as they dared to the sick, and to the perspicacious, who, like Buck, laid claim to ill-health.

The rest of us were left with five thin, bare planks which, put together, covered no more than two feet six inches. To sleep on that was impossible, so the boards had to be distributed along the length of the bunks to form a grid. This had been sufficient, with the help of cardboard, to support a palliasse when, at Heydekrug, half the boards had been confiscated, but it was not enough to support a human body, especially as, the ends of neither boards nor bodies being secured, in the night the boards tended to slip away in both directions from our behinds. Then we simply folded in the middle and fell through on to the floor, or on to the man in the bunk beneath. Some slept two to a bunk, combining their bedboards, but the bunks were so narrow that little comfort was to be gained.

In the daylight gloom of the barrack, men were everywhere sitting upon upturned kegs, like smugglers in their clandestine caves, but the existence to which we had been put was no joke, and Dick, in despair, confided to his diary: "Without his pit to sit on or lie in the kriegy is finished."

THERE was malice in the wind that clawed the freezing snow and whirled it against my face. Half-closing my eyes against the pain of it, I did not see at first the silent assembly behind Barrack C4. It was the movement of fists that caught my attention.

In the centre of a tight little knot of men huddled against the wind, a group that was tense and silent, expressionless but somehow approving, were three army men. Two were poised like distance runners waiting for the gun, taut and purposeful. Between them the third man, who was not near middle age and tough, as they were, but a boy not long a prisoner, floundered in the snow, striving to keep himself from falling. The snow, stinging his face, seemed to revive him, and he too struck a pose of expectancy.

One of the two who waited, a big New Zealander, closed tight his fist, and with it clubbed the bruised, grey face of the man in front of him. The youngster was trying not to defend himself, was giving himself, almost gladly, to the flogging, but, involuntarily his arms tried to fend off the blow. He did not fall, and now the other man stepped forward, and crashed a fist into his body.

Only when I had seen the second blow, and watched the man coil slowly into the snow, did I believe that I had seen the first. How long it had been going on I did not know. The nonchalant pitilessness of it was frightening. As if sensing disapproval, the man in front of me turned. "He stole bread."

The man in the snow lay still, and I saw that his hands

were red and sore with the cold; the executioners crouched like boxers ready to be photographed; the watchers were spring-tight and motionless. And about this macabre tableau, that might have been a frieze from a pagan temple, the wind whipped in cold ecstasy like the breath of some supernatural sadist.

I saw the boy get to his feet again, drawing on some deep-laid reserves as men do whose will drives them to some near impossible achievement. He knew, and the men flogging him knew, and we who were watching him knew, that his punishment was not quite complete. Deep had gone the knife, but it wanted a fraction yet to the hilt. I heard but did not see the last two blows. I raised my head.

He lay in the snow as if he had never risen from it, and every shuddering line of him was designed by his agony. His whole attitude bespoke humiliation, and misery, and a longing for an end of everything, which was beyond our comprehension who had not endured such fires of retribution.

The trek cart from the sick-bay arrived, sleigh runners having replaced its wheels, and he was flung on to it. As the makeshift sleigh was hauled away, a man picked up from the snow where it had lain trampled the "red badge of courage", the parachutist's béret, brushed the snow from it, and ran after the sleigh. Gently, almost apologetically he placed the béret on the unconscious but convulsing chest of the man of Arnhem.

I went round a corner and was sick. More than ever one was aware of the rawness of the moral quick of hungry men, more than ever aware of the thinness of the walls containing man's core of violence. Shaken by the ordeal I had just witnessed, I hoped that it would be an end of internecine brutality in the camp. For if ever there was need for tolerance, for sodality, it was now.

"Jesus!" exclaimed Toby, leaping from his bunk. "What goes on?"

A procession of sorts was forming outside C5, the R.A.F. barrack opposite; we could hear savage jeering, and guessed that someone had stolen food, and was to expiate his crime. A room-mate of the thief entered our barrack, refusing to take part in the procession, but countenancing it, approving it.

"It isn't as if it was the first time. He was caught before," he said. "I mean, what can you do with a bloke like that?"

"Learn him," replied a member of our room, grimly, but using the antonym in an effort to sound not pompous. Our visitor looked relieved. "That's what we thought."

Hard by the latrine was a concrete trap-door beneath which was the cesspit. Each week the "honey wagon" drew up alongside and siphoned the excrementitious mess into the tank, reducing the level without ever clearing it altogether. Now the well beneath the trap-door was brimming, and it was to this that the sinner was frogmarched. Fully clothed, he was thrust into the foulness, and when it was thought that he had been punished enough, he was allowed to clamber out, and told to go to the little wooden shed near the gate, between Barracks C5 and C6, where a jet of ice-cold water was aimed at him, and kept upon him, so that he must have been numb to the marrow, and slowly the filth and the stench of the filth were washed away.

I had seen only the beginning and the end of this episode, and I felt that however mean the man's theft, his courage in facing the punishment even the young paratrooper had not surpassed. Upon the soldier his comrades had visited cruel fists, but man has always held his fists to be honourable weapons. The men who castigated the airman chose not to touch him, but, for his ineffable humiliation heaped upon him the waste of their own bodies, than which nothing is counted more despicable.

There were other instances of similar punishment; we heard of them but I saw none of them. In normal days cases of theft were most rare, but now, in the bitter, hungry winter men were impelled, often to their own horror, to some aberration, and the community, unwontedly savage, tended to magnify the smallest dishonesty. All over the compound there were cases of theft, pitiful, pathetic, pettifogging little thefts, not many when one considered that here were ten thousand men, all desperately hungry, but enough to make one wonder what would happen if one's own friends succumbed to sudden temptation, or if one were to succumb oneself.

An answer came to this. Bill Bowhill, the room leader, took me aside, and I guessed when I saw how troubled he was that a theft had been reported. He told me about it. The thief was a boy of about twenty, well educated, well mannered. Normally thoughtful, kempt and smiling, he had slowly let himself drift until he had become the antithesis of these things. He looked peaky and sly, and very unhappy. He had stolen potatoes, three potatoes, for which he had forfeited the respect and the affection of his friends. It was not the first offence, and, suspecting him, they had laid a trap for him.

"What do you think we should do about it?" Bill asked.

"Pep talk," I suggested.

"No rough stuff?"

"No rough stuff."

"That's what I was hoping you'd say," Bowhill confided. "The fellows he stole from have left it to me, and agreed to tell no one about it. I wanted to get a sort of cross-section of opinion in the room—you, Dick, Toby, Buck, Morris, Fisher, and maybe one or two more. Don't tell anyone else."

Reflecting upon Bowhill's cross-section, I wondered whether he was not carefully excluding less tolerant men. It is possible that he took aside every man in the barrack and elicited their opinions as individuals, knowing well that if he stood in front of the seventy men in the room, and announced: "Men, there is a thief in the room? What shall we do with him?" the response of the mass would have been different, indeed.

The snow leaned in thick, white, viscous slabs against the walls and doorways, its blatant virginity tedious, and the fences were bony and black upon it. Roofs were leaking increasingly, the water green-sliming the grey walls. Influenza was rife, and there were many cases of septicaemia.

The index finger of Dick's right hand swelled to the size of a sausage, and, all through the night, throbbed alarmingly. Next day he was admitted to the sick-bay and the surgeon's scalpel released the poison flow. During the next week Toby and I visited him several times, but by the next Sunday I was in the same "ward". Like Dick I had endured a night of pain, and, by morning, my hand was so bloated that only the tips of the fingers protruded. I was frightened; one man had died of septicaemia already.

Captain Todd, handsome as Dr. Kildare, in spite of being dressed in a rubber apron instead of a white robe, operated on my hand, and eventually I began to drift out of my unconscious state. I was back in the ward and had a prize hangover from the injection into the vein. Dick teased me, whistling to make me lift my head, and laughing when I had to let it fall back on the pillow.

In the evening Toby came to see us. It was the 29th of January, and he brought news that the Russians, whose crushing advance had been fermenting excitement among us for several weeks past, were now less than one hundred miles from Berlin. They had sealed off East Prussia, taken Memel, taken Warsaw, Cracow, Lodz.

When the dressings were removed from my hand for the first time, I looked at the bloody, suppurating, fat flesh, and felt sick. I had to bathe it in hot water, and soon gouts of pus, like pieces of rope, dull Naples yellow in colour, knotted and convoluted, began to ooze from the several wounds. Day after day this went on, until, in a way, I began to enjoy it, measuring the knotty strands to see if I could break my own record for length.

Dick was sent back to the barrack and several more men with the same complaint were admitted. Some men lost the use of fingers, but, although mine was a bad case, and although it was several months before the wounds did heal properly, ultimately I suffered no disability.

I woke in the middle of one night, and, hearing the wind's strident lament, was glad that I was comfortable and warm in the sick-bay. The light was on, and there was a stretcher on the floor, near the door. Upon it lay one of the men who had been in Block 40 at Sagan, and, because this story is not altogether to his credit, I shall call him "Shorty" Burns. He had been brought in from the main compound, his hut mates having signalled to the guard that they had a medical emergency.

The medical officer on duty was treating the emergency in a strange way, slapping the face, first the right side, and then the left, and intoning: "Get up, Burns. Get up. Get up, Burns, get up, get up, get up."

Burns held his head in both hands and moaned: "Oh, my swede, oh, my swede."

I was frightened for him. Even though I guessed that the doctor was convinced that he was malingering, I felt frightened. He might be wrong. Then Burns admitted it was a try on, and the doctor told him that he might remain until the morning.

We jeered him then, we the sanctimonious sick, holding to our right of possession, denying to one who was not entitled to it the haven that was ours. Not entitled? In his way he was as ill as we. But we ostracised him.

He was with us all the next morning. "Anyone spare me a fag?" he asked, almost defiantly. There was silence, then I gave him two, receiving his thanks churlishly. When he was leaving us to return to the compound I said: "Don't forget you owe me two cigarettes, Shorty."

"I won't forget," he said.

His only sin had been to seek the makeshift sanctuary of the sick-bay when life in the compound had, all at once, become too much for him. His ruse had brought people from their beds and they had had to carry him through the snow. One could hardly approve, yet had we the right to damn him?

The cigarettes came back to me with a note of thanks in words that were not ungenerous as mine had been.

CHAPTER

24

WHEN I came out of the sick-bay, still shaken, and with my right arm useless, I enjoyed lying back listening to Dick rashly promising his father's port and cigars to celebrate the homecoming which we planned, though we scarcely believed in it. It was fascinating to hear men talk of their post-war gastronomic ambitions, to remark the differences between the ideas of the imaginative who saw themselves feeding on soufflés lighter than the touch of a tit's wing, and the dullards who, unable to escape from their environment, were content to plan stocks of bully beef and Canadian biscuits.

While I had been away Dick and Toby had made their bunks and mine more tenable, nailing the bedboards to cover the lower part, and fashioning a kind of half-hammock from dubiously acquired sacking for the remainder. The hammock they had filled with pieces of spruce and fir and pine brought by the wood gatherers from the forest. It was still uncomfortable to sleep in, for the boards began just under the hip and threatened to grind through the thin flesh into the bone itself. Or so it felt.

Over his bunk Dick had erected a strange canopy. It consisted of frail uprights, and a rough mesh of pieces of string, and flattened cardboard boxes. Designed to steer leaks from the roof away from bunks, pieces of crude guttering suspended by wire and string ran in a crazy sequence, connecting and interconnecting, dripping from one to another, each drip sounding a different note but often in the same juxtaposition so that it became an irritating tune.

In the hut was a gramophone, but there was only one record the more popular side of which, "Oh, what a beautiful morning", was played continuously. In the early hours we would hear the German soldiers singing their matutinal rounds in the woods, and the music came hauntingly upon the grey air.

"What have those bastards got to sing about?" someone would mutter, and go to sleep again.

I had no canopy over my head, and no guttering. There was no more material to be found, and, in any case, with my right hand refusing to heal, it was all I could do to lever myself on to my bunk. Every few minutes a large drop of water fell from the roof, and I became convinced that someone was aiming it, for no matter how I moved my head the drop always hit me between the eyes.

A tiny black flake fell from the roof into the eye of Arthur Porter who had the bunk on my left, across the narrow gangway. The doctors were unable to remove the matter, and he was told he would have to wait until he got home. Home! There was Arthur's young wife of whom he talked often, for he had been married only just before he was shot down, and that had not been long ago. But he was destined never to reach home, and when he died the little black chip was still embedded in his eye.

The compound was a mudheap. The long freeze-up had ended on February 1st, while I was still in the sick-bay. On that day a thousand Fortresses had flown over the camp to attack Berlin, in daylight, and, every night, fleet Mosquitoes stung the capital. Everywhere the news was good. The compound was a mudheap and conditions were miserable, but we were beginning to think it would not be for long, now. "It won't be long now." The letters of years had reached us ending with that empty encouragement. Now we might have believed it, but there were no letters.

Heydekrug and Thorn had fallen to the Russians long since. Now we heard that Sagan was invested. And it was strange to think that all these camps, in each of which we had visualised liberation, had fallen to the Allies. Where, we wondered, were the officers who had been at Stalag Luft 3. The German radio gave an answer: "R.A.F. officers at Sagan were given the choice of remaining and falling into Russian hands, or of marching to the West. Without hesitation they marched, carrying those who were unable to walk; without hesitation they marched away from the terrible Russians."

On the last train to leave Sagan before the Russian trap finally closed, the Germans, with superb honesty, put a box addressed to Dixie Deans at Fallingbostel. In it were the fountain-pens and cigarette-lighters confiscated the day we arrived at Sagan. My fountain-pen was handed to me, and Alan Scanlan put it in working order. With it I have written the whole of the first draft of this story.

The compound was a mudheap and it was difficult to move between barracks, but Stan Parris and his octet went willingly to play in any hut that wanted them. "Soft Lights and Sweet Music," Parris told me he wanted to call his session, and asked me to do a poster. I obtained materials and painted a glamorous lady in a low-cut gown, using a photograph of Miss Rita Hayworth for inspiration, and around her I placed caricatures of Parris, Happy Hale, and the other instrumentalists. "Soft Lights and Sweet Music!" I worked in the grey daylight to the incessant accompaniment of "Oh, what a beautiful morning . . ."

The octet played in our hut one evening, and the only light came from a single fat-lamp, because the Mosquitoes were flying to Berlin, and whenever there was a raid the Germans turned out the lights. But the music was sweet, coming out of the darkness and reaching each man in the privacy conferred by darkness, so that he could yield himself to whatever sentimental association the familiar melodies had for him.

The rain had come again; we could hear it blustering

outside, and we could hear, too, the brave Mosquitoes bustling to Berlin; these extraneous sounds seemed to enclose the music and yet were part of it, as a frame encloses and is part of a painting. Afterwards we gave the octet coffee and a word of thanks, and they went out into the blackness and the wetness, into the mud that slimed over their boots, into the rain that slugged against their faces.

Sometimes the room committee would arrange a lecture, and the words would ride upon waves of moving darkness like paper boats in a storm drain. Such entertainment silenced for a time the bickerings, the recriminations which were becoming ever more frequent. For too long we had lived on twice-daily swede soup and ersatz bread. In the soup was the potato ration so reduced that it barely thickened the soup. Now, at the beginning of March, the bread ration was cut from a seventh to an eighth of a loaf. For too long we had gone wet and cold and lived in darkness, and for too long the Englishman had been deprived of his cup of tea than which, in times of crisis, he recognises no more effectual palliative. German coffee, compounded of acorns and charcoal, was no substitute, although we once made a very enjoyable can of coffee when a special issue of grounds was made. The barrack-room, normally sour with the reek of swede, a miasma that clung to the whole of the camp, was filled with a rich aroma. Then we discovered that for seventy men we had used the ration of seven hundred.

Dixie was worried about the ten thousand men in his charge. Our armies were advancing in the West, but how long would it be before the Germans cracked? We were not in any condition of advanced emaciation like the inmates of the concentration camps, nevertheless we were suffering from malnutrition; the flesh of thighs and upper arms atrophied a little more with each day, hip-bones resembled incipient wings. We could still laugh about it, but always present were the dread of an epidemic and the lesser fear of being put to march eastward when we had not strength enough for the ordeal. Already, if one sat down and watched detachedly the life of the camp, it was as if one watched a slow-motion film. A few hardy types plodded round the circuit, each step seemingly the outcome of a ponderous thought. Even the gestures men made as they talked were stilted.

As the German transport system was methodically being paralysed the Red Cross had established a new depot at Lubeck to provision camps in Northern Germany, and we had seen photographs of the gigantic white Diesel lorries which were to be used.

Deans decided that we must get parcels. Letters brought only promises to supply food when the Diesel lorries were available. He would go then, himself, to see what he could arrange. The Commandant was persuaded to provide a panel van, its Russian driver and a German officer, and to allow Deans and Alfie Fripp, the man in charge of Red Cross issues, to travel to Lubeck.

Ironically they took with them Red Cross food, chocolate, cigarettes and soap taken from damaged parcels, too little to be worthwhile even sharing among the sick, but enough to bribe German officials.

At a country pub along the road they lunched well, enjoying the atmosphere, for the country pub is a friendly place in whatever land it is set.

In Lubeck, which they reached late at night, they were accommodated in a German services club and slept in a dormitory with enemy soldiers on leave, drunk, most of them. Deans and Fripp, amused by the situation, could not help but appreciate the possibility of an explosion were their identities discovered, but the night passed uneventfully.

In the morning they called on the Red Cross representative, a Swede, who assured them that stocks of parcels were good. They were, however, in the hands of German shipping agents to whom they next went. As many parcels as they wanted they could have, the manager of the firm told them, but they would have to arrange transport, themselves. They were directed to the Transport Officer for the area.

His office was in a huge block of offices, and they entered without optimism, for they had seen, on the way, some of the bomb damage. Half the old town had been gutted in the incendiary raid of March 1942, when for the first time the R.A.F. really took the gloves off. No German official in Lubeck was likely to have much sympathy for R.A.F. prisoners whatever misfortunes had befallen them.

The transport Officer gave them, as expected, a categorical "No". To show that he was not being unreasonable, the German pointed to a wall-map thick with multi-coloured pins. These indicated where, and, according to the colour, to what degree railway lines were damaged. Scarcely a line was open in the area.

Told that Fallingbostel was open to passenger traffic only, Deans suggested that one, two, or even three trucks could be tacked on at the rear of the train. This was vetoed at once. Alfie Fripp placed a tin of coffee on the table, and a bar of soap. They gave the German some chocolate "to give him the taste of it"—as Deans put it.

The man had a family, a wife weary of the latherless soap, children who had never tasted chocolate—and there was the coffee. He would not agree to three trucks but they settled for two, with Deans and Fripp insisting that they should be French rolling-stock, the largest in use on the German railways.

Returning to the shipping agents they arranged to have the parcels loaded, then, after lunching with the Red Cross man, elatedly they set out for Fallingbostel.

The Russian, an erratic driver, knocked a German dispatch rider off his motor-cycle, but the escort officer was asleep, and did not waken, and the Russian drove on. The dispatch rider leaped to his feet, and shouted curses after them. He seemed little hurt, and Deans was relieved.

In the van were two hundred parcels, so that the sick were

able to have a little more than usual, but it was not until March 30th, Good Friday, that the two trucks arrived with 6,000 Canadian parcels, an issue of half a parcel per man. On that day nerves were strung tight.

Patten had crossed the Rhine on March 21st, and at last, on the 23rd Montgomery crossed. For us there was only one Rhine crossing—that of Montgomery, and the excitement of that occasion burst upon the camp like a starshell. Day after day the B.B.C. news had been of artillery barrages, and the ceaseless patrol of Mitchells and Marauders, of a smoke-curtain "lifted momentarily" at this corner or that, and we had grown tired of it all.

It seemed that Montgomery's armies would never move. A picture of the General was nailed up in the camp. Above it, in invocation, was the word "Wanted". We were increasingly anxious that the Germans should not put us on to the roads, and indeed it seemed that they were planning to leave us to our liberation. Prisoners near Kassel already had been freed.

A thousand Americans marched in having footslogged hundreds of miles from the east. They were put into one of the B compound barracks, untenanted until now. Eight hundred men from Tychow, former K Lager men, came, and hundreds more were lodged at iiB. There were 2,000 men in tents. The camp simmered. But still the Montgomery forces were no more than a "massive build-up" behind a smoke-curtain.

A German rode through the compounds on a bicycle; he had a ladder hooked over his arm, and carried a pot of paste, and a number of folded sheets. Professionally he slapped the bills on to the stone walls. It was Germany's new propoganda line:

England will find herself isolated against a Soviet Europe and a Soviet Asia from the Atlantic to the Pacific. Only co-operation between the nations of Europe and the British Empire can safeguard the existence of Europe, of her tradition, and her civilisation, against aggression from Siberia.

The very existence of the British Empire will be secured and a permanent peace guaranteed for our continent after a long period of bloody, fratricidal war.

The heavy type was blood-red. There were maps showing the areas over which the Germans conjectured Soviet power would extend.

We too had maps, and on them defined the allied advance admitted by the Germans. Dick would sit studying his map, almost willing the armies to move, I would think. But when he looked up it was to make a remark about essentially practical things.

"Today the Tactical Air Force . . ." began the news bulletins which meant that nothing important had happened, and we cursed the Tactical Air Force.

In the food locker there was a crust of bread, a little sugar, a speck of German jam. Toby would peer in, mutter as he thought he saw a particle of dust, and briskly remove the bread and the tins, so that, for the twelfth time that day, he could clean the sparkling woodwork.

"Can't you leave it alone, Toby?"

"No, I can't. This is no time for dirty food cupboards."

"But it isn't dirty. You've only just cleaned it."

"If it wasn't dirty I wouldn't be doing it. Some people wouldn't recognise a smut on their nose." When the news reader had gone, leaving a picture of a vast pall of immovable, unchanging smoke on the far side of the Rhine, Toby cleaned the cupboard harder than ever.

German workmen came and put a skylight in C6-2. The only one in the camp, it was directly over my bunk. If only it had been there a few months earlier so that we could have wrested a little light from the winter grey. There was a flurry of movement as we reacted to the increased light like ants when their tunnellings are suddenly exposed.

"So this is humanity," Toby chuckled, standing on his bunk, and gazing down upon the scene.

"You'd better inspect the food cupboard, Toby. More light now."

"You're damned right." He leaped down.

Dick and I were planning a car journey when we returned to England. "If you return," said Toby. "If that bloody smoke-screen of Montgomery's hasn't suffocated his entire goddammed army I'll go hopping."

Mike Featherstone was collecting in his log-book the "potted philosophies" of acquaintances he thought might have something interesting to say. After George Kirk showed him a long poem I had written he brought in his log-book for my contribution. Having log-books brought to me was no new experience but usually I was asked to "draw something funny", this at a time when I no longer believed in humour.

I took the commission seriously, and put down the things I had been mulling over for months, reducing life to some kind of algebraic equation. It would not read very convincingly, now.

More men were bashing the circuit than had done for many months. Some were hardening their muscles in case of a march, others had simply come out of their winter hibernation, forgotten creatures, blinking and bearded.

Gardener, a fresh-faced young man, who had spoken in the Shakespeare Day celebration at Heydekrug, was to be seen, as he had been for some months, with a small dog on the lead. The dog had survived the winter; somehow it had eaten, somehow not been eaten. Gardener walked it round the compound as if the circuit were a Kensington street.

Montgomery crossed the Rhine.

CHAPTER
25

GOOD FRIDAY! Excitement raged like a fire, like a fever. The arrival of the food parcels inspired optimism in the beginning, but were then almost forgotten. I lay on my bunk with elation squirming inside me as every few minutes someone tumbled down the front step with news heard from "a reliable source". We waited, minute by minute, for liberation.

By the end of the day the Americans were to the south and east, the British to the west of us. In Hanover there had been fierce tank battles. From all around us sounded explosions, lending verisimilitude to the stories, although it was only the Germans blowing up bridges.

During the night the fire was doused, the fever abated. There was no denial of a single one of yesterday's rumours, nor was there need for denial; truth was stark. We were emotionally exhausted, physically weak.

Day followed day; no nearer came the battle. Stories reached us of panic in Fallingbostel, but there was no sign of it among the Germans. Rumours always followed pattern, it appeared.

The Volksturmm, the German Home Guard, took part in an exercise just outside the camp. They were old men, crawling round the hillocks, wriggling forward on flaccid stomachs, running, painfully bent. A group of them settled into some bushes for a smoke, and we kept them posted of the whereabouts of their officers and N.C.O.s, enjoying the ensuing game of hide-and-seek. Were these ancients all that stood between us and liberation? It would seem so for we refused to believe that we could be moved.

We were wrong. On Thursday, April 5th, it was announced that we were to be marched into the Northern Redoubt, the area of Denmark and Schleswig-Holstein in which the Germans planned to hold out indefinitely. C compound was to go almost at once. There was little time to sort out personal possessions; obviously we could carry the barest essentials. So I threw away my folio of sketches, my manuscripts, and my diary which was by now a very thick wad of cards.

Dick suggested that we hide in another compound—"The longer we hang on the better our chance of being overrun. They won't march B compound yet." I argued against it. Better I thought to stay with our own crowd; we might be singled out among a crowd of soldiers for specially unpleasant attention. Flimsy arguments. What really worried me was a premonition that if we moved in any but the appointed direction we would be beset by tragedy. The other three were determined not to march with C compound. "I think you're being bloody silly," Dick said. "If you want to leave us at this stage it's up to you, but I'm going to do all I know to stay here, and the others agree with me."

I hesitated. "We've always decided things on a 'majority rules' principle. Come on, old son."

We heaved our kitbags on to our backs and trudged across the central area to B compound. Dick had a friend in one of the barracks who said that we could spend the night there. Other airmen with the same idea were trying to find somewhere to camp. Most of them, finding no welcome, returned to their own compound, and joined the marchers. We were told to get out too, then grudgingly allowed to stay at the behest of Dick's friend. It might be a good idea to go outside out of the way, we thought.

Under the bunk belonging to Dick's friend I put a Red

Cross box containing a scone made from a little flour bought with ten cigarettes saved for an emergency. When C compound had been marched away we revisited our own room. The army men had been there first. Already the letters, the diaries, the manuscripts I had left were scattered about the floor. Even then I could have saved them. Unhappily we returned to B compound.

"Why don't you blokes find somewhere else?"

"You should have marched with your own compound."

"You men have no idea of comradeship, none at all," shouted Dick.

"He's right, really, Dick."

Ron turned on me. "He's not right. We were asked here by Dick's friend." Toby was muttering goddams to himself, muttering and cursing, puffing up with anger like a bantam cock.

My scone had been stolen from the box under the bed and it mattered. I did not feel that it had been taken because someone was hungry, but because we were not wanted.

"Dick," I tugged his sleeve, "let's see if the Yanks will have us."

The Americans were quartered in the last barrack in the compound. Because there were no bunks, they had been given palliasses which were spread over the stone floor.

"You guys mind if we join you?" Toby asked.

"Hell, no."

They made room on their palliasses for us. They told us about their march; they had had it rough, but preferred it to camp life because they had been able to get hold of plenty of food. "Boy, those Jerry chickens sure are tender. We got hold of most everything one way or another. Our trouble was that it was kinda cold, and a few of the fellers handed in their chips. There was one guy we carried for Christ knows how many miles, and then we found he was dead and we left him. I guess he had it coming to him, anyways."

During our afternoon foraging we had found some dried peas in the cookhouse. We boiled some of them now, but they remained hard and were tasteless. There was nothing else to eat.

When it was dark one of the Americans produced a mouth-organ, and played, mostly requests, for about three hours. Here and there a cigarette glowed, a fat-lamp flickered.

"Sorry, kid, I don't know that one, but if you'll string along with me for a minute I'd like to play this little 'Blues' number."

"Silver Wings in the Moonlight?" he said, again. "It's kinda corny, but what the hell . . ."

We sang. Most of the songs were sentimental, but the Americans sang unashamedly, nostalgically, contentedly. And in the shadows we sang too, and were moved. It was a warm, a friendly gathering, relaxed, yet full of emotion. A padre could have come in and talked about God, and had the best congregation of his life, because the thoughts of these men were imbued with a peculiar reverence. Maybe some of them were thinking about God anyway.

Gunfire sounded continuously, and the crunching of bombs. Overhead was the deep monotone of aircraft, and a few incendiaries fell into the camp. One quickly burned through the roof of a barrack in A compound, spurting and spitting, all blue and yellow, and there was the tang of flaring tar. The blue went and the yellow became remote. Uneasily we slept.

We knew that R compound was to march before B, but we had forgotten that the Germans, who for some reason thought airmen more useful as hostages than soldiers, would want the Americans. Before we realised it the barrack was surrounded.

A formation of Fortresses flew overhead. Flak ripped into one of them and blew it to shreds. Pieces fell from the bellying smoke, that eternal exclamation mark to tragedy, and among them it seemed was a man, for suddenly there was a tiny gleam of white. The smoke spread in a thinning haze, then vanished; the Fortresses flew on, leaving the Mediterranean firmament unbroken to the horizons save for the parachute, which was as tiny and as clearcut as a seed pearl. The guards watched, fascinated, and we shouldered our kitbags and stole away.

Later we returned to the empty room and stayed there for the rest of the day and the night. I had acquired a billy with a handle, and in this boiled dried peas until after midnight. When we transferred our kit into A compound, in the morning, I forgot to take the peas. The Germans were marching to round up B compound. Toby yelled a warning as I dumped my kit and ran back.

Seizing the billy from the stove I rushed towards the gate. The guards were not twenty yards from it. Behind me a German officer bellowed, and, glancing over my shoulder, I saw that his pistol was pointing in my direction. Through the fence I glimpsed Dick and Toby looking grave. As hard as I could I ran, and waited for the bullet to hit me. Again I heard the officer shout, but it sounded further away. A last effort took me through the gateway and I almost knocked the feldwebel leading the squad of guards. Absurdly I murmured "Sorry", pushed past, and entered A compound.

Then I saw what had distracted the officer. There was a hole in the fence between the two compounds, and an orderly queue waited to go through. The officer was ordering the queue not to move, but men were still passing through the gap. Toby walked to the fence. "Tickets please. Have your tickets ready," he called.

Fifty or more prisoners were with us in A compound. It was in this compound that the Germans had planned to segregate the Jews, but the obstinate Deans had managed to thwart the move. From our side of the fence we watched the army men in B compound herded into column. When they were all in the road we were winkled out. Toby, Dick,

Ron and I were the last four prisoners to move out of the camp. So it had been at Heydekrug, also.

The men in sick-bay did not go at all, and as we passed I saw George Kirk, who had been suffering from some ailment of the blood, and called good-bye. To him I could have entrusted my papers, but the idea had not occurred to me.

A sense of freedom possessed us as the camp went from view, as we passed beyond the pine trees. After a few miles we halted on a country track, and a van arrived with tins of meat paste which were promptly handed out. Near us stood a guard who shouted "*Schweinhunder Englanders, Schweinhunder Englanders*", repeating it, almost singing it.

We tramped slowly and without rhythm, sometimes on metalled roads, when, instead of the flinty clatter and ring of busy boots in marching unison, there sounded the rasping and shuffle of feet grown leaden, and sometimes along tortuous ways across the fields, along cart tracks heavy with dust which, rising sluggishly from our boots, thickened the air of our breathing.

Burdening straps wore into our shoulders until we longed for some other pain so that we could forget this one, and then pain burned the feet and we wished the old pain back again. This was the first day and we marched but fifteen miles.

As we came near a village hazed with evening smoke we were met by officers who took charge of small parties and marched them down farm lanes, eighty men to one farm, a hundred to another, two hundred to a farm where the barns were large. The main body marched on. More farms, more men were guided to shelter. The high-gabled farmhouses looked attractive with their grey stone walls, and red-tiled roofs, the lofty barns, in which we imagined the softness of strewn hay, hospitable.

The last hundred of us, mostly army men, trudged along a lane where wagon wheels, in iron clasped, had driven deep, and horses had stamped their crescent spoors. In adjacent fields the first frail spikes of corn stood in Lilliputian battalions, and the cows peered with sympathy for a moment before treading away with joggling bells.

We were the last into the barn, where, as we peered into the gloom, the floor seemed to writhe as men manœuvred for space. We tried to make a way through, and there were angry shouts of "No room, no room", and a closing up of ranks. "No room at the inn," tired Toby cracked. Behind us the guards prodded the doors closed. In a moment we would be in darkness. I longed for the irenic scene outside, away from the egregious mob.

"Make for the ladder," Dick urged, and we picked a way through the sprawling crowd, ignoring the abuse, the obscenity, kicking away hands that clasped at our ankles, stumbling over legs that barred our path. We climbed to the loft where we found ourselves alone in masses of hay. Below, the noise subsided at last.

During the night Ron developed diarrhoea, and by morning was very ill and weak. The farmer, ordered to distribute potatoes, grudgingly dealt us each three, the size of strawberries, from a large black hat. So we dug up his clumps of turnips and sugar-beet, and for breakfast ate pieces of sugar-beet charred in a minute fire. Ron felt that he must have food, though we advised him against it.

We were on the road again. The day before, my greatcoat, strapped to my pack, had weighed unbearably, so now I wore it, and soon was wrapped about in clamminess. Others were having the same difficulty, and greatcoats and blankets were tossed foolishly away. At the first halt I strapped the coat on to the pack again; its sudorific folds I could tolerate no more.

Sporadically I ate dried peas though the dust had got under the lid and lay thickly upon the viscous mess. We did not talk except to encourage Ron who was in torment. When he had to leave the column we waited with him at the side of the road, and the column shuffled, dragged and shuffled, trudged and dragged and shuffled past, and there was no pity in any one of the dust-grained faces. Necks were thrust tautly forward to counteract the pull of shoulder-straps, heads jerked and bobbed like swans seeking food.

The guard who had remained with us became impatient and urged Ron to hurry. The column was past us now and we watched the gap apprehensively, too weak to catch up very far.

We were marching again, trying to overtake those strange shapes in front, the swaying, bulging bags, the swinging, clanking pans, the stumbling legs, the unlifting feet.

Bombers went scudding over the treetops, low over the road, their bowels exposed! Black shapes tumbled. "Overgrown bloody pigeons," a soldier grunted. A mile away the earth heaved. What was the target? A marching column perhaps? Did they know who we were?

In a field to our right a smartly-dressed young German officer was standing, map in hand, planning a defence position. He appeared to be relishing his little bit of what remained of the war. His subordinates scampered with every wave of his arm. Did he know who we were?

Some of the marching guards were elderly men, and for them, too, this was drudgery. Two prisoners broke from the column, stumbled down the embankment, making for the wood, jogging like cart-horses. A frying-pan and a panni-kin hanging on strings from the pack of one of them clashed and jangled, clashed and jangled. A guard took steady aim, then lowered his rifle. For almost half a minute he could have had the escapers in his sights. Then they vanished among the trees but the jangle and the crepitating of the affronted forest sounded for long afterwards.

Half an hour later one of the guards staggered drunkenly and would have fainted, but two or three prisoners took his rifle, and his satchel, and carried them until he re-covered.

The day's march was mostly across open country, and

the roughnesses of the ground, the unexpected bump and hollow sometimes jerked the breath from our lungs. Towards evening I knew that I could never take another step, and then I did, and then I did, and then I did. Ron's pallor was frightening. Did he plan each step or did he move in delirium?

"The weariness, the fever, and the fret—the weariness, the fever and the fret—the weariness . . ." I said it slowly, over and over, planting my feet to the rhythm of it. It was like a tune you can't get out of your head.

Ten miles we had toiled in the day. That was all. We heard cheering and saw, in a farmyard, men from another compound. They had not marched that day, not because they were being rested, but because so many prisoners on the roads were disorganising the German lines of communication. There seemed to be innumerable farms, and the barn into which we were herded was much larger than the one we had left in the morning.

Again we made straight for the loft, and put Ron to bed in deep hay, where at once he slept, exhausted. It was still light, and we went into the barnyard, and lit a fire in which we cooked our few potatoes, and charred more sugar-beet and turnip. Toby produced a bottle of used tea-leaves and we made a feeble brew.

A railed enclosure behind farm machinery at one end of the barn held a great mound of potatoes. At the opposite end, near the ladder leading to the loft, three farm horses were tethered. When the barn doors closed upon us sentries were posted in the potato enclosure, and they sat playing cards around a lantern. We could hear the horses stamping on the brick floor.

We lay in the straw and allowed weariness to take possession of us, stretching pleasurably against the contraction of muscles. We talked desultorily, and listened to the sounds of the night outside, and wished the barn doors could be opened for the darkness was coiling and unravelling, then flattening and greying, mysterious and viable, and the walls of the barn closed on us and receded so that we felt contained in a gigantic breathing lung. We slept.

And then, it seemed but a moment later, I came awake and was frightened. The straw beneath me was seething, and I sensed the convulsion of the timbers about me. Ron moaned. An aeroplane thundered overhead, then the noise of it was overlapped by great, jagged shocks of sound. Bombs. Again the building buckled, folded, straightened, shuddered.

From below came the terrified screams of horses; they were rearing. The tearing, rasping, shredding of a rope. Hooves smashed upon bricks, thudded, thudded. A great body hit the wall with the force of a bursting dam, gathered itself, wheeled, fought through the darkness. Men shouted in terror, hammered the door. The maddened animal ploughed through them, thudded, thudded, crashed again. Fists beat the door, beat and beat the door, but no help came.

Stunned momentarily, the horse checked, and men found courage, seized it, soothed it, led it gently to its rail, tied it. And only then were the bars drawn on the outside. The doors opened and the darkness was no longer engulfing; into the barn seeped the pale light of the stars.

A lantern was snatched from a guard silhouetted in the doorway. From the loft we watched the light moving slowly round the barn, and the soft yellow of it picked out the heaps of men and the scattered packs. Bruises and abrasions there were, but not a single broken bone. The lantern moved over to the horses, and we could see prisoners patting the trembling flanks of the beasts, stroking their noses, whispering in the way that men have who love animals.

In the morning we were told that we would not be marching that day. The farmyard abutted the road, and we could watch the men who had been quartered elsewhere in the neighbourhood begin their day's slogging. One had acquired a broken-down pram in which his kit was piled, and he pushed it along comfortably. Column after column straggled past; bent low as they plodded up the hill, and long after they had disappeared over the brow we could hear their voices and the scrape of their boots on the road.

In spite of the vigilance of the sentries prisoners stole eggs and skittled the farmer's chickens. Feathers littered the barnyard, and spitted birds were cooked in the flames of a dozen fires. Leaning on his white picket fence the farmer watched sourly, and protested to the guards who shrugged characteristically. Certainly they had orders to prevent theft, but they had seen nothing of the thefts. They had no orders to stop prisoners cooking, nor to inquire whence had come the fare.

When, transcending all other aromas, that of roast pork filled the air, the farmer disgustedly went indoors. To have to watch one of his young pigs barbecued by his unwelcome guests was more than he could endure.

The four of us aspired to nothing more than potatoes. While Dick argued with the sentry guarding the pile in the barn, I crawled beneath a tractor and plundered potatoes from within inches of their feet, stuffing them into my battle-dress blouse. When I could carry no more I backed out and Dick was able to move away from the angry German who had unslung his rifle and was threatening to use it.

Water we could get only from the farmhouse kitchen, and into the home of that German family streamed the English prisoners. The family sat around their table in stoical silence, acknowledging with a movement of the head the polite requests of the prisoners to fill this receptacle or that.

"Sorry to bother you," said one man, "but we were only able to get a boiling fowl."

The farmer, though he could not understand what had been said, remarked the apologetic tone, and answered in German. He did not blame the prisoners; they had to eat and drink. But certainly he would claim compensation from the authorities who had failed to organise provisions for the marching columns.

As we sat round the fires in the evening a feldwebel went from group to group. "Tomorrow you will march back to Fallingbostel." A breeze shuffled through the thickening trees, and stirred the smoke of our fires, and it struck chill so that we huddled into our coats. As the feldwebel went his round silence followed at his heels.

"Fallingbostel always seemed like Hell at the time," said Toby at length. "I reckon we'll soon see if I was right because as sure as God made little pussy cats it's to Hell that we're going."

"It seems an improbable tale," Dick wrote calmly in his diary. "More likely we're going to be murdered."

CHAPTER
26

Ron, a forlorn figure with the other sick, waved to us from a farm wagon. The white picket fence of the barnyard separated us, and we wondered if we should ever see him again. We were ready to march back the way we had come, back towards Fallingbostel, back into the woods where murder so easily could be done.

It was not long before we realised that our fears were needless. Our middle-aged guards were not the sort of men upon whose consciences the idea of murder rested lightly, and they were, they said, cheerfully facing the prospect of becoming our prisoners. They explained that the many prisoners on the road were interfering with the transport of supplies to German troop concentrations in the area who were preparing to resist the invaders. Those who had gone on the day before were clear of the supply routes.

Fifteen hundred of us there were, marching buoyantly now, boots thumping the road and thudding on the soft earth of the woodland tracks. That was at first, but we wearied. Two days we had taken on the way from the camp; we had now to march back in a day. The route was a little shorter, yet the road seemed endlessly to unwind. We ceased to be a homogeneous body, but struggled and straggled in raggle-taggle groups, in ones and twos, and sixes and sevens, here prisoners in a close-knit knot, there a guard, uncaring, resting his back against a tree. We craved fat and sugar, and Toby produced a small packet of German fat which we shared, eating avidly.

In the woods we lingered, treading gently the crazy paving

of leaf shade and sunlit brown earth; upon the open roads we tried to hurry, shuffling a little more quickly, and I tried to repeat to myself "Fallingbostel, Fallingbostel, Fallingbostel" because the word was quick-rhythmed like the parting tune of a theatre orchestra, but exhaustion countered the rhythm, just as the slow pressure of the crowds in the theatre bottle-necks will not allow the feet to comply with the heard melody, and again it was the "weariness, the fever, and the fret—the weariness, the fever, and the fret . . ." that dictated my step.

And then, from the crepuscular shadows, the untidy black lace of wire appeared, and the sentry-boxes, square set on their straddled legs. At the gate we learned that there was nowhere to sleep; thousands of prisoners of many nationalities had been dumped in the camp; they had been marched across an ever-narrowing Germany from west to east, and east to west, until at last the Germans had given up and left them. Nearly a thousand Yugoslavs had been on the road for seven months, and in the bitter winter death had whittled down their numbers.

A shanty town mushroomed on the open ground of the compounds. Bricks, pieces of wood, tarpaulins were found from somewhere and fashioned into little square huts like children make to "play at houses". Toby, reconnoitring, decided that the woodshed could be cleaned out, and made habitable, and we transferred our packs from the delouser, upon the concrete floor of which we had spent the night, broke into D compound where the palliasses were stored, and where there were also double-decker bunks stacked high, and soon were warmly housed.

In the guard-boxes the *postens* stood with their rifles, their machine-guns, and watched us cut holes in the fences through which we went to look for food and water. Some food was in the camp, mostly dried peas, and we took possession of a whole sack. In the nearby fields, beyond the camp cemetery, were potato clamps, and, not far away, a food magazine where there was grain, and a huge store of Turkish dried fruit.

The camp water supply had failed, and we had to go half a mile to a well. Toby and I took a large tub which, after queueing for an hour and a half, we filled brimming. Resting frequently, we heaved the tub as far as the gap in the fence. When we bent to it again I could not lift it. Angrily Toby accused me of not trying, but he forgot that he was naturally stronger. We quarrelled with great bitterness. In the last few months there had been friction between us, exacerbated by my own imaginings, but it was the first time that we had exploded in this way.

For a few minutes we hated each other, then, when nothing was left to say, Toby waited impatiently, but without further criticism until I was ready to complete the journey. With the quarrel the smouldering differences of the months were consumed. Back at the woodshed we found a recovered Ron.

But now I was fighting the same complaint, and the diet of peas and potatoes did not help. Some men had obtained eggs, having foraged adventurously in hostile, defended country near the camp, or having bartered with guards, many of whom were trying to ingratiate themselves. Dick, Toby and Ron had each been given an egg by friends, and Dick suggested that I should ask John Holborow for one. Diffidently I went to him, and was almost relieved when he said, "Sorry, Cal, old boy, but they aren't mine to give away."

I heated some water on the open fireplace we had built and took a keg of it to the side of the building where there was a narrow strip of grass. Naked, I stood sluicing my body, prizing the feeling of warmth and cleanliness.

"Christ, Cal! You're thin." It was John Holborow who with his friend had happened to walk that way. While I was dressing Holborow came in. "My friend told me to give you this. Sorry I couldn't when you asked me." I thanked him and rushed outside with the egg. The others were smiling.

"Give it to me," said Dick, excitedly, "I'll do it for you. How long shall I give it?"

We took it in turns to cook, if boiling potatoes and dried peas euphemistically can be so described. Disconsolately, one midday, I was watching the potage seething like a witch's gruel, when I heard a song—gay "Tarantella!" It was a trained voice that I heard, a tenor with the timbre of Josef Schmidt's. I could not see the singer. "Tarantella" stopped, and the singer began, "Your Tiny Hand is Frozen." A young Yugoslav in a tattered uniform appeared from behind the woodshed, and slowly walked across the centre compound until he disappeared into B compound. All the time I could hear his voice, and shivered at its beauty so incongruous-seeming in all the surrounding ugliness. Hackneyed the aria might have been, but I did not care. When I could hear him no longer it was not easy to believe that the man had passed at all.

When I looked up a shy Russian was standing beside me, a little man with dark eyes gleaming in an otherwise stupid face. There were thousands of them in the camp, gregarious Mongols, illiterate, with small intelligence, and little personal identity; in their millions they were man-power. He smiled when he knew that I had seen him, and looked towards B compound then back to me, as if he understood why I had been so engrossed. He gestured with the box he had in his hands towards the bag of dried peas. I nodded, and quietly he scooped up handfuls.

His visit decided me to go into C compound, most of which the Russians occupied. Watched by the curious inmates, I walked into the room where we had lived. It was swept, and there was an immediate impression of neatness, but the place swarmed with lice. To the Russians it must have seemed strangely impertinent of me to stroll in and search under their beds, and they did not understand the gestures by which I tried to convey that once I had lived here, occupied this bed, and that I was seeking lost possessions. I found none.

Outside the door of the hut was a pile of rubbish, and I turned some of it over with my foot, uncovering the manuscript of a novel I had been writing. I brushed the lice from it, and some of the mud encrusting the pages. Of the mass of work I had done in Germany it was all that I salvaged.

Walking back to the woodshed I met Jack Connelly, and stopped to talk. How long did he think we should have to wait for liberation?

"Oh, Monday morning," said Jack, calmly, and I thought the idea typical of a schoolmaster for whom Monday morning is always the new beginning.

On Monday morning I was peeling potatoes while the Seventh Armoured Division fought around the camp. Men lined the fences, sat on the posts, and sometimes a tank crashed from the woods, the lid opened, a cheery voice said "Won't keep you long", and then the tank thrust a way into the woods again, and the woods which had always been silent except when the Germans had sung their rounds in the cold mornings, and when the whining wind had stirred the trees in melancholy, now were filled with noise, and shot through with the red and black of flame and smoke. I went on peeling potatoes.

Armoured cars appeared at the main gate, and the *postens* surrendered their arms to the camp police. The police had been organised several months before by Deans as one of several steps he took to give effect to orders received from General Eisenhower. The messages were broadcast in a series of codes, at a certain time, on a special frequency. "Nobby" Hall, one of the very early prisoners, had long before been given code words in letters from his wife who, like several other wives, had gladly co-operated with the authorities, although at times the instructions had caused anxiety. It had seemed to the wives that their husbands were engaged upon perilous work of some kind.

Hall did not have all the keys, and some of the codes he could not break; the position was improved when a newly captured soldier arrived with two more of the key words committed to memory.

Our leaders could have used the transmitter which Bristow had ready, but it was planned to use it only in direst emergency, as for instance if the Germans began a massacre, and it was never assembled. Its immediate detection would have been inevitable.

All of these activities were known only to the few prisoners involved, and when, with the liberation, the police force appeared, they were known as "Carter's coppers", Captain Bonham-Carter having assumed nominal command of the British prisoners in the camp.

The majority of the planned force still marched, far away, but sufficient had returned to the camp for an efficient unit to be formed.

Hall, himself, had broken away from the column and had been recaptured by S.S. men who had treated him with kindness. Fallingbostel was the best place for him, they declared, and saw that he got there. They died next day, four hundred of them, as they had told him they would die, defending a small town.

The potatoes boiled, and I watched the water frothing. Past me men went running, Englishmen, Frenchmen, Poles, Yugoslavs. I heard not a single voice, only the urgent pounding of feet. The roar of the feet enclosed me like a wall, and I stood up and watched the running men who seemed caught up ineluctably in some current of magnetism. I would not be of them, I would not.

I watched the men running. Quite suddenly I realised that I saw only the same backs; I too was running.

Cheering prisoners surrounded the armoured cars, their arms held above their heads, flexed, the wave arrested by the pressure of the crowd. The crews of the cars were signing autographs on scraps of paper, on old letters, in books. Half a mile away the war went on, and it came to us on the tank radio, above the cheering . . . Germans were resisting in a woodland ambush; a tank was sent . . . twelve prisoners had been taken; would someone come and collect them . . . two cars were racing eastward, German senior officers in flight; they were to be headed off . . . Stalag 357 was liberated; it was the crew of the car talking, and the answer came . . . Good show. Give 'em our love. . . .

I stood to one side a little, watching, listening. This was the liberation of dreams, the liberation exactly as we had imagined it, but I could not believe in it. A Yugoslav officer rushed forward, seized the great padlock from the main gate, hurled it to the ground, jumped on it as if it were a living and an evil thing that had to be destroyed.

It was theatrical and absurd. "These emotional, ruddy Continentals," I thought, and laughed, laughed, laughed . . . wept. From my wallet I took the pencilled map on which I had followed the advance of the allied armies, and pressed through the crowd to the leading car.

As I write, the map is on the table in front of me, and scrawled across it, in pencil, is "Percy Venn, Lower Henlade, Taunton, Somerset", and the date, April 16th, 1945.

That day the thousands of our comrades who were still marching, by whom "the weariness, the fever, and the fret" still were endured, crossed the Elbe.

CHAPTER
27

AGE-FRAIL when he had acquired it, the bicycle that Dixie Deans had ridden indefatigably during the long march was near collapse. The most imminent danger was the tyres, which had blistered badly, like so many of the marchers' heels. There was no chance of replacing a burst tyre.

From village to village trudged the columns, from barn to barn. Flagging kriegies jettisoned more and more of their belongings; some had no kit at all. Rations were stingy, and they lived mainly from their farmyard plundering, but even this was limited by their own numbers, and the vigilance of farmers and guards.

Several times Bill Bowhill slipped away to nearby villages to barter treasures of his own or of his friends for food. Once he took a new pair of shoes for which the owner, who had carried them all the way, wanted three loaves of bread and a chicken.

Bill called at a house where an elderly couple gazed covetously at the shoes. They would give him eggs, bread, milk, onions; alas, they had no chicken. The man's eyes fell upon the pet rabbit in its hutch. There was the rabbit, he said, tentatively. Bill nodded. The deal was agreed, but who was to kill the animal? The German was reluctant, Bowhill could not face it. At last the old man killed his pet.

When Bowhill told the woman it was his birthday she went to her larder and came back with bottled cherries. Long forgotten delicacies were these to Bowhill and to the soldiers who stopped him in the street. They took the cherries, amiably allowed him to keep everything else. Back at the barn Bowhill and his friends stewed the rabbit in an old enamel bucket, and afterwards were violently ill.

The columns grew swollen as prisoners from other camps marched into the area, but all along the route men slipped away, hoping to reach the front lines. Some dashed openly and audaciously into the woods, others hid in the barns where they had slept, and saw the columns go on without them.

In this way Doug. Hurditch and Alistair Benn made their escape. Hurditch subsequently flew to Australia and New Zealand as second pilot when the *Aries* made its record run. He stayed in the Air Force, took part in exploratory polar flying, later flew jets in Malta before becoming chairborne at Australia House in London. Now a wing commander, he is back in Australia commanding a fighter squadron.

The many marched on, the Elbe, last boundary of hope, now behind them, the forlorn hostages of a cause in decay. Oberst Ossmann, the Commandant, travelled in his Opel and invited Deans to ride with him. Instead, mounted on that decrepit bicycle, Deans rode from column to column. Although marching in the same general direction, the columns were on roads miles apart, and the Camp Leader had to find a way across open country, often where there was no track, and where the only people he saw were enemy troops. He was alone.

In a narrow lane he overtook a German army column, and the soldiers watched with astonishment the neatly uniformed English airman ride past. He was not even challenged, but an encounter with two German officers produced a vigorous challenge. One wanted to shoot him and his insistence was disturbing. Deans was invited to give one good reason why he should not be shot, and talked with such conviction that he was permitted to ride on, although he was for the first minute or so, very conscious of what he felt to be his enormous breadth of back.

Afterwards he persuaded the Commandant to issue him an *Ausweis*, a pass, which reduced the hazard, but in no sense gave security; scraps of paper do not always command respect from the Germans. That he might desist from his lone journeying did not occur to him. To ride with the Commandant was not the way he wanted to lead.

He encouraged the weary, looked for those who were ill, and somehow bludgeoned the Germans into providing transport for them or taking them into hospital. Every bit of information he could glean from the Commandant he passed on. The hectoring guard, the bully, he watched carefully, ensuring that there was no brutality, for the lash of his tongue cowed the most domineering braggarts. They were trained to react to the voice of authority, and authority was epitomised in his voice, and in his presence.

At night he rode round the villages to the barns where the prisoners were quartered, ameliorating discomfort where he could, and what rations there were came only because he badgered the Germans until he got them. Often, dissatisfied with the lot of his men, Dixie would seek out the Commandant who, each evening, unerringly selected the finest house in the area in which to establish his headquarters.

There would be a cellar where the bottles had lain for many years in tranquil dust, awaiting a reverent hand and a worthwhile occasion. Vintages mellow and smooth there were which were meant to be dispensed by a gracious host, and savoured by fastidious guests. But the hosts were gracious no more, the guests not fastidious. There was only eagerness to drink as much of the wine as possible before the British troops came to help themselves. Little time was left for their libations and the parties were riotous.

Deans saw a good many well-lined nests, and met the sleek, fat birds inhabiting them, but there was no denying the genuine charm of the most sumptuous of these houses, the castle of the famous Bernstorff family.

It was impossible not to be affected by the contrast between the two worlds, the world of the desperate dinner-parties, and the world of stolen barnyard fare. Determined to get more and better food for the men, and remembering the scheme of land lorry distribution, Deans persuaded the Commandant to drive him to Lubeck. They made the journey at night.

The war was writhing to its end, but the scheme which, a few months ago, would have saved much suffering, was only now getting under way. Nevertheless, to Dixie at this moment, news that trucks were available was all that mattered. If there were to be regrets for the might-have-been they could be saved for less exigeant days. Arranging for the trucks to leave almost immediately, he returned to the prisoner columns bearing a message that the men had thought never to hear again: "Parcels are on the way."

Electric the effect upon morale. To many the coming of parcels in these circumstances was a plain miracle, and, in a mood for hyperbole, they invested Deans with the qualities of a saint. But Deans was no saint, only a superb leader, only a man living his greatest, his most selfless moments.

It was to the village of Gresse on 19th April, that the huge trucks, painted white, with the Red Cross symbol in vivid contrast, brought their cargoes of parcels, and to Gresse streamed the columns from the neighbouring villages. Twelve thousand men there were in that German village, and the villagers smiled, for how could humans fail to be moved by the joy of so many. To each man went two parcels. Patently he could not carry them complete, but he could select the most sustaining items, and the additional weight in his pack would ride lightly on revitalised shoulders.

To relieve the congestion in Gresse, it was agreed with the Commandant that the men should march for a kilometre or so, then halt to sort out the parcels. They carried a parcel under each arm, and so cumbered even a kilometre was a gruelling experience.

All along the road they stopped, tore open the cardboard

boxes, and bent to their packs. They ate as they stowed tins in their kits, ate as, reluctantly, they discarded more tins, and they ate still as they marched on, leaving on the verge a confusion of tins and packets, meat enough to fill the bellies of an army, prunes sufficient to empty its bowels.

Above them wheeled a flight of Typhoons. Allied aircraft had trailed them along the way as albatrosses follow a ship in southern waters, vanishing at nightfall to reappear in the morning. Sometimes, when they attacked targets near the columns, the men laughed a little uneasily, yet was it always a thrill to appreciate the Allies' complete mastery of the air.

Interestedly they watched the wheeling Typhoons, never guessing the mistake, the unpardonable, pitiful mistake that the Typhoon pilots were making. The fighters peeled off to begin an attack, and, suddenly, the prisoners knew about the mistake. Some rushed to lay out strips, prepared for this emergency, to identify the sprawling columns, others waved handkerchiefs, or threw themselves down in ditches, or ran into the fields. But the Typhoons swooped, remorselessly hurling anti-personnel bombs and rockets into the scattering ranks. One after another they attacked, until seven of them were circling ready to make another run as soon as the eighth had attacked. But the eighth fighter climbed steeply, and no doubt the stick was hard back against a stomach turning over, for the eighth pilot had seen what his comrades had done.

In a few tragic, shattering seconds it was over. Slowly men's heads were raised from the ditches, and again lowered. Upwards of sixty prisoners lay dead or dying; another sixty were wounded. Some of the guards, too, had been killed.

Sixty men! Measured against the carnage of years the toll was infinitesimal. Night after night Bomber Command had lost 60, or 100, or 200, even 400. Sixty infantrymen had been sacrificed to capture Fallingbostel. The sea had claimed sixty sailors a thousand times and more, and in London, when the bombs fell sixty civilians died countless times.

But these were men killed when liberation was a matter of days—and killed by their own airmen. They were men who had been enduring hardship with stoicism, who, but minutes before, had been vouchsafed a moment of pure happiness. Johnny Shierlaw would never play cricket again; Arthur Porter died with that irritating little piece of roof still in his eye.

Slowly Dixie Deans walked among the carnage, and with the help of their friends identified most of the dead. They were buried there at Gresse, and Deans helped to dig the mass grave and to lift the remains into it. In the makeshift hospitals the list of fatalities was growing. The German medical people did all that they could, but they were ill-equipped, and shock and gangrene killed.

Slowly the columns wound across Luneberg Heath. The sick list was increased by the hour. Shock had vitiated the strength of many; the unaccustomed food had caused acute diarrhoea in many more. To suffer the "squitters" on the march was intolerable torture.

Deans decided the march had gone on long enough, and set about persuading the Commandant to his way of thinking. The Commandant had clear orders to march the prisoners into the redoubt planned by the fanatical Nazi bosses. Against that he had been informed that the British were to halt on the western bank of the Elbe, while the Russians were to attain the opposite bank.

That Ossmann's impression was inaccurate Deans knew, for John Bristow was carrying the "canary" housed in a billycan. Bristow's magic set worked off either electric mains or battery, and every day of the march he had succeeded in picking up the B.B.C. news which was then filtered through the columns.

Deans pointed out to the Commandant that to the prisoners it did not much matter who liberated them, but what future had the Commandant if he were taken prisoner by the Russians? He also explained that if they went no further the British would reach them first. After reflection the Commandant agreed to allow Deans to carry out his plan to contact the British front line, to urge more discretion in the bombing of troops on the march, and to arrange transport for the sick. To facilitate this the Commandant gave Deans a letter, dated April 30th, authorising him to pass through the German front lines. He also handed him a map with the disposition of P.O.W. columns marked.

The journey was to be made by bicycle, but Deans felt that his ramshackle model was unlikely to go very far, so he borrowed a new machine from a young German officer, faithfully promising to return it. A little unteroffizier, Charlie Baumbach, who had been the Commandant's official interpreter until a few days previously when he had been relieved of his duties, in disgrace, for drinking himself into insensibility, was assigned to accompany him. Neither Deans nor Baumbach had any idea of the way modern armies fight, and Dixie foresaw trouble. He obtained permission to take a military expert, a British lieutenant captured a few days before, and the trio set off.

As a cyclist Charlie Baumbach was a complete failure. He kept dropping behind, and every few miles the others were compelled to wait for him. They could not afford to lose him for he carried the precious documents.

It was no easy task to find a way across the Elbe-Trave Canal; Oberst Ossmann had recommended that they cross the bridge at Potrau, but it no longer existed. They cycled for many miles along the bank before finding a bridge intact. Riding day and night, constantly on the fringe of the fighting, frequently they had to hurl themselves and their machines into roadside ditches as shells exploded nearby. At each village they inquired where they could find the German front line H.Q. but invariably it was said to be in the village ahead of them. They were passed from unit to unit, and always the cannonade was close to them.

In one lovely little village an old woman rushed out and greeted them in rich Cockney. She had long been married to a German. The three weary cyclists she had taken for the vanguard of the British army, but, on finding they were not, she implored Deans to give her husband a letter absolving him of connivance with the Nazi war aims, but Deans refused, with little sympathy.

Caught in heavy mortar fire in a village further on, they propped their bicycles against the front wall of a house, and dived for shelter. Emerging when there were no more explosions, they found that all but the front wall of the house had disintegrated. Their bicycles were undamaged.

They came at last, at dusk, to a village where the front line hospital was situated, and were told that the elusive headquarters definitely were in the neighbouring village. The German Commandant was willing to permit Deans to go there at once, but insisted that he should be blindfolded, a condition Deans considered futile. Badly in need of a rest, he decided to wait until the morning, and sat down to an excellent meal.

Charlie Baumbach was sent on to warn H.Q. that a V.I.P. was on the way, but returned with the news that the village had been captured. Deans could now afford to wait, and, elated, joined in a party. He had not long been asleep after making a merry way to bed, when he was roughly awakened by British paratroopers. They were convinced that his story was phoney and his uniform a fake, but he was taken to their commanding officer, and passed on right through the local hierarchy. Not even the Divisional General was anxious to have Deans on his hands for long; the young N.C.O. was not abashed in the presence of generals, and he complained very bitterly of the Typhoon action.

Deans told General Barker, the Corps General, in whose presence eventually he found himself, that as an experienced pilot himself, he considered that the attack was indefensible. He could not believe that the prisoners in their variegated clothing, with packs on their backs, with armed guards patrolling the flanks of the columns, could possibly have been mistaken for retreating troops had any serious attempt at identification been made. Barker said that the danger to the many thousands of prisoners marching eastward was appreciated; the pilots had disobeyed explicit orders not to attack marching columns until they were quite certain there was no mistake. It must be thought that the Typhoon pilots were recklessly negligent, but they, perhaps as much as the survivors, will be haunted for the rest of their lives by the memory of the tragedy at Gresse.

Ambulances would be sent to collect the sick and the wounded, General Barker promised—if Deans could get the German Divisional Commander to agree to it. The General looked at his watch, and decided that it might be expedient to call off the air raid on the German H.Q.

"There are two thousand of our men quartered in that village," Deans told him huskily.

The bicycles had been stolen; the promise to the young officer could not be fulfilled. The General suggested that, after all, Deans might remain with them. His job surely was done. But Deans did not think so. The General supplied him with a Mercedes Benz, the bonnet of which Deans draped with a Red Cross flag borrowed from the hospital, and, in style, he returned to his incredulous fellow prisoners.

"God stone the crows," said an Australian. "Talk about miracles. Now he's turned a bike into a flaming Mercedes Benz."

Deans was due to report to General Barker at ten the following morning, to inform him of the German Commander's decision. Now that he had the O.K. from the British the Commandant was ready to go with him to obtain sanction from German Area H.Q. They went in the Mercedes because the Commandant's Opel would not start.

General Oetken refused to give a safe conduct to the British ambulances, but Deans did persuade the Divisional Battle Commander to evacuate the village where the sick were housed, and although it was not possible to report at 10 a.m. as instructed, he resolved to try to get through with what news he had. His *Ausweis* redated—it was now May 2nd—he drove away. The army lieutenant went with him, which was fortunate because it was he, and not Dixie, who spotted the big gun of a tank protruding from the woods at a bend in the road. If they had not stopped that gun would have stopped them. Deans and his companion scrambled from the car, and the British tank officer, watching through glasses, recognised them, having seen them in the Mess at H.Q. the previous day.

The tank commander explained that he was on reconnaissance with orders to proceed until he encountered opposition, and Deans told him that he had just passed a farmhouse where the Germans were preparing to hold out.

"Look, I'm just a kriegy, a harmless sort of bird," said Deans. "I'll go and see if I can talk them into surrendering."

A stubborn unteroffizier was in command, and was bent on fighting it out. Warning that the opposition would be a tank did not shake his resolve to die for his Führer, but Deans sensed that his men were less convinced of their ultimate duty; also, he quickly won the support of the farmer by evoking a vision of his farmhouse shattered by fire from the tank. The unteroffizier was obdurate. The argument was still in progress when Deans observed the tank crew outside. He signalled them in, and the unteroffizier did not have to die after all.

The army was advancing so rapidly now that the ambulance question was no longer important. Deans drove his Mercedes Benz from one pocket of resistance to another, persuading the defenders to lay down their arms without bloodshed. His supreme moment came when, overtaken at last, the Commandant formally surrendered his arms to him, remarking that in doing so he felt that his honour demanded no more.

Throughout the prisoner-of-war camps were men like Deans, men who were inspiring leaders in these strange communities, never sparing themselves though, often, gratitude was lacking. And yet I believe that among these he was outstanding. As prisoner after prisoner was repatriated, and made his report, the eulogies poured in to Air Ministry. His work was recognised, so very inadequately, by the award of an M.B.E. as if he had done a good job organising a district National Savings Campaign. Deans was unconcerned—his reward is the knowledge that thousands of men in all parts of the world remember him, still, with ineffable affection; messages come to him in letters and postcards, and sometimes on tape recordings made at reunions in many lands, and men stop him in the street, and say: "Hello, Dixie, you wouldn't remember me, but . . ." and more often than not, though probably he had nothing to do with them personally during those years, he does remember them.

He does feel, however, that when awards to prisoners were made, N.C.O.s got less than justice. Some officers received awards for simple administrative work, whereas men like Bristow got nothing.

After the war Deans left the R.A.F., went up to Oxford, and is now in the administrative section of the London School of Economics. Much of the old vitality is gone, for he gave so much of himself that little was left. He lives quietly in Surrey, with his wife and two children, and he will talk about the four and a half years he spent as a prisoner of war. But you come away realising that you have heard a lot about George Grimson, Allan Morris, John Bristow, Ron Mogg, Cyril Aynsley and many others, but of Dixie Deans—nothing, nothing at all.

CHAPTER
28

THE car at the door of the woodshed—a Hanomag—was ours. It had belonged to the vet in Fallingbostel, but he would never see it again. Perhaps he found a bicycle to carry him when he had to tend sick animals.

In the garage yard where a tank-maintenance unit was quartered were half a dozen cars. The Germans had removed some of the mechanism in the hope that the British would not be able to use them, but with the help of the tank mechanics we soon got them going. The sergeant in charge, with whom we had become friendly, said that we might as well take the cars before they were officially commandeered. The sergeant hated the Germans, and could not understand that we did not. "They've broken your spirits," he said, "and I'm not surprised. I never imagined that they'd keep prisoners in pigsties like that. Well, I hate 'em more since I've seen what they've done to you."

We were a little embarrassed by all this, but soon realised that they had been trained to hate, that if they had not hated they would probably still have been trying to break from the Normandy beachhead. Once the war was over the hatred died fast enough.

When we had replaced the missing engine parts, found tyres and tubes, and reconverted it from a charcoal-burning to a petrol-burning system the Hanomag was ready—except that the battery was flat. Watched from an upper window by a German woman whose eyes glowed with loathing, we tied the car to the back of a tank and were towed into the street. Dick was at the wheel, and as we raced down the cobblestoned road behind the tank there was so much noise, so much vibration, that he could not tell whether the engine was going or not. It was a short towrope, and we could see nothing ahead but the vast structure, and, swinging from the rear, just in front of our windscreen, three dead chickens.

There were hundreds of cars in the camp. Every car in every village within miles had been taken. Some men even raided villages still in German hands, and were recaptured. Others took not only cars but German uniforms, which they wanted for souvenirs, and were taken prisoner by our own sceptical forces. So much of a nuisance did kriegy motorists become that Fallingbostel was put out of bounds. Only our Hanomag was permitted to drive into the village, and then only when our friend Joe was a passenger.

Ron had first got to know Joe, a Yugoslav who spoke English which was a mixture of Fowler and the New Testament. A group of Yugoslav air force officers had broken the monotony of their prison days by learning English from these sources alone, and if they spoke with quaintness, their understanding of the language was remarkable.

"My friend Joe here wants to paint our names on the Hanomag," Ron said the day after we got the car. "He knows where he can get some white paint and a brush.

Joe lettered the names of the four of us on each side of the car and added Ex-P.O.W. and the star which all allied vehicles carried. It was strange that the first person to call us Ex-P.O.W.s should have been Joe, the Yugoslav, and we wondered where he had learned the significance of the prefix.

The following afternoon he asked us if we would drive him into Fallingbostel, where he had an appointment.

"We'll try," Dick said, "but you may have to walk half-way. We aren't supposed to go into the village." Promising to be back in half an hour, Joe went off to get ready. He was in quite a flurry, and we wondered if somehow he had found a girl. When he returned from B compound he was resplendent in the uniform of a General of the Yugoslav air force, and his appointment was to discuss the future of his countrymen. "I am not of the profession of painter of names, you see," he said.

We became his official chauffeurs, but one of us had to stay behind whenever the car went into Fallingbostel; there was not room for more than four. Often I was the one to drop out, because I did not feel well, and because there was plenty of life in the camp. I was the only one of the four of us to see Ralph Reader's Gang Show, which suddenly appeared, without prior publicity, took over one of the wooden huts, built a stage, and gave a show without any fuss. When I began to laugh I realised that I had not laughed for a long time, and my cheeks hurt as if a thick plaster of make-up was cracking.

When we decided to drive on a food foraging expedition the four of us went in the Hanomag. The army had brought in a little food, but, so far, only the spearhead of the force had reached Fallingbostel and penetrated beyond. Soon the R.A.S.C. was to bring enormous lorry loads of food, American K Rations, and, unbelievably, white bread. Meanwhile we looked for eggs and chickens, and cared not a jot which came first.

Five kilometres from the camp we saw two boys wearing the familiar German Army type cap. On their backs were small, neat packs. Dick stopped the car and beckoned them over. "*Soldaten?*"

"*Nein. Nein.*"

"How old are you?" One was thirteen, the other fourteen. There was no doubt that they had been in the forest prepared to carry on Germany's resistance. Perhaps in their pockets they had the directive of Canaris, onetime chief of German Intelligence, to the "Werewolf" Organisation, the new Resistance movement. Some of its comments are not without interest: "We need not fear peace conditions similar to those we might have imposed ourselves," wrote Canaris, "since our opponents will always be divided and disunited. We must strive to introduce into the coming peace the seeds of future dissension. . . . We shall be called upon to furnish our enemies with a few squads of workers, to return a few objects of art, and to hand over our obsolete machinery; and we can always say that the bulk of the stolen articles they lay claim to have been destroyed by their bombings. We must begin immediately preparing a dossier on the loot 'destroyed by Anglo-American bombs'."

The boys stood in the road, and we wondered what to do with them. "*Nicht soldaten*," they repeated. They had been in the forest, but now they were going home. It was apparent that concern for their families had driven them from their snipers' hideout in the woods. They were only boys, and doubtless they had been fanatically eager to kill the enemy, until they wearied of playing at real soldiers, grew impatient at seeing no enemy, and wanted to be home again. And perhaps it was lucky for some British soldiers that they had wearied, those boys, for other boys were killing British soldiers, not always from ambush, but shooting them at point-blank range as they reached into a pocket for chocolates or gum.

We ordered them to keep walking towards Fallingbostel, and we drove on ahead of them. Two hundred yards further on we saw a British corporal guarding the entrance to a drive. We told him about the two boys. The corporal looked as if he thought he should first arrest us.

"Thanks, chum," he said, finally. "Would you mind driving in and telling the C.O. I'll nab 'em if they come past me here."

We found ourselves in the yard of a prosperous farm where a R.A.S.C. unit had settled itself comfortably. A sergeant asked us our business, made us welcome, and hurried into the house to find the C.O. The boys were no longer any concern of ours.

The R.A.S.C. men were eager to ask questions, and we

stood in the centre of the farmyard, answering them. All around us were trucks and vans stacked with food, all sorts of wonderful-looking food. This unit had just given lunch to troops in the area, but they had left trays half covered with apple pie, with salmon pie, with huge slices of cold meat, and there were hillocks of sliced bread and fresh fruit.

Politely we explained about the march, and how we had been brought back, and the manner in which we had acquired the car, and politely we tried not to look at all the trucks of food. I knew what Toby was thinking. He was wanting some of that apple pie more than he had ever wanted anything before. To me a trayload of salmon, almost untouched, looked about the most appetising thing on earth.

"You blokes are thin, aren't you?" said the man leaning against the tailboard of the apple-pie van. "Bloody thin. You'll need plenty of real good food in you."

Toby tried to look directly at the man, and not at the trays of apple pie behind the man's head. "I reckon," said Toby.

It was Ron who said: "Look, corporal, I know this is a hell of a cheek, but could you spare just one little bit of that apple pie each. Not if the troops have to go without, of course." He laughed, nervously. All four of us must have looked strained as we waited for the answer, for the soldiers stopped talking, and glanced quickly at each other, behaving a little like people who have asked after someone and only then learned that he was dead.

"That's the leftovers. You can have as much as you like."

"You're not kidding?" asked Toby, both hands poised high.

"Let's fix you a real meal," said the corporal.

"No, thank you. Just apple pie. Lots of it. I'm fed up with dried peas," Toby replied.

"Christ!" The corporal reached for plates, and a large ladle.

We ate enormously, and though we were later to regret it, we had never enjoyed food more. The Hanomag came in for some admiring attention, and a couple of cans of petrol were stowed in the boot.

"We can give you enough juice to get to Paris or Brussels," offered another corporal, but we declined. Many prisoners were driving looted cars back (and some sold them handsomely in Brussels), but the captain in charge of the area, whose friends we had become, had said they were a great hindrance, pointing out that the war was not over, yet. In deference to our friendship with him we felt that we should wait for official transport.

Again, the following day we drove into the country, this time without Toby, and seeing about a hundred Russians in single file, carrying boxes on their heads like native porters on safari, we scouted the area until we found the food magazine from which the booty had come. The boxes contained sultanas, and we loaded a box into the car.

In a woodland lane which we hoped would lead us to a farm, we suddenly came upon six German soldiers sprawling under the trees, their rifles stacked a few yards away. "Let's get to hell out of it," I muttered, but Dick stopped the car, and Ron was out and standing with a rifle pointing at the Germans before they were properly awake. All but two of the rifle magazines we emptied, then Dick went off in the Hanomag to get transport for the prisoners, and Ron and I began to march them back to the camp.

They did not know whether the war was ended or not, and did not seem to mind that for them "the war was over," the well-worn words of captors which Ron uttered now with an obvious relish.

After they had drunk at a horse trough we marched the men along the same road which we had tramped as prisoners a few days before. There was no sign of Dick, and we reached a crossroads. Ron wanted to go one way, which was shorter, I the other because I was sure it was the road that Dick would take. We marched a few hundred yards my way, but Ron was dissatisfied, and the Germans sided with him in a fierce argument. The weight of opinion against me, we reversed, but had not gone far when an army van arrived with the Hanomag behind. Dick had punctured on the way back.

"Get in," snarled a handsome sergeant-major with an Errol Flynn moustache and assurance enough to take Burma single-handed. The Germans climbed into the truck, and we travelled with them as guards. The Hanomag nosed just behind.

On our return I was informed that I was wanted by Australian photographers, newsreel cameramen, and war correspondents who had just arrived, and so I had a good story for them. It appeared in Australian papers with the drab headline: "The Tables Turned."

Alex Stewart and Frank Bagnell were not the first cameramen to come into the camp. British newsreel men had arrived the day of the liberation, and had interviewed some of the prisoners. An Englishman spoke, a Welshman and an Irishman, but curiously no Scot was available. Peter Thomas became "Jock McPherson", and with a realistic accent, put the Scottish viewpoint on liberation. Also interviewed was George Booth, shot down with Larry Slattery on September 3rd, 1939. Late in 1941 Booth was one of those who were at a French port ready to be repatriated when negotiations fell through. The chance did not come again for his injuries had been repaired by the time the first exchange of prisoners did take place in 1943. He was a prisoner for five years and almost eight months. Slattery, who had been given the number "1", and was therefore the first prisoner of war of either side, was still on the march, and so became the man who had longest been a captive.

Polish prisoners heard that the concentration camp to which the women captured in the Warsaw insurrection had been taken, had been liberated, and they went off anxiously to find relatives. They came back, dazed, horror-struck. The army had overrun Belsen.

We remembered now the strange stench which had sometimes drifted to the camp, a stench which we knew was the reek of death, and which we believed had come from shallow graves in the camp cemetery. A few prisoners went to see Belsen; we did not. Now Germany seemed unclean, and we wanted only to be out of it, and I thought I should never want to go back.

But our departure was not to be for a few days yet. Each day a few hundred men left the camp, the first captured being the first to be evacuated, and we moved into bunks now vacant in the more convenient cookhouse. All cars, save ours, were commandeered by the army. The captain wanted the Hanomag, but allowed us to keep it on condition that we drove him around the area, and helped him to keep in check the Russians who were roaming the countryside. There were a number of cases of women living alone inviting British prisoners to sleep with them, for then the little Mongol invaders—who certainly had no reason to respect anything German—would go away with a smile.

The captain was also worried about some of our own irresponsibles.

"I wish you would persuade anyone with arms to hand them in," he said. "If there are any incidents the Jerries will take it out on your own friends still in their hands."

As proof of good faith we took him to one end of the cookhouse, where there were, under a tarpaulin, machine-guns and mortars brought in by souvenir hungry prisoners. Having expected nothing more lethal than a pistol, the captain believed that he was dreaming.

In his honour, and in honour of his batman, we had a party in the kitchen. On the table was the finest linen, the finest cutlery, enchanting wineglasses, and, stacked on shelves, cases of wine. All had been looted from the nearby mansion of a German general.

"And you were the men who helped me make those poor little Russians take back a few boxes of sultanas," remarked the captain, and ordered a van to take our surplus to the officers' mess.

Toby cooked a chicken to perfection, and I cooked a sultana pie.

"My God! Not more sultanas," exclaimed the disillusioned captain.

Wine flowed, and the captain loosed a few revolver shots through the roof, and had to be prevented from shooting at a German cap which Toby wore when he re-entered the room after going out for air.

Someone, whom I remember only as a blessed voice, stood on a box, and read out the names of the men to leave the camp on April 26th. Dick, Toby, and I were to go; Ron Kennett had still to wait. The box, as it happened, contained documents, valuable records packed by Dixie Deans. The army undertook to get them back to England, but somehow lost them, a deplorable bit of carelessness.

We climbed into the army truck and, uncomfortably packed, drove out of the camp. Soon, unclean Germany would be behind us. In convoy we went, escorted by motorcyclists, waved on at road junctions. All about us was evidence of the dying holocaust, wrecked homes, burnt-out shops, pale, sad-looking women, German prisoners going single file along the roadsides. The trucks whined like falling aircraft. Hour by cramped hour we went, and the aching whine was unceasing.

Near Diepholz we turned into a field where there were hundreds of tents, with duckboard floors and camp beds. Men queued at the Red Cross tent for the first of a number of hand-outs, but I could not be bothered to queue, now. Later I was told that the Red Cross unit was an Australian field unit, and they wanted to see me. The man in charge was a Melbourne barrister, John Nimmo, the gentlest of men, who is now one of my dearest friends.

We talked until 4 a.m. He wanted to know my plans for the future, but the only thing I was sure of was that I should never marry. A few weeks later he arrived smiling at the little Norfolk church where I was married to Margaret, my pen-friend of the last two years. At the reception we ate— of all things—Red Cross food. The Air Force sent a photographer, and he was none other than Flight Lieutenant Alex Stewart whom I had met at Fallingbostel the day we had taken six prisoners. Dick was best man. Dick is himself married, has two children, the elder of whom, Anne, is my god-daughter, and he teaches at Winchester House School, Brackley, where the boys, to break the monotony of lessons, are wont to ask: "Sir, please tell us about when you were a prisoner."

From Diepholz we went to Borghorst, where we spent the night and most of the day following. In the Mess was a visitors' book which included the names of kriegies who had gone through, some piled in German ambulances, some in cars, some even on a farm tractor.

The army had taken over the town. There was a big N.A.A.F.I. canteen, and the "Monty" cinema. We went to the cinema, but were too restless to stay more than a few minutes. Indeed it was some months before I could sit a film through. We were impatient to go. This was still unclean Germany. We were to go to the airfield at Rheine to be flown to England. The day dragged on, and we despaired. The trucks came at last, all but one, the one in which we were to travel. When it appeared, after all the others had gone, the driver was apologetic, almost maudlin. He admitted, with touching candour, that he was drunk. No more planes were to leave after six o'clock, and we urged him to hurry. The man drove like fury, the truck whined and swayed, threatening to capsize, and after we had gone seventeen miles, the driver confessed that he had lost the way, and was more maudlin than before. His shame was such that we contained our disappointment, and assured him that we should not mind another night in Germany.

He swore that he would get us to the airfield on time, and again we set off, finding the way at last. But it was long after six when we reached the airfield. The driver hunched over his wheel, and cried. The airfield was a desolate place. Broken twisted aircraft and the burnt-out skeletons of aircraft littered the ground. Some had nosed into shell craters, and their tails jutted forlornly.

No more aircraft were to fly to England that day, but a Dakota was warming up at the end of the field. It would take us across the countryside pockmarked by Montgomery's barrage from the other side of the Rhine; we would fly across the great river barrier itself, the ultimate crossing of which had begun the drive of liberation, and on across the low countries to Brussels. From there we should have to begin another journey, but Germany, unclean Germany would be behind us.

The pilot of the Dakota, a nervous little man, came over to us.

"I can't take off, yet. There's broken glass, and Christ knows what all down the field. You men had better get cracking, and pick it up."

We spread out, and heads bent, painstakingly plodded down the field, stooping whenever we saw a piece of glass or sharp metal. On my left was an Arnhem parachutist, on my right a man who had crashlanded a burning aircraft. Slowly we trod the grass back to the Dakota, and heaped our little armfuls of broken glass at the feet of the nervous pilot.

THE END

AUTHOR'S NOTE FOR 1981 EDITION

If I were now to write of those days in Germany, I should produce a much more reticent book. The original text must stand, but an epilogue of some kind is appropriate.

Shortly after *No Flight from the Cage* appeared in 1956, and partly because of it, the Royal Air Forces Ex-Pow Association came into being. With counterparts in Canada and New Zealand, it sustains the extraordinary bonds of kriegie friendship. We set up our own Charitable Fund, also The Larry Slattery Memorial Fund which helps musically gifted children as Larry did in his lifetime. The moving spirit in forming the Association, he is one of many deceased friends. Others are Ken Bowden, Stan Parris, Rev. Norman Hennessey, Air Commodore Massey, Group Captain 'Wings' Day and Canadian Andy Rodgers.

Massey and Day gladly served as active vice-presidents with Dixie Deans, still revered by men everywhere, as President. His career blighted by multiple sclerosis Dixie is now wheelchair-bound, but with the help of his indomitable wife Molly he has flown to reunions in many parts of the world. His capacity to inspire men, some now in high positions, is undiminished.

Old kriegies have distinguished themselves in many fields. Roy Dotrice is an international star; Peter Thomas was a member of Edward Heath's cabinet; Cyril Aynsley retired from the *Daily Express* as Chief Reporter, and Doug Hurditch from the RAAF with the rank of Air Vice Marshal; T. B. Miller is Professor of History at a Canadian university.

Dick, Toby and I remain close. Dick is now a headmaster and the boys find it less easy to divert him into reminiscence. Drawn from his carapace, Toby is in charge of Canada Packers food laboratories in Vancouver. Frank Hunt, an elegant seventy, teaches the violin. His wife is a concert pianist, his son principal oboist of the Philharmonia Orchestra.

I return often to Sevran where Helene Buvelot, now in her seventies and unhappily a widow, still lives. She has never told me the full story of her grilling by the Gestapo. Jean Lelong, too, I never fail to see.

On a recent visit to Australia I stayed with the family of my pilot, Russ Jones, whose mother (now ninety-three) has written to me every Christmas since 1942.

John (now Sir John) Nimmo recently retired as a judge of the federal Court of Australia. A great humanitarian, he has left his stamp on social legislation in Australia. He remains the wise friend of both Margaret and myself, though our marriage ended long ago. In the translation from wartime youth into peacetime adulthood we grew away from each other, but parted friends.

From Pow experiences I learned much and I do not regret those years. Yet, it was a very long time before I conquered a restless preoccupation with the past and found what I was searching for in my wife, Dee, and her two children, Michael and Amanda.　C.Y.